G000320789

Corporate Citizenship in Africa

Lessons from the Past; Paths to the Future

Corporate Citizenship in Africa

LESSONS FROM THE PAST; PATHS TO THE FUTURE

EDITED BY WAYNE VISSER, MALCOLM McINTOSH
AND CHARLOTTE MIDDLETON

2006

Published by Greenleaf Publishing Limited
Aizlewood's Mill
Nursery Street
Sheffield S3 8GG
UK
www.greenleaf-publishing.com

The paper used for this book is a natural, recyclable product made from wood grown in sustainable forests; the manufacturing processes conform to the environmental regulations of the country of origin.
Printed in Great Britain by William Clowes Ltd, Beccles, Suffolk.
Cover by LaliAbril.com.

British Library Cataloguing in Publication Data:
A catalogue record for this book is available from the British Library.

ISBN-10: 1-874719-55-1
ISBN-13: 978-1-874719-55-7

Contents

Part I
Introduction and overview

1

Corporate citizenship in Africa

LESSONS FROM THE PAST; PATHS TO THE FUTURE

Wayne Visser

Universities of Nottingham and London, UK

Malcolm McIntosh

Universities of Bath, UK, and Stellenbosch, South Africa

Charlotte Middleton

National Business Initiative, South Africa

2005 saw a renewed interest in development and Africa, both regionally and internationally, most notably with the publication of *Our Common Interest*, the Commission for Africa's Report chaired by the British Prime Minister with representatives from across Africa. This led to a special focus on Africa at that summer's G8 Summit at Gleneagles in Scotland, where, among other initiatives, the USA agreed to reform, to some extent, its aid budgets to poor countries. This was, of course, before hurricanes Rita and Katrina hit the southern states of the US later in the year, exposing significant levels of poverty and neglect within the world's richest country. The G8 meeting was preceded by Live8,[1] which was seen globally by some 3 billion people, making it the world's single largest event. Prior to this concert 30 million people signed a petition to the G8 lead-

1 www.live8live.com

ers. As this book goes to press discussions are taking place on reform of the United Nations; one of the issues is how Africa could be better represented on the Security Council and other UN bodies.

Despite this progress, much of the literature on Africa remains problem-focused, seeing Africa either as a moral dilemma for the rest of the world or as good aid money poured down the drain. This attitude is propped up by a plethora of statistics that show how Africa remains a marginal region in global terms: with 12% of the world's population (around 750 million people) in 53 countries, Africa accounts for less than 2% of global gross domestic product (GDP) and foreign direct investment (FDI), and less than 10% of FDI to all developing countries. Of the 81 poorest countries prioritised by the International Development Association, almost half are in Africa. And, even within Africa, there is highly skewed development, with the largest ten economies accounting for 75% of the continent's GDP.

But there is also a growing desire to develop a better understanding of the world's second largest continent and to celebrate the life of its people, literature, poetry, music, sport and social structures. And, despite generally negative press, there has been significant progress on the continent over the past decade. Fifteen countries, including Uganda, Ethiopia and Burkina Faso, have been growing on average more than 5% per year since the mid-1990s. And FDI rose to US$8.5 billion in 2004, up from US$7.8 billion the previous year. At the same time, Africa's new generation of leaders, through initiatives such as the New Partnership for Africa's Development (NEPAD), the African Union and the East African Community, are taking responsibility for development.

Higher quantity and quality of scholarly research is obviously needed, but so too is a change in media perceptions outside Africa so that its richness is reflected on television screens around the world. *Our Common Interest* pointed out that Africa is different, that Africa's development must follow a different path because of its history. For instance a snapshot of Africa in 2005 tells us that:

- Most people in Africa have never received or made a telephone call, but now 75% of all telephones are mobile phones
- Nine out of ten Africans are proud to be African (whereas less than four out of ten British people are proud to be British)
- Railway lines in Africa tended to be built to bring raw materials to ports for export to Europe, rather than connecting centres of populations as elsewhere in the world
- The boundaries of many countries were set by European colonial powers with little regard for geography, local communities or resource distribution
- Agriculture in many African countries is still determined by exports to the rest of the world, often in commodities such as coffee, sugar and cocoa, which have volatile prices
- The largest growth in trade in the last five years has not been inter-African, or to North America, or to Europe, or to Japan, but to China
- Banks outside Africa hold some US$80 billion in assets stolen from Africans by their leaders

- For every US$2 Africa receives in aid it pays US$1 in debt repayments
- Estimates suggest that, if Africa could gain an additional 1% of the global trade, it would earn US$70 billion more in exports each year—more than three times what the region currently receives in international assistance
- Every European cow is subsidised by US$2 a day—the equivalent of the daily income of half the population of Africa
- One million South Africans live in the UK
- There are more African scientists and engineers working in the US than in the whole of Africa
- Trade with the world has fallen from 6% in 1980 to 2% in 2005

Business has been central to Africa's development for centuries, and there are questions that must be asked of its role, both past and present, if we are to understand where to go next. This book and its stories are a contribution to understanding the role of business in Africa, specifically in relationship to the role that business has and hasn't played in Africa's under-development.

The track record of big business in Africa is mixed at best. There is certainly no shortage of examples of specific corporate complicity in political corruption, environmental destruction, labour exploitation and social disruption, stretching back more than 100 years. Equally, however, there is voluminous evidence of the benefits of business generally, bringing capital investment, job creation, skills transfer, infrastructure development, knowledge sharing and social responsibility programmes to countries throughout Africa.

Despite this polarisation of the debate, there is general agreement that the private sector remains well placed to make a significant positive contribution towards improving social, economic and environmental conditions in Africa. Recognition of this role is especially evident in the recent spate of publications on business's potential to impact on development and poverty alleviation. These envisaged corporate contributions are most often discussed in terms of corporate citizenship or corporate social responsibility (CSR). Hence, corporate citizenship is enmeshed in the debate about Africa's future. Arguably, Africa is the continent where the social needs are greatest and where the benefits of economic globalisation have been least felt.

What makes corporate citizenship in Africa not only fascinating, but also of critical importance, is that the continent embodies many of the most vexing dilemmas that business faces in its attempt to be responsible, ethical and sustainable: When do local cultural traditions take precedence over global standards and policies? How far do companies' responsibilities extend in providing public services? When does involvement in local governance become an unhealthy intrusion into the political process? How can business avoid creating a culture of entitlement and dependency through its charitable activities? Do global companies have a right to impose Western ideas of ethics on African societies that have their own, often different, sets of values (a question that Rajak's chapter in this book contemplates)?

The essence of these debates is in the question: Corporate citizenship or CSR according to what (or whose) definition? And is it a definition that is relevant to the African context? For example, Visser (2006) argues that the relative priorities of CSR in Africa are different from the classic, American ordering suggested by Carroll's (1991) widely accepted four-part CSR pyramid, where economic, legal, ethical and philanthropic responsibilities are assigned decreasing importance, respectively. If we accept Carroll's model for the moment, then in Africa, economic responsibilities still get the most emphasis, but philanthropy is often given second highest priority, followed by legal and then ethical responsibilities by corporations.

However, there is a strong case to suggest that Carroll's model itself is inadequate for describing the complexities and dynamics of corporate citizenship. If this is true elsewhere in the world, it is even more so in Africa where conflicts and contradictions tend to be the norm, rather than the exception: how to reconcile job creation and environmental protection, short-term profitability and Aids treatment costs, oppressive regimes and transparent governance, economic empowerment and social investment?

The limitations of the Carroll pyramid can also be illustrated by the ambiguity of classifying corporate activities into his four layers. For example, would Aids treatment be regarded as primarily an economic responsibility (given the medium- to long-term effects on the workforce and economy), or is it ethical (because Aids sufferers have basic human rights), or is it philanthropic (after all, it is a public health issue, not an occupational disease)?

De Jongh and Prinsloo (2005) concur, emphasising that the challenges facing corporate citizenship in Africa involve messy, 'on the edge of chaos' scenarios. Hence, rather than tinkering with Carroll's pyramid, perhaps we should be looking for alternatives that better describe the reality of corporate citizenship? Indeed, in attempting to understand the citizenship practices of a multinational mining company in Africa, Hamann *et al.* (2005) find complexity theory to be a much more useful model than Carroll's CSR pyramid. In addition to complexity theory (McIntosh 2003), other refreshing perspectives that hold promise for providing a better understanding of corporate citizenship in Africa include holism (Visser 1995; Visser and Sunter 2002), chaos theory (De Jongh and Prinsloo 2005) and spiral dynamics (Beck and Cowan 1996; Van Marrewijk and Werre 2002).

Encouragingly, Africa's academia is beginning to respond. In 2003 the Sustainability Institute at Stellenbosch University offered a week's course on corporate citizenship as part of an MPhil in Sustainable Development which is also open to the general public.[2] Also in 2003, the University of South Africa established its Corporate Citizenship Unit, and in July 2005 held the first academic conference on corporate responsibility on the continent attracting scholars from across Africa.[3] Shortly afterwards *The Journal of Corporate Citizenship* produced a special issue on Corporate Citizenship in Africa.[4]

This book is a further contribution to the evolving academic voice on corporate citizenship in Africa. The chapters have been broadly grouped by theme, beginning with the Introduction and overview, followed by sections on *Leadership and governance*,

2 www.sustainabilityinstitute.net

3 *1st Southern African Corporate Citizenship Symposium: Priorities for Research and Teaching on Business and Sustainable Development*, Unisa Graduate School of Business Leadership, Midrand, South Africa, 21–22 July 2005.

4 *Journal of Corporate Citizenship*, Issue 18 (Summer 2005), Special Issue on Corporate Citizenship in Africa, edited by Wayne Visser (International Centre for Corporate Social Responsibility, UK), Charlotte Middleton (National Business Initiative, South Africa) and Malcolm McIntosh (Universities of Bath, UK, and Stellenbosch, South Africa).

Community and environment, *Health and HIV/Aids*, *Industries and sectors*, *Supply chain and SMEs* (small and medium-sized enterprises) and, finally, *Globalisation and conclusion*.

Visser's chapter ('Research on corporate citizenship in Africa: a ten-year review [1995–2005]') sets the scene by providing a brief analysis of corporate citizenship research focused on Africa over the past ten years. He concludes that the volume of published research is still extremely low, most papers focus on business ethics and the coverage is almost exclusively on South Africa. Hence, there is great scope for expanding the amount of research on corporate citizenship in Africa, as well as improving the diversity of its content and its geographic reach.

The *Leadership and governance* section brings together four excellent chapter about the importance of strategic and top-management commitment for embedding corporate citizenship. Lynham, Taylor, Dooley and Naidoo ('Corporate leadership for economic, social and political change: lessons from South Africa') tell the story of the remarkably progressive actions of a few business leaders in helping to bring about South Africa's transformation to democracy. The chapter discusses the implications of this somewhat atypical business behaviour in terms of models of leadership and the role of business in furthering sociopolitical goals.

Hansen and Ryan ('Follow the rising polestar: an examination of the structures governing corporate citizens in South Africa') look for leadership in a more institutional sense, using the notion of a polestar as the central guiding principle that informs different kinds of governance structure. This chapter explores two polestars—the shareholder polestar and the stakeholder polestar—and argues that South Africa has moved from the former to the latter, which is a more appropriate approach in the African context.

Wanyama, Burton and Helliar ('Corporate governance and accountability in Uganda: a stakeholder perspective') offer another national perspective, examining the extent to which stakeholders in Uganda perceive the country's present corporate governance framework to be effective in providing confidence about the business sector. The research study concludes that, although progress has been made, gaps in accountability and perceptions of corruption still hamper attempts to develop stronger corporate governance mechanisms.

Finally, in this section, Snyckers ('Evading corporate social responsibility through tax avoidance') raises the often ignored dilemma of companies pursuing conflicting strategic goals: in this case, trying to minimise tax payment on the one hand and claiming to be good corporate citizens on the other. The chapter argues that tax compliance by companies in Africa should be central to any discussion and practice of corporate social responsibility and presents a way in which to conceptualise and justify this relationship.

The next section, on *Community and environment*, presents three chapters that emphasise the social and ecological dilemmas often faced by business in Africa. Egels-Zandén and Kallifatides ('The corporate social performance dilemma: organising for goal duality in low-income African markets') use the case study of a rural electrification project by ABB in Tanzania in order to illustrate the corporate social performance dilemma faced by many multinationals in Africa: namely, how to simultaneously achieve stakeholder legitimacy and economic growth. The chapter finds the dilemma is dealt with in practice by a partial decoupling of the project's structural and output social performances.

Hayes ('Grounding African corporate responsibility: moving the environment up the agenda') finds that, in Africa, the environment gets a relatively low priority when compared with corporate responsibility agendas in Europe and North America. The chapter builds a strong case for why the environment is an essential ingredient of corporate responsibility within a developing-country context and highlights various institutions and mechanisms that can play a role in moving environment up the African agenda.

Stiles, with Pierre Chantraine ('Voluntary initiatives and the path to corporate citizenship: struggles at the energy–environment interface in South Africa'), adds an industry-sector dimension to the environmental management debate, looking at voluntary initiatives in the context of energy and environment. The chapter finds that a recent initiative, which involves a voluntary accord on energy efficiency, provides the best available example of the historical antipathies between government and business, and between business and the environmental community.

In the section on *Health and HIV/Aids*, all three chapters adopt a case-study approach to illustrate the extent to which progress has been made (or not, as the case may be) in this critical area of corporate citizenship. Kilbourne and Porter ('The ethical governance of health: a case study of worker health in Kenyan floriculture') present a stakeholder survey on the ways in which worker health and well-being are interpreted and prioritised in the supply chain. The chapter concludes that worker health and welfare standards are not sufficiently governed or sustainable when applying transnational ethical standards without brokering a multi-sectoral approach that includes a local context of support.

Hartwig, Rosenberg and Merson ('Corporate citizenship, Aids and Africa: lessons from Bristol-Myers Squibb Company's Secure the Future') use the conceptual framework of corporate citizenship to evaluate the performance of a US$100 million project in the pharmaceutical industry aimed at finding sustainable solutions for women, children and communities affected by the HIV/Aids epidemic in Southern Africa. The chapter finds that early and continued stakeholder consultation with government officials and other local stakeholders, and transparency of goals and processes, are among the critical success factors.

Peterson and Shaw ('De Beers: managing HIV/Aids in the workplace and beyond') look at the HIV/Aids challenge from the perspective of a company and industry that is having to actively manage its impacts on business. The chapter shares successes within the De Beers HIV/Aids Programme, and speaks frankly in new areas of focus, lessons learned, and of ideas for HIV/Aids management into the future, including its implications for the African context of corporate citizenship.

The *Industries and sectors* section presents four perspectives on three sectors: mining, oil and telecommunications. Puppim de Oliveira and Ali ('Can oil corporations positively transform Angola and Equatorial Guinea?') counter popular arguments about 'Dutch disease' or the 'resource curse' that are usually associated with the oil sector. The chapter points to the emerging social responsibility and environmental movements, as well as improvements in regulation in Africa, to show how oil development could be a positive force in the continent's emerging markets.

Reichardt and Reichardt ('Tracking sustainability performance through company reports: a critical review of the South African mining sector') turn the spotlight on the sustainability reporting practices of resource companies, arguing that stakeholders need consistent and comparable performance data in order to make informed judgements. The chapter concludes that most South African mining companies are still not using the annual or sustainability report as an effective tool to build stakeholder relationships and trust.

Rajak ('The *gift* of CSR: power and the pursuit of CSR in the mining industry') looks at the same sector through a more philosophical lens and explores how CSR, seen through the metaphor of a gift, creates benefactors and recipients, which in turn builds structures for patronage and dependency. The chapter questions whether the corporate shift from philanthropy to responsibility is fact or fiction.

Finally in this section, Muthuri and Mwaura ('The digital divide and CSR in Africa: the need for corporate law reform') critically review the use of information communication technologies (ICT) as a development strategy for the continent. The chapter contends that initiatives geared towards bridging the digital divide and promoting e-government could be enhanced by reforming corporate laws in order to recognise corporate social responsibility.

The *Supply chain and SMEs* section presents three case studies to show different ways of involving smaller companies in the pursuit of corporate citizenship goals. 'T Hooft ('Up-lifting power: creating sustainable consumer-driven supply chains through innovative partnerships in Ghana') describes the creation of a public–private partnership called the Africa Sustainable Assistance Project in Ghana. The chapter distils the lessons of overcoming organisational and cultural challenges through multi-stakeholder co-operation.

Beczner, Gower and Vizzoni ('Women's gold: finding a market for Dagara shea butter') present the thinking behind a proposed project that has the goal of creating a sustainable business in Burkina Faso. The chapter explores and evaluates the various international supply chain options that would allow the establishment of an economically viable business that simultaneously creates social value and secures environmental protection in a culturally rich community.

Tesfayohannes ('Elements of SMEs' policy implementation in sub-Saharan Africa: the case of Botswana') examines why the development of SMEs has largely failed as a strategy for achieving economic diversification and sustainable development. The chapter proposes various elements of an SME policy implementation framework that would be needed to improve the effectiveness of SMEs as a corporate citizenship strategy in Africa.

In the final section, *Globalisation and conclusions*, two chapters link the corporate citizenship debate in Africa to the wider context of globalisation. Orock ('An overview of corporate globalisation and the non-globalisation of corporate citizenship in Africa') takes a critical perspective on the role of big business in Africa. The chapter argues that the marginalisation of Africa from the benefits of globalisation is largely due to the unwillingness of many multinational corporations to globalise their notions and practice of corporate citizenship from their Northern 'home' to their African 'host' countries.

Finally, McIntosh ('Treading lightly: creating harmony and co-operation in Africa') offers some reflections on what it will take for business in general, and corporate citizenship in particular, to become a significant force for positive change on the continent. The chapter concludes that companies are going to have to take their social responsibilities and the ecological limits of the planet far more seriously if they are to improve their legacy in Africa and ensure sustainability, not only on the continent but also around the world.

Africa must determine its own future, but it cannot do so unless the outside world and its diasporas pay more attention to the issues. So this book is directed to Africans *and* others, living both on the continent and abroad, who share an interest in and a passion for Africa and want to play a role in helping to tackle its challenges and embrace its opportunities. We hope that this set of thought-provoking chapters on corporate citizenship in Africa serve as a useful contribution to the growing scholarly interest in a subject that has received significant attention around the world in recent years, but only scant attention on this vast continent.

References

Beck, D., and C.C. Cowan (1996) *Spiral Dynamics: Mastering Values, Leadership, and Change* (Oxford, UK: Blackwell).

Carroll, A.B. (1991) 'The Pyramid of Corporate Social Responsibility: The Moral Management of Organizational Stakeholders', *Business Horizons* 34: 39-48.

Commission for Africa (2005) *Our Common Interest* (London: Commission for Africa).

De Jongh, D., and P. Prinsloo (2005) 'Why Teach Corporate Citizenship Differently?', *Journal of Corporate Citizenship* 18 (Spring 2005): 113-22.

Hamann, R., P. Kapelus, A. Mackenzie, P. Hollesen and D. Sonnenberg (2005) 'Corporate Citizenship, Collaboration and Local Governance as a Complex System: Lessons from Mining in South Africa, Mali, and Zambia', *Journal of Corporate Citizenship* 18 (Spring 2005): 61-73.

McIntosh, M. (2003) *Raising a Ladder to the Moon: The Complexities of Corporate Responsibility* (London: Palgrave Macmillan).

Van Marrewijk, M., and M. Werre (2002) 'Multiple Levels of Corporate Sustainability' (unpublished).

Visser, W. (1995) 'Holism: A New Framework for Thinking about Business', *New Perspectives* 7: 41-43.

—— (2006) 'Revisiting Carroll's CSR Pyramid: An African Perspective', in E.R. Pedersen and M. Hunicke (eds.), *Corporate Citizenship in Developing Countries* (Copenhagen: Copenhagen Business School Press).

—— and C. Sunter (2002) *Beyond Reasonable Greed: Why Sustainable Business Is A Much Better Idea!* (Cape Town, South Africa: Tafelberg Human & Rousseau).

2

Research on corporate citizenship in Africa

A TEN-YEAR REVIEW (1995–2005)

Wayne Visser

Universities of Nottingham and London, UK

Corporate citizenship in Africa is a critical area of scholarly enquiry, driven by the legacy of colonialism and apartheid, the human needs of the continent in the face of widespread poverty, and the trend towards improved social responsibility by multinationals in a globalising economy. Despite this growing importance, however, very little research has been done on corporate citizenship in Africa. In his introduction to the *Business Ethics: A European Review* special issue on Africa, Rossouw (2000: 225) claims that 'the first signs of academic life in business ethics on the African continent can be traced back to the 1980s', but concedes that it remains fragmented and limited.

One of the reasons why this academic discourse is both interesting and important is that corporate citizenship in Africa has its own unique features, distinctive from other regions in the world. Rossouw (2000) suggests three areas that characterise business ethics in Africa: (1) on the macro level, the influence of Africa's colonial and neo-colonial past; (2) on the meso level, the moral responsibility of business towards the reconstruction of African societies; and (3) on the micro level, the way in which individual businesses deal with affirmative action to overcome the consequences of historical racism, sexism and economic exclusion.

Visser (2006) argues that, in terms of Carroll's (1991) pyramid model of corporate social responsibility, in which the layers denote relative emphasis assigned to various responsibilities, Africa exhibits a different ordering from the classic model. Specifically, economic responsibilities still get the most emphasis, but philanthropy is given second highest priority (as opposed to legal responsibilities in the classic Carroll pyramid), followed by legal (as opposed to ethical) and then ethical (as opposed to philanthropic) responsibilities. Furthermore, he suggests that, given the ethical dilemmas faced by companies in Africa, a more dynamic and sophisticated model of corporate responsibility may be more appropriate, such as one drawing on complexity theory (McIntosh 2003).

In the first study of business ethics as an academic field in Africa, Barkhuysen and Rossouw (2000) found 77 courses and seven centres located in six countries: namely, Egypt, Ghana, Kenya, Nigeria, South Africa and Uganda. Furthermore, they identified 167 relevant publications, including 130 articles and 26 books. The majority of articles were written by South African authors, followed by authors residing outside Africa, as well as some from Kenya, Uganda and Nigeria. The content was heavily focused on descriptive and normative ethical issues.

In a review of academic research on corporate citizenship in South Africa, Visser (2005) found that, of the pre-1994 publications, most deal with the ethical investment issues relating to apartheid, while, of the post-1994 articles, many focus on the individual ethics of South African managers. Other areas of focus have included specific South African sectors (most notably mining and chemicals), socially responsible investment, stakeholder theory, small and medium-sized enterprises, corporate environmental management, sustainability reporting, corporate governance and general corporate citizenship.

While not strictly comparable owing to methodological differences, this chapter builds on these previous contributions in two ways: (1) by broadening Barkhuysen and Rossouw's exclusive focus on business ethics; and (2) by expanding Visser's previous geographic focus on South Africa.

Research method

This research is based on an electronic search of the online databases of journals in the area of corporate citizenship. Some journals—such as *The Journal of Business Ethics*, *Business Ethics Quarterly*, *Business and Society* and *Business and Society Review*—justified inclusion based on their influence, as measured by the impact factor published by the Social Science Citation Index (SSCI), and their ranking in the top 20 journals by impact factor over a number of years. This is the same as the selection approach used by Lockett *et al.* (2005) in their review of corporate social responsibility articles published in management journals.

Since these are all US-based publications, other journals were selected—including *The Journal of Corporate Citizenship* and *Business Ethics: A European Review*—to improve the geographic balance, as well as being respected journals in their own right. Finally, a number of journals—such as *Corporate Social Responsibility and Environmental Management*, *Business Strategy and the Environment*, *Organisation and Environment* and *Corporate Environmental Strategy*—were included to improve the thematic coverage of the environmental aspect of corporate citizenship.

Of course, there are African-oriented corporate citizenship articles published in other journals—for example, in the *International Affairs* special issue on Corporate

Social Responsibility in Developing Countries (May 2005; volume 81, issue 3) and in the *Development* special issue on Corporate Social Responsibility (September 2004; volume 47, issue 3). However, this review specifically targeted corporate citizenship journals to see how much African research has penetrated the core corporate citizenship academic discourse.

Table 2.1 shows the volumes and dates that are covered by the research for each journal. In the exceptional cases where these do not extend back to 1995, it is either because they were launched more recently—such as *The Journal of Corporate Citizenship*—or because they were unavailable online as far back as 1995—such as *Corporate Social Responsibility and Environmental Management, Business Strategy and the Environment, Organisation and Environment* and *Corporate Environmental Strategy*.

Journal	Volumes	Dates
Journal of Business Ethics	14(1)–60(1)	Jan 95–Aug 05
Journal of Corporate Citizenship	1–18	Spr 01–Sum 05
Business Ethics: A European Review	6(1)–14(2)	Jan 97–Apr 05
Business and Society Review	92–110(2)	Win 95–Sum 05
Eco-Management and Auditing/Corporate Social Responsibility and Environmental Management	3(1)–12 (3)	Feb 96–Sep 05
Business Ethics Quarterly	5(1)–15(3)	Jan 95–Jul 05
Business and Society	34(1)–44(2)	Apr 95–Jun 05
Corporate Environmental Strategy	5(2)–9(4)	Win 98–Dec 02
Business Strategy and the Environment	5(1)–14(4)	Mar 96–Jul/Aug 05
Organization and Environment	10(1)–18(2)	Mar 97–Jun 05

TABLE 2.1 Journal volumes included in the research on corporate citizenship in Africa (1995–2005)

The terms used for the electronic search were all the country names of Africa, as well as Africa itself. By implication, these would have to have been mentioned in either the title or the abstract in order to be selected for analysis. It is therefore possible that a few articles on corporate citizenship in Africa may have been missed if the geographical specification was not explicitly mentioned. Despite these limitations, however, the 51 articles identified represent a fairly comprehensive selection of academic research on Africa published in corporate citizenship journals over the past ten years. A full list of the articles is included in the Annex.

Key findings

Table 2.2 shows that publication of corporate citizenship research on Africa has occurred chiefly in two journals: *The Journal of Business Ethics* (JBE), which accounts for 37% of all articles, and *The Journal of Corporate Citizenship* (JCC), which accounts for 27%. This has been largely determined by the publication of special issues focused on Africa, accounting for 5 of the 19 articles, or 26%, for JBE (special issue; volume 9, issue 4; 2000), and 10 of the 14 articles, or 71%, for JCC. Although the absolute number of articles appearing in JBE is higher than JCC, the proportion of total articles published is lower, since JBE has 12 issues per year compared with JCC's four.

Journal	Number of articles	Percentage of articles
Journal of Business Ethics	19	37
Journal of Corporate Citizenship	14	27
Business Ethics: A European Review	6	12
Business and Society Review	3	6
Corporate Social Responsibility and Environmental Management/Eco-Management and Auditing	3	6
Business Ethics Quarterly	2	4
Business and Society	2	4
Corporate Environmental Strategy	2	4
Business Strategy and the Environment	0	0
Organization and Environment	0	0
Total	51	100

TABLE 2.2 Journals publishing articles on corporate citizenship in Africa (1995–2005)

The collective weight of the ethics-focused journals is the most likely explanation for the thematic dominance of business ethics as a research topic, accounting for 42% of all articles, as shown in Figure 2.1. It may also be that corporate citizenship debates have historically been framed in terms of ethics because of high-profile issues such as the injustice of colonialism and apartheid and the prevalence of corruption and fraud on the continent. It is expected that other themes, such as stakeholders, social responsibility and health and safety (including HIV/Aids) will move up the agenda as corporate citizenship increasingly addresses these issues in an African context.

Echoing previous studies, South Africa continues to dominate the geographical focus of African corporate citizenship research, representing 57% of all articles, as shown in Table 2.3. The secondary emphasis on Nigeria can be explained by the high media profile generated around corporate citizenship issues and the oil/petrochemical sector, especially focused on Shell and its impacts on the Ogoni people. It is both a sad indictment and a great opportunity that only 12 of Africa's 53 countries have had any corporate citizenship research published on them in core corporate citizenship journals.

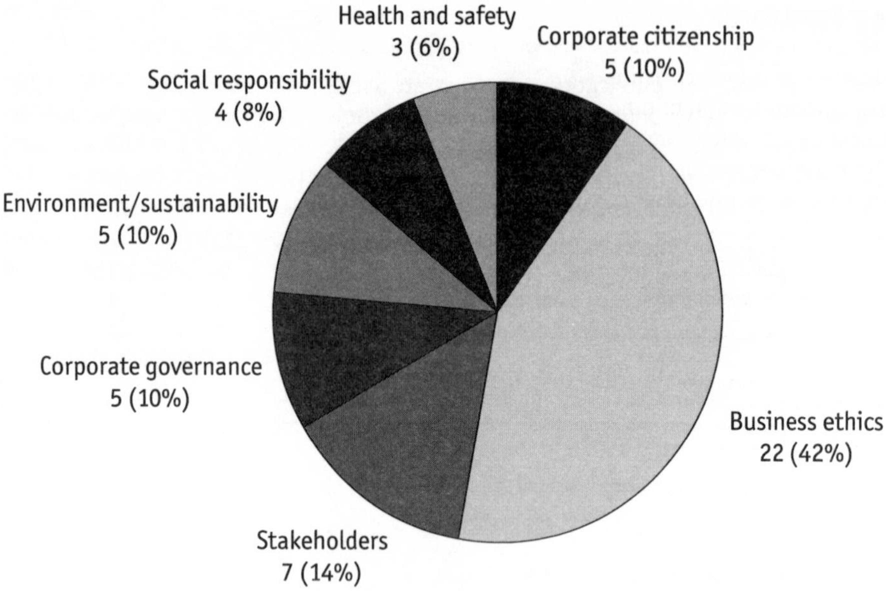

FIGURE 2.1 Thematic focus of journal articles on corporate citizenship in Africa (1995–2005)

Country	Number of articles	Percentage of articles
South Africa	28	57
Nigeria	8	16
Africa (general)	6	12
Cameroon	1	2
Côte d'Ivoire	1	2
Egypt	1	2
Kenya	1	2
Mali, South Africa and Zambia	1	2
Mauritius	1	2
Sudan	1	2
Tanzania	1	2
Zimbabwe	1	2

TABLE 2.3 Geographical focus of journal articles on corporate citizenship in Africa (1995–2005)

The most significant finding on industry sectors (Table 2.4) is that nearly two-thirds of articles (61%) have no sector orientation at all. Of those that do focus on particular industries, it is unsurprising that traditionally high-impact sectors such as petrochemicals, agriculture and mining feature heavily, while attention to areas such as education and finance is encouraging. Once again, this indicates the huge scope for new and enlightening research that critically examines the role of particular industry sectors in practising corporate citizenship.

Industry sector	Number of articles	Percentage of articles
No sector focus	31	61
Petrochemical*	5	10
Agriculture	3	6
Education	3	6
Mining	3	6
Electricity	2	4
Financial	2	4
Motor	1	2
Professionals	1	2

* Includes one article with both a petrochemical and process industry sector focus

TABLE 2.4 Industry-sector focus of journal articles on corporate citizenship in Africa (1995–2005)

Conclusion

This chapter has been included as an introduction to the book in order to frame the debate about corporate citizenship in Africa. Hopefully, the brief listing and analysis will serve as a reference point on which future scholars can draw in their own studies. There are clearly massive opportunities to increase the scale and coverage of corporate citizenship research in Africa, and especially to incorporate more thematic, geographic and sector diversity. Let us hope that, when a similar review is conducted in another ten years, the field will have developed considerably in breadth, depth and quality. For nowhere is a contribution to knowledge more urgently needed than in the pursuit of ways to effectively address the human and ecological development of Africa.

References

Barkhuysen, B., and G.J. Rossouw (2000) 'Business Ethics as an Academic Field: Its Current Status', *Business Ethics: A European Review* 9.4: 229-35.

Carroll, A.B. (1991) 'The Pyramid of Corporate Social Responsibility: Toward the Moral Management of Organizational Stakeholders', *Business Horizons* 34: 39-48.

Lockett, A., J. Moon *et al.* (2005) 'Corporate Social Responsibility in Management Research: Focus, Nature, Salience, and Sources of Influence', *Journal of Management Studies*, forthcoming .

McIntosh, M. (2003) *Raising a Ladder to the Moon: The Complexities of Corporate Responsibility* (London: Palgrave Macmillan).

Rossouw, G. (2000) 'Out of Africa: An Introduction', *Business Ethics: A European Review* 9.4: 225-28.

Visser, W. (2005) 'Corporate Citizenship in South Africa: A Review of Progress since Democracy', *Journal of Corporate Citizenship* 18: 29-38.

—— (2006) 'Revisiting Carroll's CSR Pyramid: An African Perspective', in E.R. Pedersen and M. Hunicke (eds.), *Corporate Citizenship in Developing Countries* (Copenhagen: Copenhagen Business School Press).

Annex
Journal articles on corporate citizenship in Africa: 1995–2005

Author(s)	Year	Title	Journal	Vol.(No.): pages
Abratt, R., and N Penman	2002	Understanding Factors Affecting Salespeople's Perceptions of Ethical Behaviour in South Africa	*Journal of Business Ethics*	35(4): 269-80
Ahmed, M.M., K.Y. Chung and J.W. Eichenseher	2003	Business Students' Perception of Ethics and Moral Judgement: A Cross-cultural Study	*Journal of Business Ethics*	43(1): 89-102
Ahunwan, B.	2002	Corporate Governance in Nigeria	*Journal of Business Ethics*	37(3): 269-87
Barkhuysen, B., and G. Rossouw	2000	Business Ethics as an Academic Field: Its Current Status	*Business Ethics: A European Review*	9(4): 229-35
De Jongh, D.	2004	A Stakeholder Perspective on Managing Social Risk in South Africa: Responsibility or Accountability	*Journal of Corporate Citizenship*	15: 27-31
De Jongh, D., and P. Prinsloo	2005	Why Teach Corporate Citizenship Differently?	*Journal of Corporate Citizenship*	18: 113-22
Dolan, C.S., and M. Opondo	2005	Seeking Common Ground: Multi-stakeholder Processes in Kenya's Cut Flower Industry	*Journal of Corporate Citizenship*	18: 87-98

Author(s)	Year	Title	Journal	Vol.(No.): pages
Egels, N.	2005	CSR in Electrification of Rural Africa: The Case of ABB in Tanzania	*Journal of Corporate Citizenship*	18: 75-85
Erondu, E.A., A. Sharland and J.O. Okpara	2004	Corporate Ethics in Nigeria: A Test of the Concept of an Ethical Climate	*Journal of Business Ethics*	51(4): 349-57
Eweje, G.	2005	Hazardous Employment and Regulatory Regimes in the South African Mining Industry: Arguments for Corporate Ethics at the Workplace	*Journal of Business Ethics*	56(2): 163-83
Fourie, A., and T. Eloff	2005	The Case for Collective Business Action to Achieve Systems Change: Exploring the Contributions Made by the Private Sector to the Social, Economic and Political Transformation Process in South Africa	*Journal of Corporate Citizenship*	18: 39-48
Gichure, C.	2000	Fraud and the African Renaissance	*Business Ethics: A European Review*	9(4): 236-47
Hamann, R., P. Kapelus, D. Sonnenberg, A. Mackenzie and P. Hollesen	2005	Local Governance as a Complex System: Lessons from Mining in South Africa, Mali and Zambia	*Journal of Corporate Citizenship*	18: 61-73
Hamann, R., N. Acutt and P. Kapelus	2003	Responsibility versus Accountability: Interpreting the World Summit on Sustainable Development for a Synthesis Model of Corporate Citizenship	*Journal of Corporate Citizenship*	9: 32-48
Heese, K.	2003	Black Economic Empowerment in South Africa: A Case Study of Non-inclusive Stakeholder Engagement	*Journal of Corporate Citizenship*	12: 93-101
Higgs-Kleyn, N., and D. Kapelianis	1999	The Role of Professional Codes in Regulating Ethical Conduct	*Journal of Business Ethics*	19(4): 363-74
Hill, R.	2001	Environmental Initiatives in South African Wineries: A Comparison between Small and Large Wineries	*Eco-Management and Auditing*	8(4): 210-28
Hummels, H.	1998	Organising Ethics: A Stakeholder Debate	*Journal of Business Ethics*	17(13): 1,403-19
Idahosa, P.	2002	Business Ethics and Development in Conflict (Zones): The Case of Talisman Oil	*Journal of Business Ethics*	39(3): 227-46

Author(s)	Year	Title	Journal	Vol.(No.): pages
Ite, U.E.	2004	Multinationals and Corporate Social Responsibility in Developing Countries: A Case Study of Nigeria	*Corporate Social Responsibility and Environmental Management*	11(1): 1-11
Jackson, K.T.	2000	The Polycentric Character of Business Ethics Decision Making in International Contexts	*Journal of Business Ethics*	23(1): 123-43
Kapelus, P.	2002	Mining, Corporate Social Responsibility and the 'Community': The Case of Rio Tinto, Richards Bay Minerals and the Mbonambi	*Journal of Business Ethics*	39(3): 275-96
Krummeck, S.	2000	The Role of Ethics in Fraud Prevention: A Practitioner's Perspective	*Business Ethics: A European Review*	9(4): 268-72
Kumar, R., W.B. Lamb and R.E. Wokutch	2002	The End of the South African Sanctions, Institutional Ownership, and the Stock Price Performance of Boycotted Firms	*Business and Society*	41(2): 133-65
Labuschagne, C., A.C. Brent and S.J. Claasen	2005	Environmental and Social Impact Considerations for Sustainable Project Life Cycle Management in the Process Industry	*Corporate Social Responsibility and Environmental Management*	12(1): 38-54
Limbs, E.C., and T.L. Fort	2000	Nigerian Business Practices and their Interface with Virtue Ethics	*Journal of Business Ethics*	26(2): 169-79
Geo-JaJa, M.A., and G.L. Mangum	2000	The Foreign Corrupt Practices Act's Consequences for US Trade: The Nigerian Example	*Journal of Business Ethics*	24(3): 245-55
Malan, D.	2005	Corporate Citizens, Colonialists, Tourists or Activists? Ethical Challenges Facing South African Corporations in Africa	*Journal of Corporate Citizenship*	18: 49-60
Mbohwa, C., and S. Fukada	2002	ISO 14001 Certification in Zimbabwe: Experiences, Problems and Prospects	*Corporate Environmental Strategy*	9(4): 427-36
Middleton, C.	2005	Turning Point: Interview with Michael Spicer, Chief Executive, South Africa Foundation	*Journal of Corporate Citizenship*	18: 21-24
Moskowitz, M.R.	1995	Company Performance Roundup	*Business and Society Review*	92: 66-75
Nepal, G.	2003	Ethical Decision-making in Business: Focus on Mauritius	*Business Ethics: A European Review*	12(1): 54-63

Author(s)	Year	Title	Journal	Vol.(No.): pages
Painter-Morland, M., J. Fontrodona, W.M. Hoffman and M. Rowe	2003	Conversations across Continents: Teaching Business Ethics Online	*Journal of Business Ethics*	48(1): 75-88
Prinsloo, E.D.	2000	The African View of Participatory Business Management	*Journal of Business Ethics*	25(4): 275-86
Rambharos, M.	2005	Turning Point: Managing HIV/AIDS at Eskom: A Non-negotiable for Business Sustainability	*Journal of Corporate Citizenship*	18: 25-28
Rossouw, G.	2000	Out of Africa: An Introduction	*Business Ethics: A European Review*	9(4) 225-28
Rossouw, G.J.	2000	Defining and Understanding Fraud: A South African Case Study	*Business Ethics Quarterly*	10(4): 885-95
Rossouw, G.J., A. van der Watt and D.P. Malan	2002	Corporate Governance in South Africa	*Journal of Business Ethics*	37(3): 289-302
Rossouw, G.J.	2005	Business Ethics and Corporate Governance in Africa	*Business and Society*	44(1): 94-106
Schrage, E.J., and A.P. Ewing	2005	The Cocoa Industry and Child Labour	*Journal of Corporate Citizenship*	18: 99-112
Schwartz, M.	1996	Business Ethics in Developing Countries: A Response to Rossouw	*Business Ethics Quarterly*	6(1): 111-15
Sethi, S.P.	1995	American Corporations and the Economic Future of South Africa	*Business and Society Review*	92: 10-18
Sims, R.L., and A.E. Gegez	2004	Attitudes towards Business Ethics: A Five Nation Comparative Study	*Journal of Business Ethics*	50(3): 253-65
Uys, T.	2000	The Politicisation of Whistleblowers: A Case Study	*Business Ethics: A European Review*	9(4): 259-67
Van Buren, H.J.	1996	Why Business Should Help Save the Rainforests	*Business and Society Review*	95: 22-25
Van Zyl, E., and K. Lazenby	1999	Ethical Behaviour in the South African Organisational Context: Essential and Workable	*Journal of Business Ethics*	21(1): 15-22
Van Zyl, E., and K. Lazenby	2002	The Relation between Ethical Behaviour and Work Stress amongst a Group of Managers in Affirmative Action Positions	*Journal of Business Ethics*	40(2): 111-19

Author(s)	**Year**	**Title**	**Journal**	**Vol. (No.): pages**
Visser, W.	2002	Sustainability Reporting in South Africa	*Corporate Environmental Strategy*	9(1): 79-85
Visser, W.	2005	Corporate Citizenship in South Africa: A Review of Progress since Democracy	*Journal of Corporate Citizenship*	18: 29-38
Visser, W., C. Middleton and M. McIntosh	2005	Introduction to the *Journal of Corporate Citizenship* Special Issue on Corporate Citizenship in Africa	*Journal of Corporate Citizenship*	18: 18-20
Wheeler, D., H. Fabig and R. Boele	2002	Paradoxes and Dilemmas for Stakeholder Responsive Firms in the Extractive Sector: Lessons from the Case of Shell and the Ogoni	*Journal of Business Ethics*	39(3): 297-318

Part II
Leadership and governance

3

Corporate leadership for economic, social and political change

LESSONS FROM SOUTH AFRICA*

Susan A. Lynham

Texas A&M University, USA

Robert G. Taylor

University of KwaZulu-Natal, South Africa

Larry M. Dooley

Texas A&M University, USA

Vassi Naidoo

Deloitte, Southern Africa

Throughout history, organised business has played an important part in influencing the nature of the society in which we live. In many diverse contexts and circumstances, business has acted in order to establish or support institutions or practices that are intended to provide redress in areas that are seemingly neglected by the functioning of government.

* The authors thank the following people and organisations for their invaluable assistance and sponsorship: Dr and Distinguished Professor Yvonna Lincoln, Texas A&M University; the Deloitte Foundation SA; Sue McLean, Deloitte SA; Texas A&M University International Office; and all those who participated in this study, particularly the late Arie van der Zwan.

A legitimate concern of business is the maintenance of stable economic and social circumstances. The behaviour of business is therefore conditioned by the need to develop the means whereby uncertainty and complexity can be accommodated (Taylor 2004). In the quest for stability, it remains important, however, that business should not neglect the need for moral rectitude, nor should its actions serve to contribute to the prolongation of indefensible programmes or unjust regimes. How, then, does business define a societal role for itself that is stability-enhancing but sufficiently independent of government in order to be clear about that which is morally defensible and that which is not? In essence, where and how are the boundaries of moral authority drawn in circumstances where business feels required to influence responsible social change? Where, and how, is such change most effectively exercised?

This chapter, and the study that it reports, is intended to provide some insights into these questions, using the lived experiences of South African business leadership in the decade leading up to the advent of democracy in South Africa in 1994. The lessons deriving from the experiences of that business leadership are invaluable in developing a case for corporate vigilance where complacence (and compliance) might be temptingly comfortable. The lessons of that time also help to define how the boundaries of moral authority for business might be determined.

The context for the study

Significant environmental conditions and forces that have accumulated over a number of decades in South Africa punctuate the context in which this study is situated. Although a complex and multidimensional context, this description can be divided domestically, regionally and internationally.

Domestically, the story of change really gained some intensity in 1976 with the riots that took place in Soweto Township, outside Johannesburg. Although these events in 1976 were seen to be quite catalytic, by 1980 the government of the day had seemingly restored a semblance of normality in the country mostly through ruthless action against political dissent. The economy prospered and business confidence was mostly restored. In accounts of the time, business seemed to be supportive of the achievement of a climate for business activity through the rigid maintenance of law and order (Gottschalk 1994). It would be hard to conclude that organised business was deeply involved in the process of change until after 1985, also the year in which a state of national emergency was declared. In tandem with the maintenance of intense security, government did pursue a programme of accelerated (but limited) reform during the early 1980s: for example, the advent of the tricameral parliament, which was flawed in that it did not include black South Africans in direct parliamentary representation. The United Democratic Front (UDF), an affiliate organisation of the African National Congress (ANC), emerged in 1983, essentially playing the role of denying legitimacy to this process of limited reform (Gottschalk 1994).

Regionally, government strategy involved concluding local security agreements, primarily with Mozambique and Angola. These agreements came into play in 1984. They were aimed at limiting the support of these countries for the ANC, in exchange for undertakings not to provide support to rebel movements and/or conduct military raids into these countries. This arrangement was meant to provide a cordon sanitaire for SA and its neighbours in order to provide some comfort to the citizens, hence to create a sense of security, albeit tenuous.

Internationally, the existence (and perceived threat) of communism was a significant factor. SA in the 1980s was seen to be regionally significant in the fight to defeat communism and therefore enjoyed support from the USA in particular. The ANC was portrayed by government to be strongly aligned with communism and its global purposes. Significant numbers of the ANC leadership were overtly communist.

Facing increasing international sanctions, as well as a moratorium on interactions with SA declared by the World Bank, World Trade Organisation and the United Nations, the political, social and economic environment of SA was, to say the least, an untenable one. It was in, and because of, this extremely unhealthy political environment that a relatively small group of SA business leaders came together to help influence and direct the political, economic and social changes necessary to bring an end to the practice of apartheid. The ensuing actions taken, and achievements made, by this group of business leaders was nothing less than remarkable, given the environment extant in SA at that time.

The study

This study presents some of the resulting insights on the role and nature of this unique lived experience of SA business leadership. Using a multi-year, interpretive and multi-case approach, the study was initiated and designed in 2002, and the first data were collected in 2003 involving three primary researchers.[1]

The overall objectives of the study are: (1) to reveal and understand the nature and role of the decade-long business leadership experience of a particular group of SA business leaders who played an instrumental role in the political, economic and social change necessary to move to a post-apartheid SA; and (2) to use the results to inform, adapt and develop leadership and change-leading theory, research and practice in the wider business, national and international contexts.

One main research question informed and directed the study: What was the lived experience of this particular group of SA business leaders during the mid-1980s to mid-1990s? Two further questions informed the findings presented here: What insights describe the nature of this particular experience of business leadership during the formative years of their involvement? And what insights exemplify the value-driven nature of this lived experience of business leadership?

The Consultative Business Movement (CBM), the organisation that is the focus of this study and from which the participants were purposely drawn, was conceptualised in

1 The team was purposely constructed to enrich the inquiry and interpretive strength of the study by including an indigenous insider (resident SA), an indigenous outsider (non-resident SA), and an outsider (non-SA) (Merriam *et al.* 2001). The study was designed to ensure validity and reliability, as advocated by Lincoln and Guba (1985) and Dooley (2002).

the early 1980s, formalised in the late 1980s, and disbanded in the mid-1990s.[2] The study participants were purposely selected, using snowball sampling (Spradley 1979; Lincoln and Guba 1985; Merriam 1998).[3]

The theoretical framework

Business leadership has taken many forms in the last several decades. It is our belief that the business leadership in this study closely patterns that espoused by *Servant Leadership*. According to Greenleaf (1977: 7), 'the servant-leader *is* servant first. It begins with the natural feeling that one wants to serve, to serve *first*. Then conscious choice brings one to aspire to lead.'

Most reviews of servant leadership highlight ten discernible characteristics (Spears 2000). However, in a recent review by the University of Nebraska Extension Leadership Development Center (Barbuto and Wheeler 2000), an eleventh characteristic, particularly relevant to this study, that of **calling**, emerged. These characteristics are briefly described as:

1. Calling: a natural desire to serve others, deeply rooted and value-based
2. Listening: being excellent listeners, receptive and genuinely interested in and valuing the views and input of others
3. Empathy: the ability to 'walk in others' shoes', understanding and empathising with others' circumstances and problems

2 The vision of a handful of influential business leaders, the CBM was 'formed by concerned business leaders with a national rather than a parochial agenda, and with a vision for SA based on strong values and principles' (Chapman and Hofmeyr 1994: 1). Its purpose was to '[challenge] SA business people to "define the real nature of their own power, and to identify how they [could] best use this not inconsequential power to advance the society towards non-racial democracy" ' (Nel 1988 as cited in Terreblanche 2002: 79). In 1994 it was awarded Business Statesman of the Year by the Harvard Business School Club of SA, the first time this award was made to an organisation rather than an individual. In 1991 it was singled out by Nelson Mandela as the organisation best suited to facilitate the multilateral constitutional negotiations leading up to the first free national election. This organisation, which eventually grew to a membership of 113, clearly 'made a real and permanent contribution to the well-being of the people and to the development of Southern Africa' (Andrews 1994: 1).

3 The participants were chosen according to their ability to inform four distinct perspectives on the business leadership experience under study: (1) those instrumental in forming the organisation; (2) those who worked for and joined the organisation after it had been formalised; (3) those involved in its role as facilitator of the multilateral constitutional negotiations; and (4) those who, although not direct members, had ongoing interactions with the organisation and provide invaluable outside-looking-in perspectives on this experience. The participant voices used to inform this write-up of the study outcomes fall within the first group. The length of each interview varied between one and a quarter and two and a half hours. Informed consent was obtained from each participant, including agreement to respect his or her anonymity. Hence no further description of the participants is presented.

4. Healing: a developed appreciation for the emotional health and spirit of others; the ability to create an environment that encourages emotional mending
5. Awareness: having a keen sense for what is happening around them
6. Persuasion: seeking to convince others to do things rather than using coercion; effective in building consensus within diverse groups
7. Conceptualisation: not being consumed by the need to achieve short-term operational goals
8. Foresight: being able to anticipate future events and understand the lessons from the past, realities of the present, and likely future consequences of a decision
9. Stewardship: preparing an organisation for its destiny, usually for the betterment and greater good of society
10. Growth: believing that all peoples have intrinsic value beyond the bottom line
11. Building community: demonstrating that true community can be created among those who work in businesses

The participant interview data bear a striking resemblance to the above characteristics. As we discuss the findings they can be easily related to these characteristics of servant leadership.

The findings

Sixteen themes, embodied in related principles and practices, have resulted from the data analysis. They are listed in Table 3.1. These themes represent our findings to date. Six of them (indicated by * in the table), those particularly reflective of the value-centred and servant-type nature of this business leadership experience, are expounded on. The remaining themes will be expanded in future research write-ups.

Serving as non-partisan conduits of political and national change (Table 3.1, theme 1)

Practices and principles describing this theme include:

- Demonstrating non-partisanship and consistently acting in a non-partisan manner
- Serving and acting as *shuttle diplomats*, shuttling between various partisan groups for the purpose of relationship building
- Consensus seeking, negotiated agreement and movement towards shared commitment, action and outcome

Theme number	Themes of responsible business leadership
1*	Acting as non-partisan conduits of political and national change
2*	Strictly adhering to explicitly agreed rules
3*	Building a community of shared vision and values
4	Listening deeply, in order to understand and empathise
5*	Acting from deeply held personal leadership values
6	Creating space to think and act fundamentally differently
7*	Earning trust and the authority to act
8	Building bridges through strategic conversations
9*	Being driven by business principles and values
10	Leveraging the power of quiet leadership
11	Taking immense risks and making personal sacrifices
12	Leading change, from the top
13	Engaging in critique followed by committed action
14	Leveraging a position of power
15	Recognising, attending to and leveraging driving forces in the environment
16	Recognising and responding to *tipping point* moments

TABLE 3.1 **Data themes: principles and practices of responsible business leadership**

Although it can be argued that this group of SA business leaders took a very political stand (Greenleaf 1977; Frick and Spears 1996)— against the prevailing apartheid system and form of government—they clearly understood that to be effective as change agents they had to act in as neutral a manner as possible to achieve their conciliatory aims. This neutrality became important in enabling the change agent and accompanying marginality role (Cummings and Worley 2001) later played by the organisation. Emphasised by all the participants, one described this stance and role: 'We never sought to be a principal. We always sought to be a facilitator. We didn't express a point of view, we conveyed points of view. This was our point of view' (IP3 05/15/03: 6).[4] This participant continued 'there was a neutrality, because we knew that, unless there was trust, we would never be communicating what was really going on'.

4 Citation information provided is required by the research methodology (Lincoln and Guba 1985) and refers to a particular study participant (the number of which is allocated by the researchers), e.g. IP3 for 'interview participant number 3'; the date of the interview, e.g. 05/15/03 for the interview having been conducted on 15 May 2003; and the transcript page number, e.g. p.1 for the transcript page on which the particular excerpt occurs and thus can be found in the research data.

Echoing a deep sense of awareness for business to become involved in political and national change, another participant shared:

> I had the realisation . . . that it was absolutely essential, if there was going to be any future for the country, and for my organisation and shareholders . . . to take a much more proactive line in terms of speaking up on issues on apartheid . . . trying to steer people away from the disastrous principles embodied in apartheid (IP1 07/16/03: 3-4).

Using the notion of *shuttle diplomacy* to describe their role, one participant explained:

> It was imperative that something was done in rescuing the country from the headlong rush into what could well have become a violent revolution . . . We sought to create an environment of shuttle diplomacy . . . to become people who could move from the far right to the far left and be trusted by both . . . to establish trust and credibility so that communication could occur (IP3 05/15/03: 3).

Strictly adhering to explicitly agreed rules of conduct (Table 3.1, theme 2)

Descriptive principles and practices include:

- Consistently acting from strict rules of dialogue and engagement—held and adhered to by all participating business leaders in this movement
- Having significant consequences to ongoing participation if rules are not adhered to

Describing related advice received during an early meeting with exiled members of the ANC in Zimbabwe, one participant shared:

> And they said to us, 'If you're going to do this, then your heads must not show above the parapet . . . because if that happens you'll be taken out. So, everything you do has got to be done so quietly that there are no documents, there's no formal structure, it's an informal gathering, working quietly' (IP3 05/15/03: 2).

Emphasising the significance of these rules to their role of shuttle diplomacy, and later shuttle brokering, this participant explained: '[The required nature of our role] led to the creation of a constitution and rules for moving forward . . . we keep a low profile, [and seek] no publicity. Had we sought that, I don't think it could have worked' (IP3 05/15/03: 6). He continued: 'no one sought publicity, no one sought any form of reward or grandeur. All were sharply conscious of the need to be a facilitator [of change], rather than a principal' (IP3 05/15/03: 16).

Building a community of shared vision and values (Table 3.1, theme 3)

Principles and practices that embody this theme are:

- Developing a shared vision of, and commitment to, a democratic, free South Africa in which their grandchildren, and their grandchildren's grandchildren, could live, thrive and prosper . . . socially, politically, culturally and economically
- Pursuing a humane and socially, politically and economically just South Africa for all

The notion of community, of people and purpose, is described in SA literature by the concept of *Ubuntu*: I am because you are, and you are because we are. It is about developing the spirit of a village, of realising a communal spirit and shared dreams (Mbigi and Maree 1995). This group of business leaders clearly coalesced around strongly shared beliefs about the prevailing environment in SA and their greater social responsibility as a result.

> We all saw a recipe for disaster if something were not done . . . South Africa was on the road to isolation. It was on a road to violence. And it was on a road to where its citizens were becoming the polecats of the world. Something had to be done (IP3 05/15/03: 3-4).

This participant continued:

> It was a terrible time of torture, of the infringement of human rights, of dignity, of humiliation, and of internal violence by the government. Something needed to happen. And we tried to see . . . Is there a little way in which we can help? (4-5).

This need to pursue a new outcome for the country, one that could be envisioned by all, was supported by another participant: 'we needed to see if there were ways in which we could influence the thinking of the [political] leaders . . . towards a change in approach that would be sensible for the country as a whole' (IP6 07/03/03: 10). 'There was a shared understanding of "we need to change" . . . we need to contribute to changing the system,' said another participant. 'There was a shared common purpose, without technical detail . . . and then a growing development of relationships of interdependencies, which then fuelled the common purpose again' (IP5 06/26/03: 7-8). This movement, he explained, was made up by a group of individuals who were 'willing to submerge their individual identities into a larger integrated identity, which had a common purpose, and which became [the organisation]' (12).

Acting from deeply held personal leadership values (Table 3.1, theme 5)

The essence of this theme includes the following principles and practices:

- Believing that everyone is due respect and dignity, regardless of who they are and what they do
- Acting with great humility, not seeking the rewards or recognition for their actions

Compelling personal values are an integral part of good leadership (Gardner 1990). Knowing what these are, and acting on them consistently, is imperative for responsible leadership (Lynham 2004). This sense of, and service to, greater humanity (Greenleaf 1991) is embodied in the personal leadership values described by the participants.

Reflecting on these compelling personal values, one participant said: 'You first have to develop adequate revulsion in what you want to change . . . revulsion [for] the system. And then, when the opportunity came [*sic*] . . . to have the courage to do something about it . . . and the humility and dignity to listen' (IP5 06/26/03: 18). Another elaborated:

> I concluded at a very early stage [in my career] that people really are the most important thing . . . [that to] be any good as a leader . . . it was terribly important to establish this sort of mutual, reciprocal confidence with people . . . to be accountable . . . to trust . . . to try to always get the best out of people . . . You can't earn loyalty and trust and support from people simply by asking them to support [you] (IP1 07/16/03: 1-2).

Another offered:

> I think we recognised that we had a set of principles and values that we wanted to uphold and maintain . . . respect for the individuals . . . productivity, communication . . . value for value . . . there was a need to try to redistribute wealth, but in a responsible manner (P6 07/03/03: 10).
>
> 'Leadership . . . [is about] going out of one's way to show respect for the individual, and to ask that individual: 'What do you think?' (25).

On this responsibility of leadership, one participant said:

> People are influenced by the lead they get . . . I think we must be vigilant all the time . . . the need for change . . . is an ongoing process . . . we can never assume [things] are OK . . . we can move on but we've also got to be vigilant in the process (IP1 07/16/03: 9, 14).

Another stressed the values of humility and the willingness to suspend judgement, to operate from a point of 'ignorance':

> [The] business leaders were willing to say 'We actually haven't got a clue how to get where we want to get to' . . . but they had a deep dissatisfaction with the status quo . . . [and they] had to be willing to go in open-handed (IP5 06/26/03: 3-4).

Vividly capturing the genre of the humility of this group of business leaders, one participant shared: 'If you don't mind who gets the credit there's nothing you can't do' (IP3 05/15/03: 7).

Earning trust and the authority to act (Table 3.1, theme 7)

The nature of this theme is revealed by the following principles and practices:

- Meeting with and being among the people—recognising that conversations had to include all, and having the patience and persistence to keep meeting and keep talking until change began to happen

- Earning the right to stand up and act on behalf of—earning and extending unquestionable trust, and the authority to act, from all parties and players involved.

The story of this business leadership experience compellingly exemplifies what Cohen and Bradford (1990) describe as **influence without authority**. We have come to think about this insight as reflecting the need to **earn moral authority to influence and act**, as illuminated by the following insights.

Recalling what was different about this leadership experience from others they had had during their leadership careers, one participant said: 'I very quickly found out that the sort of behaviours that I used in my business to get people to start moving and take action and think differently didn't work'. He explained,

> In a hierarchical structure your authority is first conveyed to you, and thereafter how well you continue depends on respect and trust . . . which you build with your people. Outside you don't have that advantage of the award of the initial authority. You have to build it from scratch, and it is unique (IP2 05/14/03: 28).

Clearly earning trust was an integral part of this business leadership experience, repeatedly emphasised in the interviews.

> It was a leadership that depended totally on mutual trust. And it was all about being trusted and accepted by the parties that were actually doing the job of changing the face of South Africa. It was a leadership that said: How can we best win the confidence and trust of the far right, the far left, the extremists, the middle players, and those who headed up the political movements concerned? . . . They had to know that whatever they told us, we would never breach [their] confidence, that we would convey it in a manner which would never be to their detriment, or disadvantage. The most important thing to achieve [was] to gain absolute trust across a unique spectrum . . . it had to be earned. There was a lot at stake (IP3 05/15/03: 10).

Said another of the effect of earning this trust:

> It [the organisation] had credibility . . . it was well regarded . . . on all sides . . . it became very much a sort of a clearing house . . . and very clear to all of us . . . that we were suddenly part of the process of change, and one knew that you could [now] influence things (IP1 07/16/03: 5).

Being driven by business principles and values (Table 3.1, theme 9)

The following principles and practices reflect the essence of this theme:

- Inventing and pursuing the vision and goal of 'socially responsible free enterprise'—bringing the importance of 'business with a social and national conscience' to the awareness of business colleagues, governing boards, and business partnerships, and driving business culture changing initiatives to this same end within their respective companies

- Understanding that business leadership has a responsibility beyond that of business performance, to the greater good of the environment, too

Without exception, the participants stressed the need to recognise that they were not operating from some altruistic intent. They made it very clear that their primary motivation was 'an abiding belief in free enterprise' (IP2 05/14/03: 23). This need to improve the business environment for the sake of better business performance and to attend to the primary stakeholder needs is echoed throughout leadership performance literature as a necessary, but not necessarily sufficient, outcome of responsible business leadership (Gardner 1990; Greenleaf 1991; Lynham 2004; Lynham and Chermack 2006). What is *not* unusual about this insight is that business leadership acted in *self-interest*. What *is* unusual is the way in which they did this—that, in the end, it was in service to a common national good (Greenleaf 1991; Bryson and Crosby 1992).

Extracts from one interview are especially revealing in this regard.

> We were prepared to go in conflict with this government over what we considered to be a very important issue called **freedom of association**. So we asked ourselves the question: What do we stand for? . . . And we came up with this way of describing it: **Socially responsible free enterprise** . . . free enterprise, but with a [social and national] conscience . . . A better environment for our businesses to flourish in. Not the environment that we would necessarily design, but a better environment, and that's what motivated us. An abiding belief in free enterprise . . . *really* [believing] in free enterprise, as being the right environmental mechanism in which the best [for all] will emerge (IP2 05/14/03: 7, 23).

These concerted efforts were not just externally focused, but first became integral to the business culture of the companies being led by these business leaders. In one company this change took the form of creating **An Island of Sanity and Security**: 'We were seeking to do in the country what we were doing in the company' explained one participant.

> There was so much tension in people's lives outside the company that the leadership of the company said: Can we not create within our company an island of sanity, of safety, and of peace and trust? Other business leaders who were involved [in the movement] did similar things in their companies . . . to differing extents, in differing companies (IP3 05/15/03: 12, 13).

Gradually, company by company, a new order of business in SA began to be fostered.

Implications

In the introduction to this chapter the need for business to operate in a stable context, but not at the expense of, or as tacit custodians of, indefensible sociopolitical practices, was identified. In a number of different national contexts, of which South Africa has been a significant one, business has appeared to be tacitly complicit in the moral transgressions of government. Such compliance does not necessarily derive from the will to do wrong. It derives rather from uncertainty about 'where' and 'how' the boundaries of the moral authority are determined and 'where' and 'how' business might play a role in influencing the nature and scope of that moral authority. 'Where' presupposes the will of business to resist being the vehicles for the agendas of governments that infringe on the emancipatory rights of groups and individuals. 'How' defines the means whereby engagement and influence might most effectively occur. The quietly constructive approach, akin to the approach of servant leadership, was the mode of South African business that provides valuable lessons for others.

The findings from this study provide a sense of the kind of business leadership likely to be increasingly needed in the future. Particularly relevant in the global context in which we live, we need to understand and learn from experiences of business leadership in diverse, complex and emerging national environments, such as South Africa. In order to do so we need to continue to uncloak leadership histories from these transitioning countries, encourage participants to share their experiences, and use this knowledge and understanding to inform corporate citizenship, organisational practice and leadership development theory, research and practice.

References

Andrews, A. (1994) *Business Statesman of the Year Award Address* (Johannesburg: Harvard Business School Club of South Africa).

Barbuto, J.E., and D.W. Wheeler (2000) *Becoming a Servant Leader: Do You Have What it Takes?* (File G02-1481; Lincoln, NE: Cooperative Extension, Institute of Agriculture and Natural Resources, University of Nebraska).

Bryson, J.M., and B.C. Crosby (1992) *Leadership for the Common Good: Tackling Public Problems in a Shared-Power World* (San Francisco: Jossey-Bass).

Chapman, N.T., and M. Hofmeyr (1994) 'The Most Exciting Five Years of Our Lives', unpublished address on the occasion of the CBM receiving the Harvard Businessman Award of the Year 1994 (Johannesburg, Gauteng, South Africa).

Cohen, A.R., and D.L. Bradford (1990) *Influence without Authority* (New York: John Wiley).

Cummings, T.G., and C.G. Worley (2001) *Organisation Development and Change* (Cincinnati, OH: South-Western College, 6th edn).

Dooley, L.M. (2002) 'Case Study Research and Theory Building', *Advances in Developing Human Resources* 4.3 (Special Issue on 'Theory Building in Applied Disciplines', ed. S.A. Lynham): 335-54.

Frick, D.M., and L.C. Spears (eds.) (1996) *On Becoming a Servant Leader* (San Francisco: Jossey-Bass).

Gardner, J.W. (1990) *On Leadership* (New York: The Free Press).

Gottschalk, K. (1994) 'United Democratic Front, 1983–1991: Rise, Impact and Consequences', in I. Liebenberg, F. Lortan, B. Nel and G. van der Westhuizen (eds.), *The Long March: The Story of the Struggle for Liberation in South Africa* (Pretoria, South Africa: Haum): 190-92.

Greenleaf, R.K. (1977) *Servant Leadership: A Journey into the Nature of Legitimate Power and Greatness* (New York: Paulist Press).

—— (1991) *The Servant as Leader* (Indianapolis, IN: The Robert K. Greenleaf Center).

Lincoln, Y.S., and E.G. Guba (1985) *Naturalistic Inquiry* (Beverly Hills, CA: Sage).

Lynham, S.A. (2004) 'A Theory of Responsible Leadership for Performance: Viewing Leadership as a System', in T.N. Garavan, E. Collins, M.J. Morely, R. Carbery, C. Gubbins and L. Prendeville (eds.), *Abstracts of the Fifth UFHRD/AHRD Conference* (Limerick, Ireland: The University of Limerick): 107-109.

—— and T.J. Chermack (2006) 'Responsible Leadership for Performance: A Theoretical Model and Hypotheses', *Journal of Leadership and Organization Studies* 12.4: 73-88.

Mbigi, L., and J. Maree (1995) *Ubuntu: The Spirit of African Transformation Management* (Randburg, South Africa: Knowledge Resources [Pty] Ltd).

Merriam, S.B. (1998) *Qualitative Research in Case Study Applications in Education* (San Francisco: Jossey-Bass).

——, J. Johnson-Bailey, M. Lee, Y. Kee, G. Ntseane and M. Muhamad (2001) 'Power and Positionality: Negotiating Insider/Outsider Status within and across Cultures', *International Journal of Lifelong Education* 20.5: 405-16.

Spears, L.C. (2000) 'On Character and Servant-leadership: Ten Characteristics of Effective, Caring Leaders', *Concepts and Connections* 8.3: 1-4.

Spradley, J.P. (1979) *The Ethnographic Interview* (Belmont, CA: Wadsworth).

Taylor, R. (2004) 'Leading in Uncertain Times', in T.N.A. Meyer and I. Boninelli (eds.), *Conversations in Leadership: South African Perspectives* (Gauteng, South Africa: Knowles Publishing): 162-79.

Terreblanche, S. (2002) *A History of Inequality in South Africa: 1652–2002* (Pietermaritzburg, South Africa: University of Natal Press).

4

Follow the rising polestar

AN EXAMINATION OF THE STRUCTURES GOVERNING CORPORATE CITIZENS IN SOUTH AFRICA

Angela R. Hansen and Victoria Ryan

Guiding and governing African corporate citizens

The Zulu word *ubuntu* bears likeness to another word used frequently in this chapter: the colonial term *citizenship*. Both words are associative, yet *ubuntu*, which is loosely translated as 'a person is a person through other persons', more fully expresses the African belief that no individual can stand alone in a strong society (Shutte 1993: 46). Cultural expectations regarding the rights and obligations of citizens in Africa are steeped in the spirit of this Zulu proverb. As we apply the concept of citizenship to African corporations, *ubuntu* is extended and we see that corporations also cannot stand alone in a strong society. Colonial expectations regarding corporate citizenship endow the right to operate profitably and the responsibility to accumulate and utilise capital to provide goods and services needed by society, fostering economic growth through business activities. The process of African reconstruction following decolonisation, in conjunction with the realities of the globalising business environment, has generated more progressive expectations of corporate citizenship in Africa. These expectations highlight additional obligations a company has to society, such as environmental stewardship, ethical behaviour, transparency and true commitment to society. Corporate governance is the set of practices through which a corporation actively manages its citizenship. Corporate governance practices are regulated by mechanisms external to the corporation, such as laws, regulations and expectations expressed by government and society.

As corporate governance regulation is essentially the external manifestation of the rights, responsibilities and obligations of corporate citizenship, it is clearly pertinent to investigate this regulation. Even more pertinent, perhaps, is the investigation of such regulation in one of the continent's newest and most influential democracies, South Africa. In this chapter we do so, but first we contextualise the immediacy and importance of progressive regulatory guidance of South African corporate citizens operating on a continent besieged by poverty and disease.

2005 brought Africa's plight to the forefront of the global mind as political leaders, rock stars, academics and everyday people bustled about to help Africa make progress towards the Millennium Development Goals. In London's Trafalgar Square, Nelson Mandela asked 20,000 concerned Britons to join the international coalition headed by Oxfam and to do their part to 'Make Poverty History'. Months later, thanks to Bob Geldof, Bono and the other voices of Live8, the same message echoed in song from Johannesburg to London. And, as America's 'rock star economist' Jeffrey Sachs toured the world promoting his Africa-focused book *The End of Poverty*, the G8 met in Gleneagles, Scotland, for what was heralded as 'the greatest summit for Africa ever'.[1] In Gleneagles the leaders of the world's wealthiest nations pledged debt relief and increased aid to African nations. The events of 2005 will play some part in alleviating extreme poverty on the African continent and spurring economic development. But how much of the development of Africa should be left to concerned Britons, the G8 and rock stars (economic or otherwise)? Aid to heavily indebted African nations is critical, but so is indigenous economic development, essentially expressed by the on-point and *ubuntu*-esque mantra of our time, calling for 'African solutions to African problems'.

The roots of African problems are many, but one in particular stands head and shoulders above the rest. According to the United Nations Conference on Trade and Development, Africa's 'debt problems and its resource requirements are inextricably linked to the capacity of African countries to generate capital accumulation and growth' (UNCTAD 2004: 1). Capital accumulation fostering economic growth, as previously pointed out, is a primary responsibility of corporate citizens in their quest for profit. South African corporations, like all others, have lived up to this responsibility and enjoy profits as a result.

South African corporations in the collective have become the largest contributors of foreign direct investment to the greater continent of Africa (Daniel *et al.* 2003: 379). This type of investment, largely driven by the northern expansion of South Africa's existing and established corporate citizens, is 'the catalysts of economic growth, particularly in developing countries' (Khoza and Adam 2005: 14). With expansion-based investment comes the propagation of South African corporate citizenship practices, and to the extent that these practices are considered normative by their host nations, the impact of South African foreign direct investment on the development of corporate citizenship practices in the rest of Africa cannot be understated. Owing to its relative economic prosperity and capacity for investment, South Africa sits poised to shepherd newly debt-relieved African countries into a phase of economic growth, drawing on operating practices formulated by South African corporate citizens. But do South

1 This quote has been attributed in online media to UN Secretary General Kofi Annan, as well as UK musician Bob Geldof. While the exact origin of the statement is debatable, the sentiment was widely shared in print media coverage of the Gleneagles Summit.

Africa's current corporate governance structures push corporations to be appropriate role models for the rest of the continent?

This chapter attempts to answer this first 'big question' by evaluating sample structures of corporate governance in South Africa to determine their **polestar**. The term 'polestar' is used here to describe the structural underpinning of a governance mechanism: the basic tenet of guidance offered to corporations. Although our investigation will indicate that some structures of governance are based on premises most closely aligned with colonial definitions of corporate citizenship, we suggest that many corporate governance structures in South Africa are progressive and espouse an enlightened definition of corporate citizenship, indicating that they stem from a markedly different polestar. We further suggest that this new polestar, oriented around stakeholders, is a most appropriate African solution and a worthy role model.

Structures of governance and the corporate polestar

Corporate governance structures exist to ensure that the scope and nature of corporate action is aligned with managers' fiduciary responsibilities. Some fiduciary responsibilities are explicitly defined by foundational laws governing corporate existence. Other structures defining corporate responsibility include non-law policies and codes of practice as well as the unspoken cultural expectations of society, which allow business to function by public consent. These three structures, although varied in their legal enforceability, collectively determine engagement protocol between business and society, and should thus emanate from a commonly accepted corporate polestar: one guiding principle that informs all governance structures.

To determine if this ideal is the case in South Africa, we look to the spirit of laws and other structures governing corporate citizens, as opposed to debating the merit of their technical legal features. In this process, we ask the second 'big question': for whom is the South African corporation governed? The answer to this question ultimately defines the role of business in society, and the corresponding nature of the citizenship obligation.

Commonly accepted interpretations of the role of business in society offer two corporate polestars. The first follows traditional economic theory viewing the primary responsibility of the corporation as its agency to the shareholder. This position does not explicitly recognise corporate responsibility to anyone who is not a shareholder. Laws and other governance structures that align with this position are considered to be descendant from a **shareholder polestar**. According to work published by the European Corporate Governance Institute (ECGI), the shareholder polestar drives the prevalent corporate governance systems in the United States, the United Kingdom and most Commonwealth countries, and 'relies on legal rules largely resulting from case law and on the effective legal enforcement of shareholder rights' (Goergen *et al.* 2005: 2).[2]

2 The body of case law is the court's interpretation of the rights and duties arising from the foundational laws of a jurisdiction. Case law develops over time and the judgements that form its basis reflect legal, social, political and ethical considerations.

The second approach to corporate governance acknowledges obligations to shareholders, but also recognises a corporation's responsibility to stakeholders. For our purposes, stakeholders are defined as the collection of players, including shareholders, who have a vested interest in the actions of a corporation based on their contractual and non-contractual relationships with it. This could include creditors, employees, customers, suppliers, the community and the environment. In this chapter we refer to governance approaches that consider this group as the **stakeholder polestar**, although it is sometimes referred to using other terminology.[3] Again according to the ECGI, this alternative polestar is exemplified by practices in much of Continental Europe and 'relies on codified law and emphasizes rules protecting stakeholders' (Goergen *et al.* 2005: 2).

In the following sections we will analyse the governance structures in place in South Africa, assessing their basic spirit to determine their polestar. We begin with an examination of current foundational laws in South Africa.

A shareholder foundation: South African company law

Perusal of the voluminous legal and academic text regarding South African foundational company law will leave the reader edified that laws governing the formation, existence and dissolution of companies exist to regulate the relationships between the company, its directors and its shareholders. The South African Companies Act No. 61 (Companies Act), promulgated in 1973, structured the nation's corporations during a dark time of systematic disenfranchisement of certain citizens within its borders, motivating economic sanction from the global community. Although the Companies Act has been amended since the apartheid era, its core tenets remain unchanged.

Although the Companies Act applies to public and private corporations, we consider the relevance of the Companies Act only as it applies to publicly listed companies. This application is most relevant for our analysis of governance and corporate citizenship, as publicly listed companies are prone to tension between diversely motivated principles and agents, thus necessitating explicit corporate governance structures. In addition, because the transfer of shares in publicly listed companies takes place in an open market demanding transparency, such companies are more closely scrutinised.

The Companies Act entrenches the position that directors are required to act in the best interests of the company, citing their fiduciary duty to exercise care and skill in managing the company for the benefit of shareholders. The scope of this duty has been

3 The terminology surrounding the debate on shareholders versus stakeholders is undeveloped. Authors writing on the subject choose their own terms and define them as required by their arguments. When discussing the issue, South Africa's Department of Trade and Industry in the Company Law Reform document recognises three approaches to the shareholder/stakeholder debate: the shareholder-centric approach, the enlightened shareholder value approach and the pluralistic approach (pp. 22-26). Goergen *et al.* refer to the market-based system (characterised by diversified shareholder base and clear responsibility to shareholders) and the blockholder-based system (characterised by blocks of homogeneous shareholders and increased interaction with stakeholders) to describe the polarity.

extensively interpreted in case law, and currently focuses on maximising long-term shareholder wealth, which may by default benefit stakeholders, but not to the extent that it reduces shareholder returns (DTI 2004b: 21-22). As such, it can be said that South African foundational company law originates from a shareholder polestar. For as long as this remains the case, directors may only act in the interests of stakeholders when a failure to do so would violate other policies and codes of practice or cultural expectations to such an extent that long-term shareholder value would be jeopardised.

Proponents of the shareholder polestar argue that the single-minded goal of shareholder wealth maximisation is preferable to a multi-constituency fiduciary duty (i.e. stakeholder polestar) because it allows directors to avoid increased agency cost (Bainbridge 1993: 1,433). Clearly, stakeholder engagement is not without costs. However, economists might argue that chronic unemployment, pandemic HIV/Aids and insufficient education and training also contribute cost to a corporation. It is not possible for any one sector to address issues and costs of this magnitude alone. Alignment with the stakeholder polestar suggests that increased agency costs may be necessary in South Africa, supporting the premise that meeting the needs of society is the responsibility of every citizen, corporate or individual.

Recognising the radical change that has occurred in South Africa in the past decade, the Department of Trade and Industry (DTI) has embarked on a review of South Africa's foundational company law. Preceding the DTI's work, the Institute of Directors in Southern Africa (IoDSA) assembled the King Commission in response to demands for more robust corporate governance structures. The DTI and publications emanating from the King Commission[4] evidence enlightened thinking about companies, their management and their interactions with shareholders and stakeholders. The implications for South Africa's polestar are important, and are examined in the next section.

Stakeholder transition begins: the King Report on corporate governance and company law reform

The King Report on Corporate Governance 2002 (King II Report) is a powerful contribution to the debate regarding the corporate polestar because it makes explicit the obligations of corporate directors. According to the report, directors are 'accountable' to shareholders of the company and 'responsible' to its stakeholders. Although the potentiality of legal recourse with regard to 'accountability' drives the King II Report to address these obligatory relationships separately, note that the words 'accountable' and 'responsible' are, in fact, synonyms. As we evaluate this structure of governance to determine its guiding principles, the implications of this synonymous obligation are significant.

4 The details of the DTI's work have been published in the discussion document 'South African Company Law for the 21st Century: Guidelines for Corporate Law Reform', Department of Trade and Industry (the Corporate Law Reform document), May 2004. The King Commission published two reports: *The King Report on Corporate Governance 1994* and *The King Report on Corporate Governance 2002*.

Calling on corporations to prove they are meeting broader obligations, the King II Report recommends expanded, more holistic corporate reporting to shareholders and stakeholders, noting that financial metrics are insufficient proof of obligations met. This type of holistic governance reporting takes into account social and environmental performance as well as financial performance, and is known as 'triple bottom line' reporting (IoDSA 2002: 9-10). Specifically the King II Report recommends that companies report annually on 'the nature and extent of its social, transformation, ethical, safety, health and environmental management policies and practices' (IoDSA 2002: 34). The King II Report suggests the use of the 'Global Reporting Initiative Sustainability Reporting Guidelines' (GRI Guidelines) as a tool to inform triple-bottom-line reporting activities. The GRI Guidelines, developed by a collaborating centre of the United Nations Environment Programme, encourage reporting on non-financial aspects of corporate performance in a way that 'achieves comparability, credibility, rigour, timeliness and verifiability of reported information' (GRI 2002: 65). This type of reporting is of keen interest to stakeholders and is a marked departure from traditional, shareholder-oriented reporting.

In addition, the King II Report defined the characteristics of good governance as discipline, transparency, independence, accountability, responsibility, fairness and social responsibility (IoDSA 2002: 10-11). The King II Report made these notions actionable through the creation of the Code of Corporate Practices and Conduct (King II Code). While the code provides a framework for addressing governance issues and guidelines for related action by public companies, financial and insurance entities and certain social-sector enterprises, it is not legally binding. It would be a mistake, however, to assume that, because the King II Code itself is not a law, it lacks 'teeth'; as we will see later in this chapter, the King II Code has been integrated into other structures of corporate governance, such as the JSE (Johannesburg Securities Exchange) Listing Requirements. This integration gives the principles a powerful market mechanism for enforcement. In addition, the King II Code inspired the call from the DTI for the reform of company law to make it more 'appropriate to the legal, economic and social context of South Africa as a constitutional democracy and an open economy' (DTI 2004b: 8).

The DTI's core message, published in the policy document 'South African Company Law for the 21st Century: Guidelines for Corporate Law Reform' (Reform Guidelines), is that the shareholder polestar is outdated, inappropriate and does not meet the needs of the country South Africa has become. Considering corporate law reform precedents in the United Kingdom, the DTI recognises that South Africa's laws must 'take account of stakeholders such as the community in which the company operates, its customers, its employees, its suppliers and the environment' (DTI 2004b: 26).[5]

Here, the DTI clearly makes the case for the adoption of the stakeholder polestar in South African foundational law to ensure that obligations to shareholders and stakeholders are met in tandem. In days to come debate will no doubt ensue regarding the exact nature of company law reform; however, these statements from the DTI indicate that the law will be liberalised, taking an inclusive approach to corporations, share-

5 The United Kingdom documents referred to by the DTI are 'Modernising Company Law', White Paper presented to Parliament by the Secretary of State by command of Her Majesty, July 2002 (UK DTI 2002) and 'Modern Law for a Competitive Economy: The Strategic Framework', Consultation Paper prepared by the UK Department of Trade and Industry (1999).

holders and stakeholders. Until then, the ill-fitting shareholder polestar will remain the premise of company law in South Africa.

Above the law: other structures for stakeholders

The DTI, as the primary regulator of South Africa's economic affairs, takes an enlightened approach to the management of corporations and to their role in society. This is evidenced by the DTI's call for company law reform as well as its response to other challenges facing South African society, such as the structural transformation of the economy after the fall of apartheid.

Under apartheid, black persons were excluded as shareholders and completely disregarded as stakeholders. The resulting disenfranchisement of the majority of the population has prompted government to formalise the transformation of businesses into entities representative of the nation's demographic structure and responsive to the needs of previously disadvantaged individuals. *The Broad-Based Black Economic Empowerment Act No. 35 of 2003* (BEE Act) is intended to 'increase broad-based and effective participation of black people in the economy and promote a higher growth rate, increased employment and more equitable income distribution' (BEE Act 2003: Preamble). The more specific objectives of the BEE Act include promoting black ownership and management of enterprises and increasing the extent to which black stakeholders benefit from access to 'economic activities, infrastructure and skills training' (BEE Act 2003: Section 2[b-c]).

To achieve these objectives, the BEE Act initiated the drafting of actionable codes of practice for BEE and the negotiation and drafting of charters tailored to specific industry sectors. Akin to the King II Codes adopted into the JSE Listing Requirements, the Draft Amended Codes of Good Practice on Broad-Based Black Economic Empowerment (BEE Codes) advance transparency by providing business with tools to report on their progress.[6] The BEE Codes provide a scorecard designed specifically for the South African context through which black economic empowerment activities can be measured. The scorecard focuses on three elements of performance: human resource development, indirect empowerment and direct empowerment. Examining the first two elements closely, it is clear that truly effective empowerment of stakeholders can be achieved via human resource development and indirect empowerment.

For example, by measuring human resources development and allocating companies 'BEE points' for their efforts, the scorecard promotes employment equity and skills development. Businesses tendering for government contracts are vetted in part on the points earned on their BEE scorecard, and are thus encouraged to build and empower a diverse workforce. The human resource development objective of BEE is a well-designed governance response to pressing stakeholder needs. The indirect empowerment provisions of the scorecard further address these needs by allocating points for

6 Several drafts of the Codes of Good Practice for BEE have been written, the most recent on 22 June 2005. Because this most recent draft has not yet officially been published, the December 2004 draft codes are referred to here. The authors have had sight of the June 2005 draft codes and the provisions that are relevant to this chapter have not been altered.

procurement from black economically empowered suppliers and for enterprise development of black economically empowered businesses.

Together the human resource development and indirect empowerment elements of the BEE scorecard constitute 60% of the points available on the card. Additionally, 10% of the points are allocated to a residual component (the definition of which can vary by industry) and are often gained through corporate social investment in the stakeholder community. Thus a clear majority (70%) of BEE points are allocated based on interaction with stakeholders—employees, suppliers and the broader community. This indicates the importance that government places on stakeholders and alignment to a stakeholder polestar.

The remaining 30% of the scorecard is allocated to direct empowerment, measuring black ownership and management of the business. The transfer of ownership to black persons, thereby creating black shareholders, may initially seem to place the importance of shareholders above stakeholders. However, considering the spirit of the legislation we suggest that this transfer of equity has the effect of diversifying the shareholder base and making it more representative of the South African society of stakeholders. It should be noted that direct empowerment, and the transfer of equity it necessitates, has been a problematic area of BEE. The lack of widely accessible financing for BEE deals has meant that a few wealthy black-owned corporations have been involved in many empowerment deals that have failed to deliver (in the short term, at least) broad empowerment or substantial economic benefit to more than an elite few.

This criticism aside, the spirit of the BEE Act and its attendant policies illuminates government's position regarding the interaction between business, shareholders and stakeholders. In its attempt to make South African business more representative of society and to create a new business framework, the mechanism of black economic empowerment and its implementation guidelines clearly drew inspiration from a stakeholder polestar as opposed to a shareholder polestar.

As support for the stakeholder polestar spreads in South Africa, evidence of its influence can be seen in the policies and procedures of even the most shareholder-oriented institutions. The JSE, as regulated by the Financial Services Board, has long formulated policies and procedures that it deemed necessary to protect the diversified shareholder base of publicly listed companies. Prior to 2003, the JSE Listing Requirements reflected this tradition and followed a shareholder polestar. However, the JSE turned the tide in 2003 and published amendments to the JSE Listing Requirements which formally expanded the role of directors to include their accountability to stakeholders. The amended JSE Listing Requirements require listed companies and those planning public offerings to report the extent of their compliance with the King II Code or to make public an explanation of their failure to comply.[7] In addition to making the King II Code broadly applicable, the JSE Listing Requirements have also been amended to make certain recommendations in the King II Report mandatory for listed companies. These include recommendations limiting the power of directors and fortifying the importance of shareholders. However, by requiring publicly listed companies to report on their compliance with the King II Code, the JSE expressly acknowledges the importance of

7 The JSE Listing Requirements make King II and the King II Code applicable in section 3.84 (Continuing Obligations), section 7.F.5 (Listing Particulars) and section 8.63(a) (Financial Information).

stakeholders as well (IoDSA 2002: 34). Through insistence on non-financial metrics reporting corporate performance in the areas of occupational health and safety, the environment, social investment and human resource development the JSE Listing Requirements follow a stakeholder polestar. An additional indication of the JSE's move towards a stakeholder polestar is the introduction of the JSE Socially Responsible Investment Index (SRI Index), where inclusion in the index is determined based on triple-bottom-line criteria. Although relatively few companies have been included in the SRI Index, the JSE's attention to social performance, as well as market demand for such an index, confirms support for inclusive principles of corporate citizenship following a stakeholder polestar.

Conclusion

Corporate governance in South Africa is a manifestation of corporate citizenship, which drives transparency, increases investor confidence and prescribes an inclusive approach to the role of business in society. Earlier in the chapter we posed two 'big questions' about citizenship and governance. First, we questioned the appropriateness of South African corporate citizenship as a role model to the rest of the continent. Second, we questioned the essence of these governance structures, querying for whom they indicate the corporation is governed: shareholders or stakeholders. As is often the case with interrelated questions of this magnitude, in order to answer the first question, we must first answer the second.

Our analysis of foundational laws, policies and codes of practice clearly concludes that the guiding principle of South African corporate governance has moved from the shareholder-oriented position promulgated in the apartheid-era Companies Act to a broader and more inclusive stakeholder polestar. This conclusion is supported by the explicit actions of the DTI, calling for company law reforms that would make directors responsible to stakeholders as well as to shareholders. Yet, even if there were no plans to reform foundational company law, the policies and codes of practice discussed in this chapter provide ample evidence of the shift from shareholder polestar to stakeholder polestar. The incorporation of the King II Code into the JSE Listing Requirements is one such compelling indication. Tipping the scales irrevocably in evidence of a stakeholder polestar are the empowerment mandates found in the BEE Codes. To score well on the BEE scorecard, companies must engage stakeholders through skills development, preferential procurement and business development. Although the stakeholder element of the BEE Codes is often overshadowed by the shareholder element due to high-profile equity transfer, it is in fact the case that 70% of all BEE points are allocated based on a company's treatment of stakeholders.

Therefore, the answer to our second question is this: South Africa's support of the shareholder polestar will draw to an appropriate close with the reformation of foundational company law allowing the governance structures put in place during the country's first decade of democracy to solidify the predominant role of the stakeholder polestar. Bearing this in mind, we can now address the appropriateness of corporate citizenship and governance in South Africa as a role model to the rest of the continent.

From a Zulu proverb we learned that a person is a person through other people, and in many ways, from our investigation of recently devised stakeholder-based governance structures we learned that a citizen is a citizen through other citizens. Individual or corporate, no one stands alone in a strong society. The interdependence of South African citizenship is intrinsically African. The cultural norms and expectations of society have been expressed through South Africa's democratically elected government. This government has facilitated the development of policies and code of practice that make corporate directors responsible to stakeholders. In so far as South Africa has become a model for democracy in Africa, it has also created governance structures that allow its corporate citizens to become model participants in business-sector-led economic development in the continent.

South Africa has shown its ability to be responsive: creating policy and putting forward codes of practice that increase transparency, engagement and market efficiency; in short, South Africa has exhibited the capacity to install robust corporate governance mechanisms that support active corporate citizenship. The lessons learned from the South African experience in corporate governance can and should be applied across the continent, as they truly represent African solutions to African problems. It is through solutions such as these that the continent currently characterised by darkness can achieve economic renaissance.

References

Bainbridge, S.M. (1993) 'In Defense of the Shareholder Wealth Maximization Norm', *Washington & Lee Law Review* 50 (ssrn.com/abstract=303780).

The Broad-Based Black Economic Empowerment Act No. 53 of 2003, Republic of South Africa.

The Companies Act No. 61 of 1973, Republic of South Africa.

Daniel, J., V. Naidoo and S. Naidu (2003) 'The South Africans have arrived: Post-apartheid Corporate Expansion into Africa', in J. Daniel, A. Habib and R. Southall (eds.), *State of the Nation: South Africa 2003–2004* (Cape Town: HSRC Press).

De Jongh, D. (2004) 'A Stakeholder Perspective on Managing Social Risk in South Africa: Responsibility or Accountability?', *The Journal of Corporate Citizenship* 15 (Autumn 2004): 27-32.

Department of Foreign Affairs (2001) *The New Partnership for African Development* (Pretoria: Republic of South Africa, www.dfa.gov.za).

DTI (South Africa Department of Trade and Industry) (2002) *South Africa's Economic Transformation: A Strategy for Broad Based Black Economic Empowerment* (Pretoria: Republic of South Africa, www.gov.za/ reports/2003/dtistrat.pdf).

—— (2004a) *The Draft Amended Codes of Good Practice on Broad-Based Black Economic Empowerment* (Pretoria: Republic of South Africa, www.dti.gov.za).

—— (2004b) *South African Company Law for the 21st Century: Guidelines for Corporate Law Reform* (Pretoria: Republic of South Africa, www.dti.gov.za).

Gilson, R. (2005) 'Separation and the Function of Corporation Law', Columbia Law School Law and Economics Research Paper Series, Working Paper no. 227, ssrn.com/abstract=732832, accessed 4 June 2005.

Goergen, M., M. Martynova and L. Renneboog (2005) 'Corporate Governance Convergence: Evidence from Takeover Regulation', European Corporate Governance Institute, Law Working Paper No. 33/2005; available at ssrn.com/abstract=709023.

GRI (Global Reporting Initiative) (2002) 'The Global Reporting Initiative Sustainability Reporting Guidelines', www.globalreporting.org, accessed 8 June 2005.

Hamann, R., T. Agbazue, P. Kapelus and A. Hein (2005) 'Universalizing Corporate Social Responsibility? South African Challenges to the International Organization for Standardization's New Social Responsibility Standard', *Business and Society Review* 110.1: 1-19.

IoDSA (Institute of Directors in South Africa) (2002) *King Report on Corporate Governance for South Africa* (Johannesburg: Republic of South Africa).

The JSE Securities Exchange Listing Requirements, JSE Securities Exchange, Johannesburg.

Khoza, R., and M. Adam (2005) *The Power of Governance: Enhancing the Performance of State-Owned Enterprises* (Johannesburg: Pan Macmillan and Business in Africa).

Mackenzie, C. (2004) 'Moral Sanctions: Ethical Norms as a Solution to Corporate Governance Problems', *Journal of Corporate Citizenship* 15 (Autumn 2004): 49-52.

Morrison, J. (2004) 'Legislating for Good Corporate Governance: Do we expect too much?', *Journal of Corporate Citizenship* 15 (Autumn 2004): 121-24.

OECD (Organisation for Economic Cooperation and Development) (2004) 'OECD Principles of Corporate Governance', www.oecd.org, accessed 8 June 2005.

Shutte, A. (1993) *Philosophy for Africa* (Rondebosch, South Africa: UCT Press).

UNCTAD (United Nations Conference on Trade and Development) (2004) *Economic Development in Africa. Debt Sustainability: Oasis or Mirage*? (New York: United Nations Publications).

United Kingdom Department of Trade and Industry (1999) 'Modern Law for a Competitive Economy: The Strategic Framework', Consultation Paper, www.dti.gov.uk, accessed 7 July 2005.

—— (2002) 'Modernising Company Law' White Paper presented to Parliament by the Secretary of State by command of Her Majesty, www.dti.gov.uk, accessed 7 July 2005.

5

Corporate governance and accountability in Uganda

A STAKEHOLDER PERSPECTIVE

Simeon Wanyama, Bruce M. Burton and Christine V. Helliar

University of Dundee, UK

The notion of good corporate governance (and departures therefrom) now dominates much of the world's professional and academic literature, largely as a result of various high-profile corporate scandals and failures. Although most of the attention has focused on cases in the world's richest nations (e.g. Enron, Worldcom and Parmalat), developing countries have not been immune from such difficulties. For example, Uganda has had several recent large-scale corporate failures;[1] consequently there have been various efforts made by government and private organisations to promote good governance in both the private and the public sector.

The World Bank, through the International Finance Corporation (IFC), set out to promote corporate governance throughout the world, and has sponsored and endorsed efforts to this end. Among the main results of these endeavours were the *Principles of Corporate Governance* issued by the Organisation for Economic Co-operation and Development (OECD) in 1999 (later revised in 2004). These, together with the *Commonwealth Principles* (1999) and the *Code of Corporate Practices and Conduct* (The King Committee Report of South Africa, 1999, revised in 2002) were used as a basis for draft-

1 Three indigenous banks (The Co-operative Bank, Greenland Bank and Trans Africa Bank) collapsed in 1999 while a fourth (Trust Bank), a subsidiary of a Kenyan financial institution, was closed in the same year.

ing the *Manual on Corporate Governance: Incorporating Recommended Guidelines for Uganda* (Institute of Corporate Governance of Uganda 2001).[2]

Semi-structured interviews with 16 individuals occupying various industrial, regulatory and judicial positions in Uganda were carried out during the month of September 2004, with the purpose of examining the extent to which stakeholders in Uganda perceive the country's present corporate governance framework as being effective in providing confidence about the corporate sector. Table 5.1 provides further details about the interviewees.[3] The aspects of the Ugandan corporate system that were examined included the legal, regulatory and supervisory frameworks, the political framework, the cultural framework, the ethical framework and the economic framework.

Interviewee	No.
Legislators and regulators	6
High Court Judges	2
Company secretary and legal counsel	1
Senior civil servant	1
Solicitor and senior partner	1
Former director, Central Bank of Uganda	1
Managing director of a bank	1
Partner, CPA firm	1
Other senior officials	2
Total number of interviews	16

TABLE 5.1 The interviewees (September 2004)

The state of corporate governance in Uganda and the relevance of Western models

The CEO of the ICGU expressed concern that the structures needed to support implementation of the ICGU guidelines were not in place, and that the level of implementation of the guidelines was poor. This interviewee also pointed out that the ICGU was trying to have an impact on the situation by: training senior management; conducting public-awareness lectures; adding value to organisations by sensitising people; and

2 When interviewed for the present study, the President of the Institute of Corporate Governance of Uganda (ICGU) suggested that the ICGU guidelines should be used by companies as a basis for developing their own internal rulebooks.

3 Each interview lasted for about one hour and was recorded with the permission of the interviewee. These tapes were later used in transcribing and writing up the results of the interviews.

developing appreciation of the fact that good corporate governance was inherently beneficial. He felt that the training and sensitisation seminars would have a multiplier effect arising from the dissemination of ideas by those taking part.

Because Western models of corporate governance dominate the literature, the interviewees were asked for their views about the applicability of such norms in a developing country such as Uganda. Most were of the opinion that international guidelines of corporate governance were of relevance to Uganda, citing issues such as disclosure, integrity and transparency as being universal in application. However, some interviewees observed that international guidelines had to be adapted to fit the Ugandan environment, since it was felt that one model could not fit all situations completely. In this context, factors such as the level of national economic development, corruption, sectarianism, poverty, lack of job security, unemployment and corporate ownership structure were mentioned as being likely to affect the practice of corporate governance. The specific impact of Ugandan culture and tradition was also cited. These issues are discussed in detail later in the chapter, in the context of societal and ethical influences on the Ugandan corporate governance framework.

The importance of corporate governance in a Ugandan context

The interviews also sought to explore opinions about the underlying importance of corporate governance. The good governance of Ugandan corporations was perceived as having a wide range of benefits, but was thought likely to be particularly important in terms of: the economic and social development of the country; creating wealth for shareholders; managing resources in a transparent manner; promoting accountability and corporate social responsibility; managing risk; attracting both local and foreign investment; protecting the interests of all shareholders—including minorities; and growth prospects in the corporate sector.[4] The CEO of the ICGU expressed the belief that good governance allows a company to examine its long-term sustainability and assess the extent to which value is being added to the company. He also pointed to its role in controlling management's handling of owners' resources, so that the entity is managed in line with the latter's objectives.[5]

In a similar vein, a Member of the Ugandan Parliament stressed the importance of good corporate governance as follows:

> If any company is not properly managed and it collapses or gets a problem, the effect of the corruption or poor management goes beyond the managers

4 The interviewees were unanimous in their view that the basic principles of corporate governance should apply to all companies in Uganda, whether listed or unlisted; the only difference would be in the matter of details to be disclosed.

5 This interviewee further expressed the hope that corporate governance improvements would address the issue of corruption, leading to better utilisation of scarce resources and enabling people to have a better quality of life and standard of living.

and owners of the company and affects either the government revenue in the form of lost taxes, or the employees who may lose a source of income.

The role of corporate governance: stakeholder versus agency perspectives

One of the striking findings arising from the interviews was that most of the individuals appeared to view corporate governance from a stakeholder perspective rather than as a dimension of conventional principal/agent theory. For example, the President of the Capital Markets Authority (CMA) of Uganda argued that: 'Businesses cannot operate in isolation since they operate in an environment where there are other stakeholders; businesses need the co-operation of these stakeholders in order to survive and operate profitably.'

Stakeholder theory extends the notion of corporate governance beyond the relationship between management and the shareholders to include other relevant parties that might have an interest in the operations of corporations. The theory is premised on the concept of a company as a 'person' that operates in a community, and on the view that 'there should be some explicit recognition of the well-being of other groups having a long-term association with the firm—and therefore an interest, or "stake", in its long-term success' (Keasey *et al.* 1997: 9).

In contrast, the principal–agent theory of corporate governance places good governance in the context of the relationship between management (as agents) and shareholders (as principals), and tends to limit accountability of management and the board of directors to the company as a whole and shareholders as a collective (Keasey *et al.* 1997).[6] The principal–agent perspective is broadly in line with the approach adopted in the Cadbury Report (1992) in the UK, which defined corporate governance as 'the system by which companies are directed and controlled' (para. 2.5) and specified the responsibilities of the board as including 'setting the company's strategic aims, providing the leadership to put them into effect, supervising the management of the business and reporting to shareholders on their stewardship' (para. 2.5). As noted above, however, the stakeholders who were interviewed in Uganda for the present study generally supported the stakeholder view of corporate governance.[7]

6 This standpoint was implied in the 'Caparo' Case in the UK where the House of Lords ruled that auditors owed a legal duty of care to the company and to the shareholders collectively, but not to the shareholders as individuals, nor to third parties (*Caparo Industries plc* v. *Dickman and others* [1990] ER 568).

7 The King II Report (2002) of South Africa appears to endorse the stakeholder view in embracing the following description of corporate governance given by Cadbury (1999): 'Corporate governance is concerned with holding the balance between economic and social goals and between individual and communal goals . . . the aim is to align as nearly as possible the interests of individuals, corporations and society.'

Accountability

The interviewees agreed that accountability to several stakeholders (i.e. not just shareholders) was an essential aspect of good governance, but they felt that very little accountability was evident in the current Ugandan environment, especially in public-sector corporations. A company secretary of a listed company made the following observation:

> In law, management is accountable to the company and to shareholders as a collective. However, if you look at society as a whole, depending on the nature of the industry, the industry is such that it has an impact on the environment, or it extracts its resources from the environment. Government uses revenues collected from these companies in the form of taxes to provide services to the community. The community is also the market for the products of the company. The company survives because of the broader society and not just the shareholders. Management has, therefore, to be accountable to society on how they utilise the environment.

The elements that featured most prominently in the definitions of accountability advanced by the interviewees included:

1. The provision of information to enable stakeholders to make judgements about the performance of management in running the company
2. Managerial ability to justify their actions and decisions in the pursuit of maximising shareholder value
3. Assurance that what is entrusted to a person is put to the rightful use for the benefit of whomever it is intended and as authorised (i.e. probity and legality)
4. Demonstration of proper stewardship of resources
5. Adherence to agreed budgets and programmes
6. The ability to demonstrate the reasonableness of policies followed (or not followed).

This multidimensional view of accountability is in line with Stewart's Ladder of Accountability (Stewart 1984). Stewart suggests that five levels of accountability exist:

1. Accountability for probity and legality, i.e. the extent to which funds have been used in the authorised manner and whether the powers given by law have been exceeded
2. Process accountability, which examines the extent of any waste in the use of resources, the adequacy of procedures used to perform the work and whether or not the work has been carried out as specified
3. Performance accountability, involving scrutiny of the performance of an officer or an organisation to determine whether or not the expected goals and objectives have been achieved

4. Programme accountability, which is concerned with the work carried on and whether or not it has met the goals set for the programme
5. Policy accountability, relating to the policy-setting process[8]

Although Stewart's Ladder of Accountability was devised to assess accountability in the public sector, it is also applicable to the private sector and can be used to study the various aspects of accountability in both private- and public-sector corporations.[9]

Both Stewart (1984) and Tricker (1983) argue that for accountability to exist there must be a relationship of power between the person giving the account and the person to whom the account is being given. These rights and responsibilities—which must be enforceable—stem from a situation where the subject has an obligation to explain his or her actions to someone who has the power to assess the performance of the subject and allocate praise or censure (Stewart 1984; Gray *et al.* 1996).[10] There are other rights and responsibilities which are not stated in statute or other forms of agreement; these may be absolute or relative and their establishment can be achieved only through debate, education and agreement (Gray *et al.* 1996). Although the form and substance of an account generally depends on the values, beliefs and perceptions of the person giving the account (Jackson 1982), the account should recognise the values, beliefs and perceptions of those to whom the account is given (Stewart 1984).[11]

One of the High Court Judges suggested that people in Uganda are 'docile', tending not to demand accountability from government or those in charge of running private corporations, and typically being afraid of expressing themselves freely; the interviewee argued that this encouraged officials to act with impunity. The same individual went on to indicate that the political history of Uganda might have affected people's attitudes in this manner, stating that:

> During the colonial times Ugandans used to exercise their rights through boycotts, but with the coming of military regimes people feared for their safety. Boycotts and any expression of displeasure were quickly quelled through the use of force against the demonstrators.

In summary, the views expressed throughout the interviews overwhelmingly indicate that there is a need for greater accountability (of many types, including those suggested in Stewart's ladder) in Uganda and that concrete action is required to achieve it.

8 Stewart (1984) argues further that the information and explanations provided by the officers of the organisation do not in themselves represent accountability, but merely provide the basis for judgement of whether the officers have been accountable in fulfilling their responsibilities.

9 This potential was acknowledged by Stewart (1984: 18) himself in the following words: 'This framework has been constructed for the analysis of public accountability, but can be used for other forms of accountability, such as managerial accountability and commercial accountability.'

10 The rights might stem from 'a constitution, a law, a contract, an organisational rule, a custom or even an informal obligation' (Ijiri 1975: ix). Rights may also be enshrined in quasi-legal documents such as codes of conduct, statements from authoritative bodies to whom the organisations subscribe, mission statements and other documents (Gray *et al.* 1996).

11 According to Gray (1994), the concept of accountability also reflects notions of fairness and justice.

The framework of corporate governance

Section I of the revised *OECD Principles of Corporate Governance* (OECD 2004) stresses the importance of an effective corporate governance framework in the following words: 'The corporate governance framework should promote transparent and efficient markets, be consistent with the rule of law and clearly articulate the division of responsibilities among different supervisory, regulatory and enforcement authorities.'

In the light of this multifaceted notion of corporate governance, the semi-structured interviews covered a range of related issues, including the legal, regulatory and political frameworks in Uganda, together with the economic, cultural, social and ethical factors that might have an impact on corporate governance practices.

The legal framework

The CEO of the Uganda Securities Exchange (USE) stressed that the interaction between the directors, managers and shareholders of a company had to take place according to the law of the country concerned and must ensure that: (i) no laws are violated; (ii) all shareholders (whether minority or majority owners) are protected; and (iii) issues of corporate social responsibility are addressed. In Uganda, the basic law governing the operation of all companies is The Companies Act, originally issued in 1948 and last revised in 1964.[12] Various laws and statutes governing different types of statutory corporation also exist; the Act or Statute establishing each public-sector corporation outlines the corporate governance guidelines that they are required to follow.[13] Some of the interviewees pointed out that there are various laws in Uganda which address corporate governance, but their implementation remains a major problem. It was also noted that some companies implement selective sections of the Companies Act while some private corporations find a way of getting around the requirements of the law. The laws that govern corporate governance in Uganda were perceived as either not being adequate or being outdated and needing revision; the Companies Act was singled out in this context.[14]

A Judge of the High Court of Uganda felt strongly about the need to protect employees and to pay living wages. This interviewee pointed out that, presently, there was no law covering the setting of minimum wages and that The Workers' Compensation Act (2000) was silent on this issue. Employers were, therefore, free to pay what they wanted and this state of affairs had led to exploitation, with some employees being paid 'a pittance'.

12 The Ugandan act is largely based on the British Companies Act of 1948.

13 Examples of such Acts and Statutes include: The Companies Act 1964; The National Environment Statute 1995; The Public Finance and Accountability Regulations 2003; The Public Finance and Accountability Act 2003; The Leadership Code Act 2002; The Collective Investment Schemes Act 2003; The Investment Code 1991; The Public Enterprises Reform and Divestiture Statute 1993; The Public Enterprises Reform and Divestiture (Amendment) Act 2000; The Capital Markets Authority Statute 1996; The Financial Institutions Act 2004; The Accountants Statute 1992; The Workers' Compensation Act 2000; The Uganda Registration Services Bureau Act 1998; The Uganda Securities Exchange Limited Rules 2003.

14 A number of respondents claimed that, in some cases, there was no proper consultation process before the passing of the statutes and laws governing various corporations.

Some of the interviewees argued that, although the courts were a mechanism for enforcing laws, the court system was overstretched, as the number of judges was not sufficient to handle all the pending cases expeditiously. Concern was also expressed that some members of the judiciary were being influenced by bribes when cases were brought before them.[15]

The regulatory and supervisory framework

The OECD Principles state the following regarding the supervisory and regulatory framework: 'Supervisory, regulatory and enforcement authorities should have the authority, integrity and resources to fulfil their duties in a professional and objective manner. Moreover, their rulings should be timely, transparent and fully explained' (Section I, D).

Some of the interviewees claimed that Ugandan regulatory authorities were not effective in enforcing regulations. The Registrar General outlined several problems that have an impact in this regard, but shortage of resources (including funds, personnel, transport and up-to-date technology) was the major problem faced by the Registrar's office in its effort to follow up what was happening in companies and to demand compliance. Moreover, the office was still using obsolete information systems that relied on paper files, which, considering the number of companies involved, made it difficult to keep track of developments.[16] Other factors mentioned in the interviews were: the inadequacy of fines designed to encourage compliance; ignorance of laws and regulations; lack of political will to enforce compliance; political interference with the officers charged with enforcing the laws and regulations; corruption; and insufficient training for those involved in implementing the rules and regulations.

On the whole, the respondents felt that there was a clear division of responsibilities between regulatory bodies, although in some areas more than one agency appeared to want to be involved. This situation often reflected the fact that different bodies were looking at a variety of consequences of the same event.

The political framework

The general consensus was that a nation's political environment affects the practice of corporate governance in tangible and substantive ways. The interviewees argued that factors such as the government's fiscal and monetary policies, as well as security, stability and the nature of political leadership all have a strong influence. Moreover, a stable and conducive political climate was perceived as being a prerequisite for providing assurance to the business community and stimulating investment and good governance practices. Some of the specific political factors mentioned as affecting the practice of corporate governance in Uganda were:

15 However, to date no concrete evidence has been brought to prove this allegation against judges.

16 The Registrar's office also experienced difficulties in verifying the information supplied by existing and prospective companies due to the geographical spread of companies and the insufficiency of resources. Most of the companies did not keep proper financial and other required records; this inevitably affected the quality of data collected. It was, however, hoped that the Registrar's office would soon set up a computerised record-keeping system.

1. Political interference with the work of regulatory and supervisory bodies
2. The protection of certain entities that have political connections when these entities do not comply with certain legal and regulatory requirements
3. The existence of political appointees who do not have the required qualifications and experience, or who cannot be held to account because of protection from major political figures
4. The awarding of tenders to political supporters, and the denial of business to entities critical of government

The interviewees did not have much confidence in the ability of the present Ugandan Parliament to enact laws that could assist in the practice of good governance. This belief reflected perceived corruption within parliament; there was also a feeling that some of its members were easily manipulated by the executive arm of government and that several failed to understand the concepts underlying good corporate governance.[17]

Cultural, social and ethical factors

The interviewees were of the view that cultural, social and ethical factors could all impact on the practice of corporate governance in Ugandan corporations. Appropriate attitudes towards integrity, political interference, corruption, bribery, conflicts of interest and accountability were all seen as being necessary for the development of a robust governance system. The specific cultural and social factors mentioned by the interviewees included: (i) pressure from extended families and the clan for financial support (which might encourage corruption and bribery); and (ii) respect for elders, allied to due deference to one's superiors and non-confrontation of those in authority. These issues were mentioned as having the potential to affect the demand for accountability. The practice of glorifying those who acquire wealth—irrespective of the means used to acquire it—was thought likely to encourage corruption and embezzlement of funds, while tribalism could lead to the employment of unqualified and incompetent personnel. The Chairman of Transparency International—Uganda (TI) gave the following explanation of why elders were respected and not questioned in some Ugandan cultures:

> The elders were considered to be wise and very fair; they would only make a decision after looking at all sides and so they would not need questioning. Some of our cultures are very democratic. In Karamoja, for instance, all important decisions are determined by the council of elders. However these days some people are appointed to positions of leadership on political grounds and do not have those qualities that the traditional elders had. Not questioning them would have a negative impact on good governance.

However, one of the High Court Judges felt that culture was not relevant to corporate governance and that good governance was a question of discipline and respect for the law. It is also evident from the comment made by the Chairman of TI that cultural val-

17 It was argued by some of the interviewees that parliament would do a better job if it had a recognised and credible opposition.

ues and social norms have changed over the years, reflecting influence from foreign cultures and/or as a process of normal evolution. More generally, the view of most respondents was that negative cultural and social elements in Uganda should be addressed so that good corporate governance and accountability can be enhanced in both private- and public-sector organisations.

The interviewees appeared to see a link between moral codes and governance practices, with each of the following ethical factors perceived as having a negative impact on corporate governance in Uganda:

1. Threats of a person being retrenched for exposing an official who was doing something wrong
2. Sexual harassment against staff
3. Compromising behaviour of management in dealing with junior staff
4. Political appointments that fail to take account of qualifications or competence regarding assigned duties
5. Recruitment (on other grounds) of unqualified and incompetent individuals
6. Corruption and bribery, particularly in the public sector
7. Insufficient disclosure of accounting information
8. Non-adherence to the codes of conduct governing corporations
9. A lack of qualities such as integrity, punctuality, honesty and accountability
10. The tendency of some politicians to demand favours from the officers of public-sector corporations; officers who refused to grant the favours could find themselves out of a job

It was interesting to note that, while all the interviewees believed that there should be similar ethical standards worldwide in matters relating to corporate governance, the applicability of those standards in developing (as opposed to developed) economies was often highlighted as a major problem. The following statement by the Chairman of TI summed up the perceived difficulties:

> If you take the level where we are and the level where the Americans or British are, they are up there, they understand and they have been exposed to some of these things early and they are very ethical in whatever they do and they have no pressures from friends and relatives who may not be as endowed or as privileged as they are. In our setting we are forced by circumstances to do things which someone in America is not forced to do. And even the system of controls in those countries does not allow you to go off the rails and get away with it. But here someone goes off the rails and may be running an institution or government and he does something and gets away with it. Though we should not have different standards for Uganda and the rest of the world, I think we should start with something that we can enforce.

The above statement highlights differences in checks and balances between developing countries and the Western world. In the Western world there are monitoring mechanisms such as the existence of a powerful, questioning media and the co-ordinated action of institutional investors. As a result, perceived unethical behaviour is regularly publicised, with ensuing action often taken against the corporate officers involved. Developing countries, on the other hand, do not yet appear to have effective mechanisms in place for enforcing ethical behaviour among company executives and board members. According to Ugandan cultural tradition, a council of elders enforces sanctions against anyone perceived to be acting against the interests of the community; inevitably, however, such tribal remedies are much less effective in the face of the sheer size and power of modern business organisations. There is, therefore, a need to develop effective ways of dealing with unethical behaviour in Ugandan corporations so as to enhance good governance; the extent to which Western modernistic norms are appropriate in this context is clearly an issue of important practical concern.

Economic factors

Economic factors such as the level of remuneration, poverty and inflation were seen as affecting accountability. For example, a member of parliament took the view that companies in financial distress might be tempted to manage their accounts (using unethical and illegal means) so as to give a misleading positive impression to shareholders, thereby reducing the accountability of managers. However, one of the company secretaries argued that fiscal policies such as tax regimes could also influence corporate governance. Specifically, if tax rates are considered to be too high, he argued, certain business people might try to evade the taxes by either under-declaring their profits (or the value of the goods that they import) or smuggling goods into the country.

One of the interviewees claimed that some board members were primarily concerned about getting paid and, therefore, simply accepted what the company executives told them about, or decided for, the company. This behaviour was seen as being likely to affect the board's oversight function. Some interviewees asserted that poor wages often underpinned any corrupt tendencies, especially if employees thought that they could get away with it. However, one of the High Court Judges argued as follows:

> I have come to the conclusion that you do not have to be rich to be honest and not every poor person is a thief or is corrupt. It is just greed that makes people corrupt. Whatever the case is, corruption should not be tolerated at all as it can only lead to disadvantages.

It was also pointed out that some Ugandan organisations that are struggling to survive under stiff competition might not follow good corporate governance practices. For example, a senior government official referred to the case of a multinational company that had resorted to means that were potentially unfair to customers:

> Last week the Governor of the National Bureau of Standards visited some stores that sell food products. When he visited Company X, which is a multinational supermarket, he found that the supermarket was using expired materials to bake bread which they were selling to customers in the store. One would not expect such a prestigious store to resort to such practices in order to make profits.

Summary

The interviews documented in this study suggest that much more sensitisation is needed to develop an awareness of the importance of good governance and accountability among a wide range of groups of stakeholders in Ugandan corporations. Several organisations, including the ICGU, are attempting to improve the situation, but the government itself is seen as perhaps needing to exhibit a greater will to tackle corruption—and encourage accountability and good governance—not just in words, but in practical actions. Political cronyism, vested interests and interference, as well as a lack of sufficient backing for regulatory agencies, appear to be serious obstacles to the emergence of improved governance structures in Uganda. A concerted effort was thought to be required to ensure that management and boards develop better corporate governance practices and enhance their accountability framework so that they become (and are seen to become) good corporate citizens.

In summary, there is clearly a need for the Ugandan authorities to address the issues identified in this study, and work towards a system of governance that will enhance confidence (both domestic and international) in the inherent accountability of the Ugandan corporate system. It is apparent, however, that many of the key players in the system perceive there to be a sufficiently widespread degree of corruption to make substantive improvement difficult. The priorities of the Western-based codes on corporate governance may therefore only have limited applicability for a developing nation such as Uganda. While the present study has limitations, most notably in the fact that only those willing to be interviewed took part, the results point strongly to a common view along the lines stated above and a need for action that is increasingly urgent.

References

Cadbury, A. (1999) *Corporate Governance Overview: 1999 World Bank Report* (Washington, DC: World Bank).

Cadbury Report (1992) *Report of the Committee on The Financial Aspects of Corporate Governance* (London: Gee).

Commonwealth Principles (1999) *Principles for Corporate Governance in the Commonwealth: Towards Global Competitiveness and Economic Accountability* (Marlborough, New Zealand: Commonwealth Association for Corporate Governance).

Gray, R.H. (1994) 'Accounting, the Accountancy Profession and the Environmental Crisis (or can Accounting Save the World?)', *Meditari* 2: 1-51.

——, D. Owen and C. Adams (1996) *Accounting and Accountability: Changes and Challenges in Corporate Social and Environmental Reporting* (Hemel Hempstead, UK: Prentice Hall Europe).

Ijiri, Y. (1975) *Theory of Accounting Measurement* (Sarasota, FL: American Accounting Association).

Jackson, P.M. (1982) *The Political Economy of Bureaucracy* (Oxford, UK: Philip Allan).

Keasey, K., S. Thompson and M. Wright (1997) *Corporate Governance: Economic, Management, and Financial Issues* (Oxford, UK: Oxford University Press).

King, M. (2002) *King Report on Corporate Governance for South Africa* (Parktown, South Africa: Institute of Directors in Southern Africa).

Institute of Corporate Governance of Uganda (2001) *Manual on Corporate Governance: Incorporating Recommended Guidelines for Uganda* (Kampala, Uganda: Institute of Corporate Governance of Uganda).

OECD (Organisation for Economic Co-operation and Development) (1999, revised 2004) *OECD Principles of Corporate Governance* (Paris: OECD).

Stewart, J.D. (1984) 'The Role of Information in Public Accountability', in A. Hopwood and C. Tomkins (eds.), *Issues in Public Sector Accounting* (Oxford, UK: Philip Allan).

Tricker, R. (1983) 'Corporate Responsibility, Institutional Governance and the Roles of Accounting Standards', in M. Bromwich and A.G. Hopwood (eds.), *Accounting Standards Setting: An International Perspective* (London, UK: Pitman).

6

Evading corporate social responsibility through tax avoidance

Telita Snyckers

South African Revenue Service

Paying taxes is one of the most fundamental ways in which corporate citizens engage with broader society; tax revenues are the lifeblood of the social contract vital to liberty and the market economy (Hutton 2002: 75).

While there is no agreed definition of CSR (corporate social responsibility) and corporate citizenship, what most do seem to agree on is that 'a business that makes nothing but money is a poor kind of business' (Henry Ford).

Business, like society, cannot thrive as an island of wealth in an ocean of poverty (Kofi Annan, at the World Summit on Sustainable Development 2002). This means taking seriously discussions around corporate citizenship and CSR, and support for the various appeals to business in frameworks such as the Millennium Development Goals, the European Union's Lisbon Agenda and the New Economic Partnership for Africa's Development.

Tax avoidance in an African context

Of course, in an African context, with many countries beset by social instability, social fragmentation and conflict, issues around tax compliance are perhaps understandably not regarded as a priority. As a result, tax compliance is relatively low in Africa, with most African countries suffering from a tax gap—the difference between the tax payable and that collected—of more than 40% (African Trade Policy Centre, Economic Commission for Africa 2004).

In view of the fact that the profits of tax evasion are made at the expense of local economies, and are often repatriated offshore by larger multinationals, the time is perhaps right to encourage a greater awareness of the importance of tax compliance in an African context, particularly by those corporates who are engaging in the CSR debate.

'African nations must generate their own fiscal resources in a sustainable manner for their growth and development strategies in order to advance their programmes of reclaiming dignity and fiscal sovereignty'.[1] Tax compliance is not only crucial for mustering the finances required to pay for government expenditures, but is at same time an important prerequisite for and is inevitably interlinked with good governance.

Avoiding the issue of tax in the CSR debate in an African context

The relationship between tax avoidance and evasion on the one hand, and corporate social responsibility on the other has not been the subject of much discourse. So, for example, much is made of issues such as reduction of corruption, collusion and nepotism, inadequate disclosure and insufficient transparency of financial statements, inadequate enforcement of existing rules, and a lack of clear separation of company ownership and management, yet the seemingly related areas of compliance with taxation obligations, not using aggressive tax avoidance techniques and transparency of reporting of tax planning measures are not mentioned in the numerous leading publications on corporate governance, corporate citizenship and CSR.[2]

For the purposes of this chapter, concepts such as corporate citizenship, corporate governance, CSR and regulatory compliance are regarded as interrelated and complementary, and are jointly referred to as **responsible business practices**.

Basic propositions and premises

It is submitted that a number of factors inform and influence a company's attitude towards responsible business practices. These include:

1 Trevor Manuel, address at the Official Launch of the Southern African Tax Institute (SATI), 23 June 2002.

2 See, for example, the PwC (2003) report on good governance, and the AA1000S Assurance Standard launched in March 2003 by UK-based AccountAbility to promote corporate accountability for sustainable development.

1. Patriotism and fiscal citizenship. A company's feeling of pride in and respect for its country, a willingness to sacrifice for it, and being loyal to it[3] must surely influence its behaviour insofar as responsible business practices are concerned. Combined with the concept of fiscal citizenship, corporates must be argued to owe an allegiance to government and its fiscal systems, with its concomitant rights and obligations.[4] The concept of patriotism is increasingly being raised in the context of fiscal citizenship; many authors now argue that aggressive avoidance (not to mention evasion) constitutes a distinct lack of patriotism on the part of corporates, and that creating offshore entities to avoid taxes is grossly unpatriotic[5]

2. Ethics. Similarly, a corporate's ethical motive, its motivation based on ideas of right and wrong, and reflected in the principles or assumptions underpinning the way individuals or organisations ought to conduct themselves, influence its attitude towards responsible business practices.[6] Ethical behaviour cannot exist in isolation, to be dusted off when it suits a corporate's specific agenda—it must permeate all of the corporate's dealings and activities, including the manner in which it chooses to engage with the tax system

3. Civil governance is a more contemporary trend in which the shifting balance of power between the state, market and civil society has led to new ways of providing societal direction. Government is part of a wider 'network', in an environment where policy-makers who want to encourage 'governing without government' should be interested in creating policies that encourage corporate citizenship (Zappalà 2003)

4. Available incentives. The triple bottom line will probably continue to be one of the main drivers of business, and understandably so. So, quite conceivably, the more incentives are made available in support of responsible business practices, the more such responsible practices will become entrenched. Tax policy constitutes a potential tool for supporting and advancing the cause of CSR (Philipps 2004); it is in this space that the CSR agenda should seek to explore how best to lobby and participate in the development of tax policy in advancement of the causes of CSR. In this regard the current incentives in the form of deductions from taxable income for CSR expenditure, are dealt with briefly later in this chapter

5. The regulatory environment. For the regulatory environment to have a positive impact on a corporate's attitude towards responsible business practices, it is submitted that the following minimum requirements must be met:

3 See the definitions in www.cogsci.princeton.edu/cgi-bin/webwn2.1; www.abateofcolo.org/Tips%20&%20Info/Civics%20Glossary.htm.

4 See the definitions in www.mdk12.org/mspp/vsc/social_studies/bygrade/glossary.shtml; www. ilo.org/public/ english/protection/migrant/ilmdb/ilmterms.htm.

5 www.cogsci.princeton.edu/cgi-bin/webwn2.1; www.politicalstrategy.org/Tactics/tactic_define_patriotism.htm.

6 See the definitions in www.cogsci.princeton.edu/cgi-bin/webwn2.1; www.cdc.gov/genomics/gtesting/ACCE/FBR/CF/CFGlossary2.htm; www.booksites.net/download/chadwickbeech/Glossary.htm.

- The cost of regulatory compliance should not be inhibitive
- There must be a credible threat of detection, and adequate punishment, in respect of regulatory non-compliance

A company's resultant behaviour can then be analysed, regulated, informed and influenced by a range of interrelated concepts. While there is certainly an overlap between the concepts listed below, they complement each other substantially:

1. Corporate citizenship. The World Economic Forum describes corporate citizenship as the contribution a company makes to society through its core business activities, its social investment and philanthropy programmes, and its engagement in public policy—the manner in which a company manages its economic, social and environmental relationships, and the way it engages with its stakeholders, which all have an impact on the company's long-term success. Good corporate citizenship integrates social, ethical, environmental, economic and philanthropic values in the core decision-making processes of a business

2. Corporate governance

3. Corporate social responsibility, for which of course there is a whole range of definitions

4. Regulatory compliance, i.e. the extent to which a corporate complies with the various regulatory requirements imposed on it

In this context, it becomes relatively easy to ensure that behaviour is directed towards four specific areas of interest, in terms of the company's impacts and relationships:

1. Economic impact. To this end, this chapter is premised on the view that tax evasion and aggressive tax avoidance undermine any positive impact that a corporate may make in respect of economic growth and sustainability, which is so critical in an African context, and run counter to the sentiments that underlie the concepts of corporate citizenship, corporate governance and CSR. (The extent and economic impact of tax evasion and aggressive tax avoidance are considered briefly below)

2. Social impact. Similarly, tax evasion and aggressive tax avoidance have a negative social impact and must similarly be argued to run counter to the sentiments that underlie the concepts of corporate citizenship, corporate governance and CSR

3. Environmental impact

4. Its relationship with all of its stakeholders. There can be little doubt that a revenue authority is a stakeholder in a corporate; it has a vested interest in the successes of corporates, in their sustainability and in their regulatory compliance. In particular, the revenue authority has a vested interest in the outcomes of the activities in which a corporate engages—they influence a gamut of fiscal policies, ranging from the setting of revenue targets, actual tax collections through to government spending and government's borrowing requirements Consequently, where a corporate chooses to disengage from the tax system or

to engage with it in an aggressive manner, it surely cannot be regarded as effecting the spirit and tenor underlying the interrelated concepts of corporate citizenship, corporate governance and CSR

The resultant outcomes of engaging in responsible business practices are arguably, then, attributable to the spectrum of aspects listed above, and include:

1. A positive effect on the company's financial performance
2. National competitiveness
3. A **social licence to operate**
4. Enhanced brand and market appeal
5. Increased opportunities to participate in government procurement, and being regarded as a preferred partner, which is of particular relevance on the African continent, with its many developmental states
6. Social policy complementarity. The social and environmental challenges facing society are too vast to be effectively dealt with by governments alone. Corporate citizenship is attractive to government because it can substitute, complement and/or legitimise governmental social effort and policies (Zappalà 2003). This interaction has interestingly been labelled by Richard Teather (2003) as what he terms a 'stealth tax': increasing tax rates comes with a certain amount of political risk. Of course, governments can achieve their objectives (and satisfy their various constituencies) in one of two ways: (1) by raising taxes and paying for the changes that they desire, or (2) alternatively they can achieve the same result by regulation, and by promoting agendas that are aligned to their own political agenda—such as a CSR agenda. If there is resistance to increased taxation, then politicians are likely to turn to the latter approach
7. Reduction in the negative consequences of regulatory non-compliance
8. Keeping regulation at bay

Combined, these outcomes result in increased revenue collections, and complement government's social policy, which in turn potentially reduces government's spending requirements.

Against this background, any efforts to evade or aggressively avoid the payment of taxes must surely now be regarded as evading corporate social responsibility. This interrelatedness is depicted in Figure 6.1.

Against this background, this chapter now turns to briefly consider:

- Acknowledgement of the role of CSR expenditure in tax policy
- Tax avoidance as a current norm
- The implications of tax avoidance in relation to responsible business practices

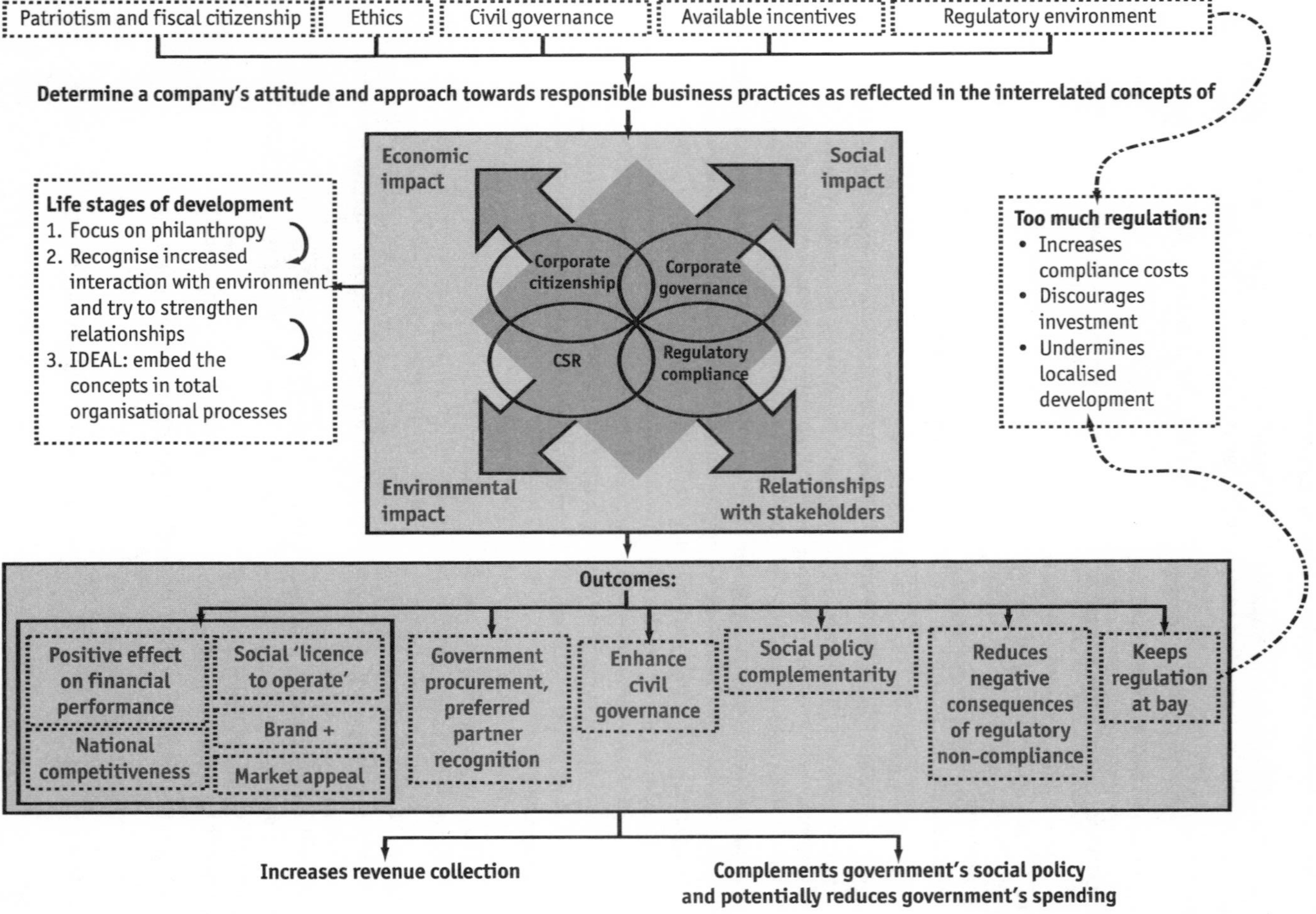

FIGURE 6.1 Interrelatedness between corporate social responsibility and tax evasion

Acknowledgement of the role of corporate social responsibility spending in tax policy

Tax policy can potentially play a positive role in supporting corporate citizenship programmes and sustainable development, by way of tax breaks and increasing deductions in respect of socially responsible spending. In the inimitable words of Lawrence Summers: 'all taxes discourage something; why not discourage bad things like pollution rather than good things like working or investment?'

Tax policy currently dictates that, under certain circumstances, CSR expenditure can be deducted from taxable income. The onus is on the taxpayer to prove that:

- The expenditure has been incurred in the production of income[7]
- The expenditure was not of a capital nature[8]
- The expenditure did not result in amounts received/accrued which are not income[9]
- The expenditure was expended for the purposes of trade[10]

Some guidance can be gleaned from recent judgements by the courts on what these requirements imply:[11]

1. Expenditure and losses must have actually been incurred in the production of income
   - Monies spent by taxpayers simply to advance the interests of their company is not expended in the production of income[12]
   - Monies spent by taxpayers from motives of 'pure liberality' is also not expenditure in the production of income[13]
2. Expenditure and losses must not be of a capital nature. Arguments supporting the contention that social responsibility spending is not of a capital nature include the following:
   - There is no question of the creation or improvement of a capital asset in the hands of the taxpayers
   - Where no new asset for the enduring benefit of the trading operation has been created any questioned expenditure naturally tends to assume more of a revenue character
   - Payments and expenditure to protect a taxpayer's earnings, to preserve it from harm, and to avert the risk of harm to an income-earning structure have been found to constitute payments of a revenue nature

7 Section 11(a) of the Income Tax Act 58 of 1962.
8 Section 11(a) of the Income Tax Act 58 of 1962.
9 Section 23(f) of the Income Tax Act 58 of 1962.
10 Section 23(g) of the Income Tax Act 58 of 1962.
11 See specifically *Warner Lambert SA (Pty) Ltd* v. *Commissioner for SARS* SCA Case number 277/02.
12 *Solaglass Finance Company (Pty) Ltd* v. *Commissioner for Inland Revenue* 1991 (2) SA 257 (A).
13 *Commissioner for Inland Revenue* v. *Pick n Pay Wholesalers (Pty) Ltd* 1987 (3) SA 453 (A).

3. The deduction will not be allowed to the extent to which the monies were not expended for the purposes of trade
   - The purpose for which expenditure was incurred is decisive[14]
   - It is easy to mistake the purpose of an act with its consequences.[15] In a tax case one is not concerned with what possibilities a taxpayer may have foreseen and with which he reconciled himself; one is solely concerned with his or her objective, or actual purpose[16]
   - To qualify as monies expended in the course of trade, an outlay does not itself have to produce a profit—such monies may well be disbursed on the grounds of commercial expediency or in order to indirectly facilitate the carrying-on of the taxpayer's trade[17]
   - Expenses incurred for the performance of a taxpayer's income producing operation, and which form part of the cost of performing such income-producing operations, are regarded as having been incurred for the purposes of trade

It is submitted that the potentially positive contribution of fiscal policy to CSR in the broader sense, and tax policy in a more limited sense, has not been canvassed sufficiently, and should form a critical part of any comprehensive discussion on CSR. In reality, the development of tax policy is currently the subject of relatively little democratic participation beyond a small circle of enthusiastic tax professionals; policy-making is potentially susceptible to regulatory capture by vested interests, effectively negating an alternative understanding of the role of relative newcomers such as CSR.

Tax avoidance: the current unpatriotic norm?

Admittedly, there is a distinction between avoidance and evasion—a line famously defined by Dennis Healey, a former UK Chancellor of the Exchequer, as being 'the width of a prison wall'. But this distinction cannot save either aggressive avoidance or evasion from scrutiny insofar as the debate about responsible business practices is concerned.

Very little work has been done in respect of tax evasion and avoidance in Africa, although we know that the average tax gap in African countries is estimated at some 40% (African Trade Policy Centre, Economic Commission for Africa 2004).

In a study carried out for the Canadian Democracy and Corporate Accountability Commission, 72% of respondents accepted the legitimacy of corporations and their right to make profits, but also wanted companies to accept a broader sense of accountability that extends beyond profit maximisation (Canadian Democracy and Corporate Accountability Commission 2002: 1). It must be argued that such a broader sense of accountability must include a commitment to paying all taxes due, with an explicit stance being taken against pursuing aggressive tax avoidance or evasion tactics.

14 *Ticktin Timbers CC* v. *Commissioner for Inland Revenue* 1999(4) SA 939 (SCA) at 942F-G.

15 ITC 1706 63 SATC 334.

16 *CIR* v. *Pick n Pay Employee Share Purchase Trust* 1992 (4) SA 39 (A).

17 *De Beers Holdings (PTY) Ltd* v. *Commissioner for Inland Revenue* 1986(1) SA 8 (A) at 36 I-J.

Seemingly, this sentiment does not reflect the current norm: that tax evasion and aggressive avoidance has become par for the course. The following examples provide a quick overview of perceptions and the pervasiveness of aggressive avoidance and evasion:

- In the case of Enron a total of 881 offshore subsidiaries were used as part of an elaborate strategy to avoid taxes (Johnston 2003). Enron generated pre-tax profits approaching US$1.8 billion but paid no income taxes and was in fact a net recipient of tax rebates
- A large number of companies, including famous brands—which were represented across Africa—such as Accenture, ExxonMobil, Hewlett-Packard, Deutsche Bank, Halliburton, Lufthansa and Deutsche Telekom, have paid legions of accounting, banking and legal practitioners to concoct schemes devised solely to launder profits to tax havens in order to avoid paying their share of taxes in the jurisdictions where they make and market their goods and services
- In the UK, 52% of the largest companies quoted on the London Stock Exchange have admitted to using 'novel tax planning ideas', a euphemism for tax avoidance schemes (Atkinson 2001)
- KPMG—which also has been amply represented across the African continent—had a complex infrastructure for devising and marketing about 500 tax-related products and acted in the knowledge that some of these products transgressed the line between avoidance and evasion. In a series of internal emails a senior US tax professional told colleagues that if regulators took action, the possible penalties were much smaller than the potential profits
- The value of assets held offshore internationally is estimated at over one-third of global GDP
- The volume of funds that pass through tax havens annually is estimated at some US$7,000 billion. This sum is greater than the value of goods and services traded through the havens, the difference being transactions of a purely financial nature (Oxfam 2000)

While tax policy could certainly be more forthcoming in respect of CSR spending, corporates have a concomitant responsibility in respect of the payment of taxes. However, driven by profit logic, and by a legal principle that suggests that taxpayers may organise their affairs in such a way as to pay the least tax possible under the law, the majority of corporates have (arguably) been structured in such a way as to enable tax avoidance in every jurisdiction in which they operate.

A number of tax avoidance mechanisms are widely known and used, such as transfer pricing, re-invoicing, offshore special-purpose vehicles, corporate inversions, dubious charitable trusts and other vehicles for tax abuse.

Aggressive avoidance and evasion tactics seem to be highly prevalent; a literature review indicates that avoidant behaviour has arguably become the norm. In fact, writers such as John Christensen and Richard Murphy go so far as to actually suggest that tax avoidance activity has become so enormous that it can reasonably be described as a shadow economy operating in the majority of globalised sectors, such as extractive industries, banking and finance, aviation, shipping, communications, pharmaceuticals, media, traded commodities and the weapons industry.

Following a series of public incidents related to unethical business practices, it seems that the court of public perception was ready to embrace a position that the ruthless pursuit of profit was out and compassionate capitalism was in (Azer 2002). Yet there are still some who question the business rationale for companies taking the moral high ground on ethical issues, as being bound to simply raise costs and divert management time.[18] Many are of the view proposed by Milton Friedman that 'business is in the business of being in business', and continue to pay homage to the doctrine of profit maximisation. So we continue to hear statements to the effect that 'The improvement on earnings is powerful enough that maybe the patriotism issue needs to take a back seat'.[19]

But, comfortingly, there are some lone voices expressing their opposition to tax evasion and aggressive avoidance by corporates. They acknowledge that the decrease in corporate tax responsibility is an indication of the rise of corporate power,[20] but are increasingly becoming disillusioned by the apparent lack of patriotism, and are now beginning to make public statements such as 'executives who want to evade taxes on income by moving their mailbox to an island and holding beach-side board meetings are entitled to a tan, not a tax break'.[21] This move towards a more patriotic view of paying taxes is reflected in the statement made to the House Ways and Means Committee in the USA, to the effect that 'we believe that it is unpatriotic for corporations to place a larger burden on other taxpayers while still benefiting from the stability and privileges this country provides'.

There is certainly a perception that corporates are particularly guilty of a distinct lack of patriotism insofar as paying taxes is concerned. To this end some are of the view that small businesses cannot avail themselves of tax havens—they cannot afford the big-name tax lawyers and accountants to show them how to do their books Enron-style—but they probably wouldn't do it anyway, because the small businesspeople do not want to renounce their citizenship.[22]

This new trend of viewing payment of taxes as being patriotic, as part of good fiscal citizenship, and as part of a corporation's social responsibility is perhaps best expressed in the words of US President George W. Bush:

> In order to usher in a culture of responsibility, corporates must be responsible, must make sure that there are no shenanigans or sleight of hands, must make sure there is an openness and disclosure about true liabilities and true assets. And if they don't, they must be held to account.

18 For example, Paul Street, Professor Emeritus of Boston University.

19 Kate Barton, Ernst & Young, quoted in *Citizen Works: Quotes on Taxes, Tax Dodging and Corporate America*, at www.citizenworks.org/corp/tax/taxdodgersquotes.php, accessed 13 April 2006.

20 Rep. Dennis Kucinich, quoted in *Citizen Works: Quotes on Taxes, Tax Dodging and Corporate America*.

21 Rep. Lloyd Doggett (D-TX), quoted in *Citizen Works: Quotes on Taxes, Tax Dodging and Corporate America*.

22 Senator Paul Wellstone (D-MN), quoted in *Citizen Works: Quotes on Taxes, Tax Dodging and Corporate America*.

Tax avoidance: impact and implications

A number of corporates operating from Africa are increasingly seeking to be domiciled offshore in countries with more tax-friendly administrations. This amounts to little more than renouncing their fiscal citizenship, which must be argued to detract from their corporate social responsibility where their true business interests lie. These fiscal termites (to borrow Tanzi's [2000] term) have enabled multinational companies to remove themselves from nationally based tax and regulatory regimes, while their capital mobility enables them to choose between different jurisdictions according to the preferential tax terms and other benefits on offer.

According to one leading developmental NGO (non-governmental organisation), the revenue losses as a result of tax competition and from non-payment of tax on flight capital amounts to at least US$50 billion annually (in respect of developing countries only, and excluding losses due to tax evasion and transfer pricing).

Tax avoidance enables companies to be economic free-riders, enjoying the benefits of corporate citizenship without accepting the costs, in the process causing harmful market distortions and shifting a larger share of the tax burden onto other taxpayers who do not have the luxury of exploiting avoidance mechanisms. Aggressive tax avoidance by companies undermines the integrity and equity of existing tax structures, it increases the administrative burden of revenue collection and, perhaps most importantly, it increases income disparities (Christensen and Hampton 2000). Local, compliant businesses, no matter whether they are technically more efficient or more innovative than their avoidant or evasive rival, will be competing on an uneven playing field.

The resulting impact on economic policy, development and sustainability is immense, compelling many countries to borrow extensively to fund revenue and capital expenditure that would otherwise be funded from tax revenues, at a substantially lower cost—borrowing that most African countries can ill afford.

No agenda to encourage responsible business practices—whether it is CSR, corporate citizenship or corporate governance—can be successful on such an uneven and inequitable playing field.

Conclusion

Ultimately, it remains to be seen whether CSR is simply yet another transitory management strategy that secures work for public relations consultants and social auditors. But any corporate that states its commitment to responsible business practices, and espouses the values underpinning corporate citizenship and CSR, cannot ethically engage in tax evasion or aggressive avoidance—to do so would be evading its corporate social responsibility.

Bibliography

African Trade Policy Centre, Economic Commission for Africa (2004) *Fiscal Implications of Trade Liberalization on African Countries*, available at www.uneca.org/atpc/Fiscal%20Implications.pdf, accessed 13 April 2006.

Atkinson, D. (2001) 'Revenue's let-off for big business', *Mail on Sunday*, 2 March 2001.

Azer, A. (2002) 'The Ethics of Corporate Social Responsibility: Management Trend of the New Millennium', available at www.chumirethicsfoundation.ca/downloads/publicpolicyfellows/azeralison/azeralison1.pdf, accessed 13 April 2006.

Canadian Democracy and Corporate Accountability Commission (2001) *An Overview of Issues*, available at www.corporate-accountability.ca, accessed 13 April 2006.

—— (2002) *The New Balance Sheet: Corporate Profits and Responsibility in the 21st Century*, available at www.corporate-accountability.ca, accessed 13 April 2006.

Christensen, J., and M.P. Hampton (2000) 'The Economics of Offshore: Who Wins, Who Loses?' *The Financial Regulator* 4.4: 24-26.

—— and R. Murphy (2004) 'The Social Irresponsibility of Corporate Tax Avoidance: Taking CSR to the Bottom Line', *Society for International Development Journal* 47.3 (September 2004).

Economist (2004) 'A Taxing Battle', *The Economist*, 31 January 2004.

Freedman, J. (2003) 'Tax and Corporate Responsibility', *The Tax Journal*, 2 June 2003.

Hampton, M.P. (1996) *The Offshore Interface: Tax Havens in the Global Economy* (Basingstoke, UK: Macmillan).

—— and J. Christensen (2003) 'A Provocative Dependence? The Global Financial System and Small Island Tax Havens', in F. Cochrane, R. Duffy and J. Selby (eds.), *Global Governance, Conflict and Resistance* (Basingstoke, UK: Palgrave Macmillan).

Hopkins, M. (1998) *A Planetary Bargain: Corporate Social Responsibility Comes of Age* (Basingstoke, UK: Macmillan).

Hutton, W. (2002) *The World We're In* (London: Little, Brown).

Malherbe, S., and N. Segal (2001) *Corporate Governance in South Africa*, available at www.oecd.org/dataoecd/9/19/2443999.pdf, accessed 13 April 2006.

Philipps, L. (2004) 'Contested Visions of Fiscal Citizenship: Innovations in Budget and Tax Policy Processes Internationally', presented at Tax Policy Research Symposium, Toronto, 2004.

PwC (2003) '17% Premium for Good Governance', available at www.pwcglobal.com/gx/eng/about/svcs/corporatereporting/WW9_Indonesia.pdf, accessed 13 April 2006.

Seidman, G.W. (2003) *Monitoring Multinationals: Lessons from the Anti-apartheid Era* (London: Sage; pas.sagepub.com/cgi/content/abstract/31/3/381, accessed 13 April 2006).

Tanzi, V. (2000) *Globalisation, Technological Developments and the Work of Fiscal Termites* (WP/00/181; Washington, DC: International Monetary Fund).

Teather, R. (2003) 'Corporate Citizenship: A Tax in Disguise', available at www.mises.org/story/1280, accessed 13 April 2005.

UN (1999) *The Social Responsibility of Transnational Corporations* (New York/Geneva: United Nations; www.unctad.org/en/docs/poiteiitm21.en.pdf).

Zappalà, G. (2003) *Corporate Citizenship and the Role of Government: The Public Policy Case* (research paper no.4 2003-04; Parliament of Australia; www.aph.gov.au/library/pubs/rp/2003-04/04rp04.htm, accessed 13 April 2006).

Additional websites visited

tdaxp.blogspirit.com/archive/2005/02/04/corporate_social_irresponsibility.html

www.aph.gov.au/library/pubs/rp/2003-04/04RP04.htm

www.business-ethics.com

www.cdc.gov/genomics

www.citizenscape.wa.gov.au

www.deakin.edu.au
www.ethicaltrade.org
www.ilo.org
www.iveybusinessjournal.com
www.politicalstrategy.org
www.smallbusinesseurope.org
www.assnat.qc.ca/eng/publications/rapports/concfp1.htm

Part III
Community and environment

7

The corporate social performance dilemma

ORGANISING FOR GOAL DUALITY IN LOW-INCOME AFRICAN MARKETS

Niklas Egels-Zandén

School of Business, Economics and Law at Göteborg University, Sweden

Markus Kallifatides

Stockholm School of Economics, Sweden

There is an emergent wave of multinational corporations (MNCs) entering low-income markets in developing countries (London and Hart 2004; Hart 2005; Prahalad 2005). Notable examples of MNCs entering low-income African markets are Ericsson, Asea Brown Boveri (ABB), Tetra Pak and The Dow Chemical Company. MNCs often enter these markets with the dual goal of gaining legitimacy and achieving growth (cf. Hart and Christensen 2002). In terms of legitimacy, MNCs strive to act as good 'corporate citizens' and to improve their legitimacy in the eyes of their most influential stakeholders in mainly the US and Europe.[1] Thus, MNCs' operations in low-income African markets become part of the trend of increased corporate emphasis on corporate social responsibility (CSR) (Waddock *et al.* 2002). In addition to legitimacy, MNCs enter low-income markets in an effort to overcome the slow growth characterising the middle- and high-

1 In this chapter, 'corporate citizenship' is defined from an empirical perspective (cf. Rowley and Berman 2000; Egels 2005). Hence, the values that MNCs further both rhetorically and in practice comprising 'corporate citizenship', and 'good corporate citizens' should be understood as a striving to improve legitimacy by furthering certain sets of values.

income markets in which they have traditionally operated (Hart and Christensen 2002).

In this chapter, we argue that this goal duality of legitimacy and growth is likely to affect MNCs' corporate social performance. Despite the potential societal impacts of the trend among MNCs to enter low-income African markets, there is little research on the CSR aspects of this trend (Egels 2005). Hence, there seems to be an unsustainable discrepancy between practice and academic research. By analysing how the drivers for MNCs to target low-income African markets affect MNCs' organisations and in turn MNCs' social performance, the chapter attempts to bridge this gap and increase our understanding of MNCs' expected societal effects in Africa.

We begin by showing, based mainly on institutional theory, that it is reasonable to expect the managerial capabilities necessary for achieving the dual goal of legitimacy and growth to be situated in different geographic and hierarchical locations in MNCs' organisational structures. We then illustrate this reasoning, and analyse its effects on MNCs' corporate social performance, in a qualitative case study of the Swedish–Swiss multinational ABB, and its rural electrification project, Access to Electricity, in Tanzania. Based on the case findings, we argue that MNCs face the corporate social performance dilemma of needing to achieve irreconcilable social performances for realising the dual goal of legitimacy and growth. The chapter concludes by discussing implications for MNCs entering low-income African markets.

Goal duality and organisational structure

There are two separate logics that MNCs need to abide by to achieve the dual goal of legitimacy and growth. In terms of legitimacy, MNCs seem to strive to respond to augmented stakeholder pressure related to CSR and to improve their somewhat tarnished reputation (Waddock *et al.* 2002). To effectively realise this intent, the stakeholders capable of conferring organisational legitimacy need to perceive MNCs' actions in low-income African markets as congruent with their values (Meyer and Rowan 1977; Pfeffer and Salancik 1978). Since only certain actors are capable of conferring legitimacy (Meyer and Scott 1983; Deephouse 1996), a key step is to identify those actors capable of conferring legitimacy in relation to CSR. Similarly to previous research on organisational legitimacy (e.g. Meyer and Scott 1983), we believe that internationally influential governmental organisations constitute the first such key stakeholder group. Additionally, and more specifically related to CSR issues, we believe that large, international non-governmental organisations (NGOs) constitute the second key stakeholder group capable of conferring legitimacy owing to their influence on public opinion (cf. Meyer and Rowan 1977; Meyer and Scott 1983; Boli and Thomas 1999). To achieve a social performance that is in line with these governmental and non-governmental organisations' demands, and hence achieve increased legitimacy, the MNC needs a manager in its African low-income market projects who is capable of presenting the firm's projects as consistent with these stakeholders' demands. It seems reasonable to expect that such managerial capabilities are most likely to be found in MNCs' international staff functions closely related to CSR.

In terms of growth, MNCs strive to realise their growth potential in low-income African markets. London and Hart (2004) argue, based on an exploratory empirical study of MNCs in low-income markets, that in order to achieve growth MNCs must leverage the strengths of the local context rather than 'Westernise' the local context to fit their existing business models. Hence, MNCs need to cast off their 'imperialistic mindset' (Prahalad and Lieberthal 1998), and develop a capability of 'social embeddedness' to successfully overcome the liability of foreignness and profitably explore low-income African markets (London and Hart 2004). This social embeddedness is achieved by leveraging the strengths of the local context, collaborating with local stakeholders and responding to local stakeholders' demands (London and Hart 2004). To achieve this, a manager is needed who is capable of understanding and leveraging the local context. Low-income markets differ from middle- and high-income markets in, for example, being characterised by an informal economy based on social rather than legal contracts, and by having poor protection of patents and brands (Delios and Henisz 2000; de Soto 2000). Furthermore, rather than, as is often assumed, necessarily being at an earlier stage of the evolutionary path to a Western-style business environment, the business environment in low-income African markets may potentially evolve along different paths (cf. Arnold and Quelch 1998; London and Hart 2004). Given these differences between low-income and middle- and high-income markets, it seems reasonable to expect that the managerial capabilities needed to leverage the local context are to be found in MNCs' local African subsidiaries closely related to the latter's operational core.

Since the managerial capabilities for achieving MNCs' dual goal of legitimacy and growth seem to be located in different hierarchical and geographic positions in the organisational structure, we propose that MNCs' projects in low-income African markets are likely to have dual project managers responsible for the projects: first, an international project manager closely related to the CSR function and in practice responsible for ensuring a social performance coherent with influential governmental and non-governmental stakeholders' demands; and, second, a local project manager closely related to the operational core of the firm's African subsidiary and in practice responsible for the operational aspects of the project.

Method

To capture how this organising for goal duality is handled in practice and how it affects MNCs' corporate social performance in low-income African markets, we make use of materials from an explorative case study of an ABB project in Ngarambe, Tanzania. The reliance on qualitative research methods is in line with the suggested methods for studying MNCs in low-income markets (London and Hart 2004), and for providing detailed descriptions of firms' corporate social performance (Winn and Angell 2000). Materials for the ABB study were collected through written documentation (e.g. webpages, email communication among the involved actors, policies, budgets, time schedules and contracts), direct observation and interviews. Thirty-four representatives from ABB and its different types of business stakeholder (e.g. Ericsson and Tetra Pak), non-governmental stakeholders (e.g. United Nations Development Programme

[UNDP], the World Bank, WWF and unions), governmental stakeholders (e.g. the Swedish International Development Co-operation Agency [SIDA] and Tanzanian government agencies), and village stakeholders, were interviewed using semi-structured interviews. With each key representative involved in the studied project in Tanzania, two to five interviews were conducted lasting on average one and a half hours. The interviews with ABB's other stakeholders lasted on average one hour. The interviews were focused on discussing ABB's Ngarambe project in general and particularly instances of conflict between various actors involved in the project. Materials were collected at three different geographic levels: international, Tanzanian and village level. Given the limited amount of written sources available at the village level, materials here were mainly collected by means of observations and interviews. In contrast, written information was heavily used at the international level.

ABB and electricity in Ngarambe

ABB's rural electrification project 'Access to Electricity' was launched at the World Summit in Johannesburg in 2002 as an ABB response to the UN Global Compact. While acting as a good corporate citizen by improving the conditions for individuals in low-income African markets and improving ABB's legitimacy in the eyes of its influential European and US stakeholders through a social initiative was part of ABB's motive for initiating 'Access to Electricity', ABB also acknowledged the currently unexplored growth potential in small-scale rural electrification around the globe. The studied sub-project in the Tanzanian village of Ngarambe was the first project under the 'Access to Electricity' umbrella. The project was launched as a not-for-profit R&D project that would provide the learning experiences essential for scaling up the 'Access to Electricity' project in a for-profit manner in other sub-Saharan African markets. ABB's chosen focus on sub-Saharan Africa was related to this region's low level of rural electrification. Of the 1.6 billion people lacking access to electricity around the globe, 500 million live in sub-Saharan Africa, making it perhaps the region most in need of electricity (IEA 2002). Additionally, 80% of those without electricity in the region live in rural areas, and 92% of the rural population lack electricity (IEA 2002).

The project's organisational structure

On an overall level, an international manager located in Sweden and hierarchically positioned directly below the ABB Senior Vice President for Sustainability Affairs was responsible for the 'Access to Electricity' project. This manager was responsible for initiating the project as a response to the UN Global Compact and selecting the village of Ngarambe in Tanzania as the site for the first sub-project (the Ngarambe project was conducted in partnership with WWF). The manager was also responsible for deciding on the use of diesel as the power source in the project, for documenting the project's aims and progress, and for communicating with international governmental and non-governmental stakeholders.

The international manager's long-term vision was to launch 'Access to Electricity' projects in several sub-Saharan countries. This was to be done through applications for subsidies to the recently created Rural Electrification Funds in, for example, Tanzania, Uganda and Senegal.[2] Due to the selection criteria of these funds and the expected fierce competition for these subsidies, ABB would have to develop a highly cost-effective business model for rural electrification to be eligible for subsidies and, hence, to be able to achieve the project goal of growth.

To develop this business model, the international manager appointed a local Tanzanian project manager for the first sub-project in Ngarambe. The local manager, an engineer in trade, had worked for ABB's subsidiary in Tanzania for several years. Within the framework developed by the international project manager (e.g. the choice of power source, partnership with WWF and the setting of the Ngarambe village), the local manager had extensive room for manoeuvring. In practice, he assumed responsibility for developing and implementing the project in Ngarambe.

The case findings illustrate the expected project structure with both an international and a local manager assigned to the project in order to achieve the dual goal of legitimacy and growth. An analysis of the communication patterns between these managers shows that the managers had a fairly sparse level of communication and that the international manager had little involvement in the practical decisions of the Ngarambe project.[3] In essence, the project seemed to proceed on two fairly disconnected geographic and hierarchical levels.

The corporate social performance dilemma

There are two main ways of classifying the 'Access to Electricity' project's social performance. First, a classification based on previously proposed definitions of corporate social performance could be made (e.g. Wood 1991). Second, an empirically derived classification could be made based on the firm's stakeholders' demands. In this chapter, we adopt the latter approach in order to be sensitive to the potential uniqueness of low-income African markets (Rowley and Berman 2000; Egels 2005).

If we analyse the demands of ABB's international governmental and non-governmental stakeholders that can be expected to be able to confer legitimacy, a fairly homogeneous stakeholder-demand pattern emerges.[4] The demands were closely related to the ten principles of the United Nations Global Compact, the International Labour Organisation's Tripartite Declaration of Principles concerning Multinational Enterprises and Social Policy, the OECD Guidelines for Multinational Enterprises, and the World Bank's criteria. The principles expressed in these documents are closely related in terms of both content and cross-references (cf. Lozano and Boni 2002). Although somewhat sketchily defined, these principles seem to constitute a fairly homogeneous

2 These Rural Electrification Funds were created by the World Bank and other international donor organisations as a way to achieve greater rural electrification in sub-Saharan Africa.

3 This conclusion is based on both an analysis of interviews with the managers and an analysis of all email communication between the managers.

4 This conclusion is based on an analysis of the interviews with ABB's influential governmental and non-governmental stakeholders as well as an analysis of the discussions at several international conferences attended by one of the authors and the international ABB project manager.

demand pallet with the ten principles of the UN Global Compact serving as a good summary of the demands. To realise the goal of increased legitimacy, we can therefore conclude that the ABB project needed to achieve a social performance well in line with the principles of the UN Global Compact.

An analysis of the Ngarambe village stakeholders' demands regarding 'Access to Electricity' shows that the villagers' demands can also be captured in the categories outlined in the UN Global Compact. However, the villagers' evaluation of these categories differed and was often in conflict with the values expressed in the UN Global Compact. Examples of differences between ABB's village and international stakeholders' demands are provided in Table 7.1. The identified conflict between international and local stakeholders' demands is probably not unique to the ABB case, since the UN Global Compact, and similar principles, were developed to overcome the 'negative' aspects that characterise, for example, Tanzanian and other low-income African markets.

Dimensions of corporate social responsibility	Demands from international stakeholders	Demands from village stakeholders
Environmental protection	Highly important	Low/medium level of importance
Women's rights	Equal to men's rights	Different type of rights
Importance of tribal and religious background	Low level of importance	High level of importance
Child labour	Low level of tolerance	Medium level of tolerance
Corruption	Low level of tolerance	Different conception of the practices involved

TABLE 7.1 **Stakeholder demands related to various dimensions of corporate social responsibility**

To achieve the 'social embeddedness' essential for realising the goal of enhanced growth by encompassing local stakeholders' demands, we can thus conclude that ABB needed to achieve a social performance in line with the village stakeholders' demands, which were partly in conflict with the UN Global Compact principles. Hence, to achieve the dual goal of legitimacy and growth by satisfying international and local stakeholders, ABB needed to be perceived as acting in accordance with irreconcilable stakeholder demands (cf. Meyer and Rowan 1977). Thus, ABB faced the corporate social performance dilemma of needing to adhere to social performances which in fact were irreconcilable.

Categorising corporate social performance: presentation and practice

To analyse how ABB handled this corporate social performance dilemma, we distinguish between the project's *structural* and *output* social performances (cf. Meyer and Rowan 1977; Mitnick 2000). Structural social performance is linked to the project's presentation (e.g. policies, reports and public statements), while output social performance is linked to the practice of the project (e.g. installation of an electricity system and recruitment of technicians). The ABB project had a *structural* performance highly correlated to ABB's influential international governmental and non-governmental stakeholders. For example, the project was launched as a response to the UN Global Compact, a commitment was made to follow the World Bank's social guidelines when applying for subsidies from the Rural Electrification Funds, numerous reports were published highlighting ABB's commitment to follow the Global Compact principles in its 'Access to Electricity' projects, and a human rights checklist is to be introduced in the next stage of the project.

The international project manager seemed to assume sole responsibility for the project's structural social performance. This is, for example, illustrated by the fact that neither the Tanzanian project manager nor the Tanzanian project team participated in creating the documentation for the project or in communicating with international stakeholders. Hence, the international manager acted as a gatekeeper to ABB's international stakeholders with all information being channelled through him. Based on our analysis of ABB's structural social performance and the interviews with ABB's internationally influential stakeholders, a tentative inference is that the international project manager succeeded in both achieving a structural social performance congruent with these stakeholders' demands and enhancing ABB's legitimacy in relation to corporate social responsibility.

The *output* social performance of the project, on the other hand, was mainly directed by the local Tanzanian project manager. This project manager was relatively successful in 'socially embedding' the project in the village context by both encompassing local stakeholders' demands and building on the strengths of the local context to develop a cost-effective business model. For example, the local manager dug down distribution cables between the engine and the houses to protect the local wildlife, distributed unofficial payments to the village head-technician and the villagers digging trenches for the distribution cables, and utilised a cheaper type of distribution cable that was safe and adequate for the purpose of the project but below national Tanzanian standards. However, the local manager also contested some of the local stakeholders' demands by, for example, installing an electricity system despite protests from the village's traditional medicine man, providing electricity based on proximity to the engine and financial capability rather than based on villagers' hierarchical position, and recruiting a Christian head-technician without permanent village citizenship rather than the village elders' relatives. All in all, the result of this encompassing and contesting of village stakeholders' demands was that the project's output social performance ended up as a trade-off between the international and local stakeholders' demands.

A comparison between the project's structural and output social performances highlights a partial *decoupling* of different types of social performance (cf. Meyer and Rowan 1977). While the structural performance was consistently aligned with the international stakeholders' demands, the output performance was more aligned with the local stakeholders' demands.

Explaining the partially decoupled corporate social performance

The main explanation for the decoupling of the project's structural and output social performances is to be found in ABB's goal duality of legitimacy and growth leading to a hierarchical and geographic separation of the loci of control for the project's social performance. While the international manager explicitly focused on the project's legitimacy and structural social performance, the local project manager seemed to have paid limited attention to corporate responsibility aspects and instead focused on successfully installing an operational electricity system in order to achieve growth. The local manager's activities can be described by the principle of 'expedient action' aimed at finding practical solutions to the problems occurring, rather than acting in a consistent way in terms of any fixed (moral, political or religious) definition of, for example, 'corporate social responsibility'; that is, typically managerial action (e.g. Jackall 1988; Watson 1994). Based on this plebeian rationale for action, it is not surprising that the output social performance was less consistent than the structural social performance and more in line with local stakeholders' demands.

Although the project's structural and output social performances were partially decoupled, there was still strong alignment between them. Hence, despite the separation of loci of control due to goal duality, the limited communication between the international and local managers, and the local manager's focus on the technical aspects of the project, several aspects of the project's structural social performance were met in output practice. The most obvious aspect of this is, of course, that there now is an electrical system up and running in Ngarambe. We see three explanations for the strong alignment. First, the local manager had been employed by ABB for several years and thus been socialised (e.g. Schein 1985) in the ABB culture of global standards and codes which, at least implicitly, encompass the principles of the UN Global Compact. Second, the installation of an electricity system is not in itself a neutral quest. The technologies used were developed in a Western setting and entail the values of their developers (Latour 1991). Hence, the technologies themselves can be seen as inclined to yield an output social performance in line with the project's desired structural social performance (Egels 2005). Third, although the international manager had limited influence over the installation of the electricity system, there were instances where he affected the output social performance. For example, the international manager decided on the use of an environmentally friendly diesel engine and stressed the 'inclusion of women' in the project.

Importantly, several of the project's strong alignments between the structural and output social performances were problematic for achieving the dual goal of legitimacy and growth. For example, the use of diesel was advantageous for reducing cost and aiding growth, but criticised by influential international stakeholders. The use of environmentally friendly engine equipment, on the other hand, was advantageous for enhancing legitimacy, but increased costs and possibly reduced the project's growth potential.

Concluding discussion

We have so far argued that MNCs seem to enter low-income African markets with the dual goal of gaining legitimacy in relation to CSR and achieving increased growth. Based on theoretical reasoning and support from the case study, it appears that this goal duality is likely to lead to a separation of the loci of control for the project's social performance in the form of an international manager explicitly focused on aligning the social performance with the internationally influential stakeholders' demands, and a local manager focused on 'socially embedding' the project to achieve growth. With MNCs' internationally influential stakeholders and stakeholders in African low-income markets predisposed to pose partially irreconcilable demands, MNCs seem to face the corporate social performance dilemma of needing to adhere to irreconcilable social performances when entering low-income African markets. Hence, there is little hope for MNCs to establish definitions of 'good corporate citizenship' acceptable to all their local and international stakeholders. We have argued that one way for MNCs to handle this dilemma, as was done in practice in the studied ABB case, is to partially decouple the firm's structural and output social performances: that is, to decouple different definitions of corporate citizenship.

In addition to contributing to our understanding of MNCs' social performance in low-income African markets, this analysis also has implications for MNCs. On the one hand, MNCs striving to tightly couple their structural and output social performances, while retaining an international and a local project manager, would need tighter coupling between the activities of the international and the local manager. A suitable measure would be to merge the international and local project managers' roles into one person (or two or more sharing the responsibilities). On the other hand, tight couplings are not necessarily desirable from any perspective. In this era of 'high managerialism' (Scott 1998), the gap between policy and practice seems to widen. Few students of corporate management realities, complex organisations, development and global relations—to name a few areas of investigation—believe in tight coupling of talk and action, or policy/presentation and practice, in an institutionalised and globalised world (e.g. Jackall 1988; Brunsson 1989; Boli and Thomas 1999; Quarles van Ufford and Giri 2003). Taking the issue of social development in a 'low-income market' head-on, anthropologist David Mosse (2005: 232) concluded:

> For policy to succeed it is necessary, it seems, that it is not implemented, but that enough people, and people with enough power, are willing to believe that it is. Failures arise from inadequacy of translation and interpretation: from the inability to recruit local interests, or to connect actions/events to policy or to sustain politically viable models and representations.

ABB activities in *and about* Ngarambe seem to have been organised in that spirit, enabling the project thus far to be considered a 'success' enjoying support from ABB headquarters, international NGOs, the Tanzanian government and the majority of the people in Ngarambe. With international and local stakeholders posing irreconcilable demands, increasingly tight couplings of social performances risk jeopardising either the project's legitimacy or growth—both of which are essential for the 'success' of MNCs' projects in low-income African markets. Hence, the complementary managerial capabilities found at the international and local African levels both seem essential for a 'successful' project.

Finally, the implication of both our theoretical argument and the empirical case investigated is that projects such as that in Ngarambe become what they become on a substantial, local, practical *output* level as a result of the interaction between the local stakeholders and the outsiders who actually arrive on location. Perhaps it matters to the outcome why they went there in the first place. More than perhaps, it matters *who is sent* to manage a particular project in low-income markets. Missionaries ('good') can become tyrants. Corporations ('bad') can become benefactors. The opposite is also quite possible. In the words of French historian of ideas Michel Foucault: 'Everything is dangerous' (e.g. Burchell *et al.* 1991). When it comes to ABB in Tanzania, the jury is still out and the verdict depends on which international and local stakeholders are allowed to define 'good' and 'bad'.

References

Arnold, D.J., and J.A. Quelch (1998) 'New Strategies in Emerging Markets', *Sloan Management Review* 40.1: 7-20.

Boli, J., and G.M. Thomas (eds.) (1999) *Constructing World Culture: International Nongovernmental Organizations since 1875* (Stanford, CA: Stanford University Press).

Brunsson, N. (1989) *The Organization of Hypocrisy: Talk, Decisions, and Actions in Organizations* (Chichester, UK: John Wiley).

Burchell, G., C. Gordon and P. Miller (eds.) (1991) *The Foucault Effect: Studies in Governmentality* (London: Harvester Wheatsheaf).

Deephouse, D. (1996) 'Does Isomorphism Legitimate?', *Academy of Management Review* 39.4: 1,024-39.

Delios, A., and W.J. Henisz (2000) 'Japanese Firms' Investment Strategies in Emerging Economies', *Academy of Management Journal* 43.3: 305-23.

De Soto, H. (2000) *The Mystery of Capital: Why Capitalism Triumphs in the West and Fails Everywhere Else* (New York: Basic Books).

Egels, N. (2005) 'CSR in Electrification of Rural Africa: The Case of ABB in Tanzania', *Journal of Corporate Citizenship* 18 (Summer 2005): 75-85.

Hart, S.L. (2005) *Capitalism at the Crossroads: The Unlimited Business Opportunities in Solving the World's Most Difficult Problems* (Philadelphia, PA: Wharton School Publishing).

—— and C.M. Christensen (2002) 'The Great Leap: Driving Innovation from the Base of the Pyramid', *Sloan Management Review* 44.1: 51-56.

IEA (International Energy Agency) (2002) *World Energy Outlook 2002* (Paris: OECD).

Jackall, R. (1988) *Moral Mazes: The World of Corporate Managers* (New York: Oxford University Press).

Latour, B. (1991) 'Technology is Society Made Durable', in J. Law (ed.), *A Sociology of Monsters: Essays on Power, Technology and Domination* (London and New York: Routledge): 103-31.

London, T., and S.L. Hart (2004) 'Reinventing Strategies for Emerging Markets: Beyond the Transnational Model', *Journal of International Business Studies* 35.5: 350-70.

Lozano, F.J., and A. Boni (2002) 'The Impact of the Multinational in the Development: An Ethical Challenge', *Journal of Business Ethics* 39.1/2: 169-78.

Meyer, J.W., and B. Rowan (1977) 'Institutional Organizations: Formal Structures as Myth and Ceremony', *American Journal of Sociology* 80.2: 340-63.

—— and W.R. Scott (1983) 'Centralization and the Legitimacy Problem of Local Government', in J.W. Meyer and W.R. Scott (eds.), *Organizational Environments* (Newbury Park, CA: Sage): 199-215.

Mitnick, B.M. (2000) 'Commitment, Revelation, and the Testaments of Belief: The Metrics of Measurement of Corporate Social Performance', *Business and Society* 39.4: 419-65.

Mosse, D. (2005) *Cultivating Development: An Ethnography of Aid Policy and Practice* (London: Pluto Press).

Pfeffer, J., and G.R. Salancik (1978) *The External Control of Organizations: A Resource Dependency Perspective* (New York: Harper & Row).

Prahalad, C.K. (2005) *The Fortune at the Bottom of the Pyramid: Eradicating Poverty through Profits* (Upper Saddle River, NJ: Wharton School Publishing).

—— and K. Lieberthal (1998) 'The End of Corporate Imperialism', *Harvard Business Review* 76.4: 68-79.

Quarles van Ufford, P., and A.K. Giri (eds.) (2003) *A Moral Critique of Development: In Search of Global Responsibilities* (London: Routledge; New York: Eidos).

Rowley, T., and S. Berman (2000) 'A Brand New Brand of Corporate Social Performance', *Business and Society* 39.4: 397-418.

Schein, E. (1985) *Organizational Culture and Leadership* (San Francisco: Jossey Bass).

Scott, J.C. (1998) *Seeing Like a State: How Certain Schemes to Improve the Human Condition Have Failed* (New Haven, CT: Yale University Press).

Waddock, S., C. Bodwell and S.B. Graves (2002) 'Responsibility: The New Business Imperative', *Academy of Management Executive* 16.2: 132-48.

Watson, T.J. (1994) *In Search of Management: Culture, Chaos and Control in Managerial Work* (London: Routledge).

Winn, M., and L. Angell (2000) 'Towards a Process Model of Corporate Greening', *Organization Studies* 21.6: 1,119-47.

Wood, D. (1991) 'Corporate Social Performance Revisited', *Academy of Management Review* 16.4: 691-718.

8

Grounding African corporate responsibility

MOVING THE ENVIRONMENT UP THE AGENDA*

Karen T.A. Hayes

Fauna & Flora International, UK

One size does not fit all

Corporate responsibility (CR) in Africa is a subject of growing interest, debate and investment. It is often portrayed as a recent introduction to the African business and social remit, driven by the presence of transnational corporations and some African companies that are adopting policies elsewhere and are looking to implement them in Africa. It is even described as a 'transplant from the developed world' (Gruner 2002).

The exception is South Africa. South Africa's sophisticated remit of CR and corporate philanthropy, or corporate social investment (CSI), is familiar to the international business community of Europe and North America. South African corporations meet stringent reporting guidelines and have well-publicised foundations. The country hosted the World Summit on Sustainable Development in 2002, and the Johannesburg Securities Exchange was the first in the world to endorse the use of the Global Reporting Initiative (GRI) Guidelines on sustainability reporting for companies (UNEP-FI 2004: 4). CR in South Africa is now subject to critiques and evaluations to determine its effectiveness (Hamann and Kapelus 2004).

* This chapter was written as part of Fauna & Flora International's (FFI) Business & Biodiversity Programme with funding from the Directorate-General for International Co-operation (DGIS), Netherlands. FFI acts to conserve threatened species and ecosystems worldwide, choosing solutions that are sustainable, are based on sound science and take account of human needs. Hicks&Hayes are independent advisers with the mission of 'developing opportunities for conservation'.

However Northern standards fail to appreciate the role that the private sector has played, and continues to play, elsewhere in Africa. The concepts that lie at the core of CR should not be described simply in terms of the structures, frameworks and reports that have become part of the formalised industry of corporate good practice. While these mechanisms are critical to provide guidelines and benchmarks, companies and countries where these are not in place should not be written off as being collectively and corporately 'irresponsible'.

The contexts in which companies in Europe/North America and Africa operate are so dramatically different that it is simply not possible to define a common baseline from which 'CR' can be conveniently described and compared. In many African countries, companies have been the key—sometimes the only—provider of healthcare, education, security and income for their employees and local communities. It would be naïve to view these often paternalistic roles as the preferred solution for any party involved. Nor would one advocate that companies should adopt the role of the state as there are myriad reasons against the possible monopolistic, unsustainable and unmandated delivery of national services.

However, many African companies, particularly in failed states, have traditionally been obliged to fill significant gaps in social services and infrastructure in order to ensure there are employees healthy enough to come to work, the resources to continue to trade, revenue to pay salaries and taxes, and generally that they fulfil their side of the social contract.

Hence, the presence, absence or effectiveness of African corporate responsibility should not be judged merely in terms of what is expected and accepted in Europe and America.

Regardless of the scale of social commitment demonstrated by African companies, whether expressed formally or not, the CR agenda in the North does differ significantly from that of Africa in terms of environmental responsibility.

Environment in the North; poverty in the South? The polarisation of the CR agenda

The natural environment is widely considered to be a critical CR issue for companies in Europe and America, promoted by environmental NGOs (non-governmental organisations), corporate responsibility bodies, and partnerships between these groups. Drivers include:

- Pressure from investors; conditions placed on access to capital
- Pressure from employees regarding corporate performance and impact; attracting and retaining quality staff; staff health and safety regulations
- Pressure from customers; managing reputation and brand
- Government directives linking environmental performance to both formal and informal licence to trade
- The business case; understanding the corporate environmental footprint; generating operating efficiencies; developing new business opportunities and improving market penetration; long-term strategic planning for sustainability in corporate resources and activities

The absence of the environment from the Southern agenda was recognised by Peter Moyo of Old Mutual, South Africa's largest financial institution, at the first annual African Corporate Citizenship Convention in 2002. He said that CR in Europe and the United States emphasises environmental issues and human rights, while in Africa where it is 'led by Africans', it 'address[es] social, political, and economic transformation and corporate governance issues first' (Gruner 2002).

Social issues are overwhelmingly at the top of the CR agenda in Africa. For many Northern companies, the concerns of extreme poverty, HIV/Aids and malaria, child labour and child-headed households, political insecurity and civil insurrection are at the far end of the supply chain or seen as the responsibility of an in-country subsidiary or partner. African companies, however, deal with such issues on a daily basis. Human needs are immediate and inescapable. Jobs are urgently required. Food supplies are insecure. Healthcare is rare and expensive. Water is precious.

While other regions have seen sharp declines in poverty levels over the last four decades, the 47 countries of sub-Saharan Africa have seen a deepening of poverty among its 689 million people. Africa is the only region in the world where the number of people living in extreme poverty has almost doubled, from 164 million in 1981 to 314 million today. Thirty-four of the world's 48 poorest countries, and 24 of the 32 countries ranked lowest in human development, are in Africa (World Bank 2005).

In all human development indices, the countries of sub-Saharan Africa perform worst. In Mali 73% of the population live on less than US$1 per day; in Angola only 30% of children go to primary school; in Swaziland 39% of 15–49-year-olds are HIV-positive; in Burundi there is one doctor per 100,000 people. The need for the private sector to participate in addressing these appalling statistics is unarguable (UNDP 2004).

This is relevant far beyond CSI or philanthropic considerations. Social and health issues, poverty and lack of education all impact directly on business performance. The true cost of HIV/Aids to business incorporates direct costs (benefits package, recruitment, training, HIV/Aids programmes), indirect costs (absenteeism, morbidity on the job, management resources) and systemic costs (loss of workplace cohesion, reduction in workplace performance and experience). Lonmin Platinum has quantified the operational impact of HIV/Aids. It calculated that, in 2003, the disease increased the cost of producing an ounce of platinum by $6. Based on HIV/Aids in the workforce peaking at 26% by 2006, it calculates that the extra cost will have reached US$11 by 2011 (Trialogue and AICC 2004: 30).

In the face of such obvious human needs, the fact that the environment accounts for just 4% of CSI expenditure in South Africa (an estimated US$13.7 million per annum) is hardly surprising (Trialogue 2003: 142-43). But with this low profile comes a growing range of serious environmental problems and it is time for a rethink.

Environment is not peripheral; it is at the heart of the matter

When Vice President Justin Malewezi launched the Global Compact in Malawi in 2003, he said:

> There is no doubt that for Malawi to grow, we must develop economically, but we must be careful that in developing our economy, we do not do so at the expense of the soil on which we walk and plant our crops, the air that we breathe, the water that we drink and, most importantly, the well-being of the people on whom we depend (*Business Respect* 2003).

There are four main reasons for the environment to be moved up the African CR agenda.

- The nature of the African continental economy
- The relationship between poverty and the environment
- The relationship between health and the environment
- The long-term impact of climate change and environmental degradation

First, Africa's primary economic sectors are heavily dependent on, and impact directly on, the environment, the healthy functioning of ecosystems, and the survival of the species that comprise those systems. Environmental sustainability and conservation are intrinsic to economic viability, to livelihoods, to the cost of doing business, to the cost of compensating for damage caused, and to continuing to have future options related to natural resource use.

Agriculture accounts, on average, for 30% of all Africa's GDP (increasing to 40% in sub-Saharan Africa) and provides 60% of all employment. It also accounts for 40% of export revenues but, with food production steadily falling behind population growth during the past 30 years, Africa has become a net importer of food (De Villiers 2003: 44). There are some startling examples of environmental dependence in African food production. For instance, Lake Malawi, with over 1,000 species of freshwater fish, provides over 70% of animal protein in Malawi (De Villiers 2003: 34). Contamination or disappearance of the continent's freshwaters and their biodiversity would be catastrophic for food security.

In the quest for new agricultural land across Africa, forests, wetlands and rangelands are all being degraded at a rapid rate. These are rarely being transformed to sustainable productivity. Rather they are being converted, used for a few seasons, and abandoned (less than 7% of the continent's crop-growing areas are irrigated) (De Villiers 2003: 100). Direct and indirect impacts of ecosystem destruction include flooding, siltation, and loss of indigenous natural products such as medicinal plants, foods, wood fuel and building materials.

Mining is key to economic development in Africa. Diamonds in Botswana, copper in Zambia, and aluminium in Mozambique have all been significant contributors to economic growth. However, mineral extraction activities raise significant environmental impact issues including waste management, water contamination, invasive associated infrastructure, acid drainage and the effective planning for mine closure.

Energy products are major sources of export revenues for Africa. The continent owns 7.4% of the world's proven oil reserves, 7.6% of its natural gas and 5.6% of its coal supply (De Villiers 2003: 70). The energy sector has profound environmental impacts through exploration, extraction, transport and consumption. To take just one example, Nigeria is the world's largest gas flarer, contributing more greenhouse gases than all other sub-Saharan sources combined. Despite national and international condemnation, the practice of flaring gas in the Niger Delta remains widespread. Flames and fumes affect people's health, pollute the local environment and destroy livelihoods as well as leading to destruction of crops and acid rain which corrodes roofs and buildings. Gas flaring is also an expensive waste of resources costing Nigeria an estimated US$2.5 billion annually in lost potential income (WGCCD 2005: 21).

The Grand Inga Hydropower scheme, if completed, would give the Democratic Republic of Congo greater electricity-generating capacity than all other sub-Saharan states outside South Africa. More than double the size of China's Three Gorges Dam, the project brings an 'inevitable high environmental price to pay' (Ford 2005). This price could be the loss of the second largest carbon sink on the Earth—Africa's lungs—as well as the river whose watershed feeds the forest and is critical to the sub-continent's freshwater supplies.

Tourism is the only export-oriented commercial sector in which Africa's market share is growing based on its clear advantage where the wild environment is the main attraction. In South Africa in 2004, tourism generated US$8.3 billion overtaking gold revenues of US$6.6 billion. Yet ecotourism is often far from being green and has potentially environmentally and socially destructive elements including pollution, alteration of natural ecosystems and undermining of traditional livelihoods. Sound environmental management is essential for maintaining Africa's natural advantage in this sector (World Bank 2002: 46).

The second reason to review the low priority of corporate environmental responsibility is the clear and direct link between poverty and the environment.

> Many parts of the world are caught in a vicious downward spiral. Poor people are forced to overuse environmental resources to survive from day to day, and their impoverishment of their environment further impoverishes them, making their survival ever more difficult and uncertain. The prosperity attained in some parts of the world is often precarious, as it has been secured through farming, forestry and industrial practices that bring profit and progress only over the short term (WCED 1987: 39).

Building on the seminal work of the Brundtland Commission, in the 1990s the United Nations convened global conferences on sustainable development, in which poverty and environment were central themes. Agenda 21, adopted in 1992 at the Rio Conference, devoted a chapter to the relationship between poverty and environmental problems. Similarly, the Copenhagen Declaration on Social Development (1995) confirmed that socioeconomic development and environmental protection are interdependent components of sustainable development (PEI 1999: 2).

Describing a downward spiral of poverty and environmental degradation does not, however, place the blame for environmental destruction on the shoulders of the poor. In many instances, it is non-poor, commercial companies, and state agencies that actually cause the majority of environmental damage through land-clearing, agrochemical use, water appropriation and pollution. Sometimes privileged groups force the poor onto marginal lands, where, unable to afford conservation and regeneration measures, their land-use practices further damage an already degraded environment. There are also many examples in which very poor people take care of the environment and invest in improving it (PEI 1999: 6). However, it is certain that the poor suffer most from the direct, physical and health impacts of a degraded environment, as well as through loss of livelihoods, resources and future options.

Therefore, while it is entirely understandable that the African CR agenda seeks to address poverty, many programmes may be addressing the symptoms rather than the underlying issues. Indeed, neglecting the environmental component of a poverty reduction programme will eventually undermine the efforts of the best-intentioned company.

In the same vein, recognising and addressing the link between health and the environment is crucial.

Poor health reduces survival rates, quality of life and capacity to carry out economically and socially productive activity. Africans suffer a higher total burden of disease than any other people and most of these widespread and debilitating diseases stem from environmental conditions. These include:

- Heat stress (the direct effect of the thermal environment on health)
- Air pollution (outdoor air quality)
- Weather disasters (such as floods, windstorms)
- Vector-borne diseases (such as malaria, dengue fever, schistosomiasis and tick-borne diseases)
- Water-borne and food-borne diseases (such as diarrhoeal diseases)
- Lack of food security
- Demographic changes that shift the balance of vulnerable populations demanding different health services (WGCCD 2005: 18)

While some of these conditions can only be addressed through global initiatives, many may be mitigated through improved environmental management of utilities including water and sanitation, the reduction of pollution and improved waste management: interventions that are well within the influence and activity of the private sector (World Bank 2002: 28).

The extinction of plant species used in traditional medicines in Africa will impact on people's ability to treat illness. The World Health Organisation estimates that 80% of the world's population in developing countries relies on these plants for primary health care. In Mali, traditional medicines have declined because many medicinal plants have been lost through persistent drought (WGCCD 2005: 6).

But the most serious issue facing the long-term viability and security of the African continent and its people is, undoubtedly, that of climate change and the impact that it will have on the fragile African environment.

Global warming is already affecting Africa. The Intergovernmental Panel on Climate Change (IPCC) predicts that, 'the effects of climate change are expected to be greatest in developing countries in terms of loss of life and relative effects on investment and economy'. It describes Africa as 'the continent most vulnerable to the impacts of projected change because widespread poverty limits adaptation capabilities' (WGCCD 2005: 2).

Currently around two-thirds of Africa's rural population and one-quarter of its urban population lack access to safe drinking water. The number of people suffering from water stress or scarcity is rapidly increasing as a result of urbanisation, increased economic development and population growth. According to the United Nations Environment Programme (UNEP) 14 countries in Africa are currently subject to water stress or scarcity and this will increase to 25 in as many years. Climate change will intensify Africa's increasingly critical water situation, along with profound impacts on reservoirs, rivers, sewage and industrial effluents and water-borne diseases (WGCCD 2005: 13).

Other impacts will include an increasing rate of natural disasters and crises, worsened environmental degradation through erosion, desertification and deforestation as well as increasing disease threats. It is estimated that in South Africa alone the area threatened by malaria will double and that 7.2 million people will be at risk—an increase of 5.2 million (WGCCD 2005:19)

It is clear that responsibility for the impact of climate change lies with the energy consumption and waste production of developed and wealthy countries. The countries that will be hardest hit, however, will have had least to do with generating the gases that distort the Earth's climate. But it is only with collaborative and concerted global effort, crucially involving the African private sector, that efforts can be made to limit the damage.

Partnerships and pressure points

The African private sector should not relinquish responsibility for environmental issues to Northern transnationals. The growth in transnationals has led to two levels of concern regarding environmental impact. First, while transnationals may respond well to international pressure for good practice or post-accident clean-ups, equally the variations in environmental control costs between North and South could lead companies to relocate their polluting productions to less-developed countries, exacerbating the risk and problems facing African nations. Second, transnational corporations may apply double standards to environmental responsibility in Northern and Southern countries (Hansen 2002: 159).

Nor should African companies assign the responsibility for addressing climate change to the wealthy-nation culprits. It is the people and the economies of Africa that are at stake and most vulnerable to the loss of livelihoods and future as a result of environmental degradation.

This chapter proposes that the African private sector should take ownership of the issues, and demonstrate leadership in this arena, by moving environment up the African corporate responsibility agenda. In so doing, there are many other actors and instruments that can be called into play.

African corporate leaders

There are many companies in Africa for whom environmental concerns are critical and investment in the environment is above average. In South Africa, Rand Water allocates over half its community giving to environmental projects (Trialogue 2003: 142) as well as having comprehensive social, environmental and governance policies and reporting processes. The Green Trust Awards in association with Nedbank Green and the Department of Environmental Affairs and Tourism (DEAT) present a Business Action Award annually to South African companies that excel in their environmental commitment and performance. Nairobi Bottlers Ltd was recognised for environmental management in Kenya's Company of the Year Awards 2005, while Honey Care Africa was recognised by the International Chamber of Commerce World Business Awards.

Private-sector associations including the African Institute for Corporate Citizenship

The African Institute for Corporate Citizenship (AICC) is an international multi-stakeholder platform providing an opportunity for business, government and broader civil society to discuss and act on corporate sustainability policy and practice in Africa. With the Sustainable Futures Unit (SFU) of the **South African National Business Initiative** (NBI) (discussed below), the AICC could take a leadership role in articulating a business case for moving environment up the corporate agenda, providing case studies, establishing benchmarks and indicators, and reporting on such issues, internationally, from an African perspective.

The NBI is a leading business advocate on issues connected with sustainable development, encouraging high-level interaction between business, government and civil society to increase understanding and sharing of best practice. The NBI works to articulate and strengthen the business case for sustainable development.

The NBI is the regional (South Africa) partner of the World Business Council for Sustainable Development, as are other African partner organisations such as the **Business Council for Sustainable Development Zimbabwe** (BCSDZ). This Council was formed by a group of leading business people who shared common concerns over environmental issues and aims to encourage a commitment by business to the phased implementation of environmental management programmes.

Another partner is the **Forum Empresarial para o Meio Ambiente** (FEMA) in Mozambique. FEMA was established by more than 50 of the country's largest private companies with a view to collectively support the private sector in environmental issues. Its purpose is to provide leadership and an effective voice for the private sector in critical environmental issues, to influence policy formulation and the development of regulations and the promotion of environmental awareness through education and outreach activities.

Association pour la Promotion de l'Eco-Association pour la Promotion de Efficacité et la Qualité des Entreprises (APEQUE) works to raise awareness of sustainable development and promote eco-efficiency among business leaders, governments and NGOs in Algeria. Its goals include the promotion of eco-efficiency among Algerian industries and to assist companies in developing industrial policies and environmental indicators.

The African Business Roundtable (ABR) was established by the Africa Development Bank (ADB). It is committed to fostering sustainable economic growth and social development in Africa by helping to create a conducive business environment for responsible private-sector investment and promoting intra-African trade and investment. ABR serves as a forum for business leaders to study issues, exchange ideas and develop solutions to mutual problems. This is a forum in which environmental concerns facing the continent should be discussed and responses developed.

Finance sector

The finance sector is a critically important determinant of social and environmental performance through its lending policies. There are more foreign banks involved in Africa than in any other region of the world (De Villiers 2003: 43).

The **United Nations Environment Programme Finance Initiative**, in its 2004 analysis of Sustainability Banking in Africa, has initiated a continental dialogue on the creation and adoption of a set of 'African Principles', based on the London Principles of 2002, to be adopted by African finance institutions and embedded in NEPAD (New Partnership for African Development). Three points refer directly to environmental protection:

- Principle 5: Reflect the cost of environmental and social risks in the pricing of financial and risk management products
- Principle 6: Exercise equity ownership to promote efficient and sustainable asset use and risk management
- Principle 7: Provide access to finance for the development of environmentally beneficial technologies

The African Development Bank has a three-year implementation plan (2005–2007) to execute its new Policy on the Environment. The plan seeks to ensure that a strong and diversified economy will continue to take account of environmental protection, and to guarantee that all developmental decision-making integrates economic, social and environmental considerations.

Other financing institutions such as the **International Finance Corporation** (IFC), the private-sector arm of the **World Bank Group**, are also critical partners in this effort, implementing both the IFC Safeguard Policies to manage the social and environmental risk of the private-sector operations it finances in emerging markets and the Equator Principles, now adopted by banks worldwide, which attach environmental performance conditions to investments in excess of US$50 million.

Government

Government has a critical role to play in terms of environmental performance through regulatory processes, taxes, incentives, subsidies, and so on. There is a role for self-regulation for enlightened companies who wish to create a strategic, competitive advantage; however this may become non-competitive if the cost of self-imposed standards increases and other, less responsible companies undercut good practice. Regulatory processes are often required to create level playing fields and to raise the performance bar for all players. Companies should actively engage with government on these issues.

NEPAD

NEPAD is an all-encompassing strategy conceived and designed by African leaders and adopted by the African Union in 2001 as its vehicle to mobilise the concept of an African renaissance. The NEPAD plan includes programmes in environmental protection and it would perform a dual strengthening purpose to find ways to dovetail corporate environmental responsibility initiatives with NEPAD's objectives. The **NEPAD Business**

Group comprises leading business organisations both inside and outside Africa that are committed to helping the continent realise its full economic potential.

Non-governmental organisations

Environmental NGOs work to increase global awareness of, and commitment to, environmental responsibility and conservation. Methods used to influence the policies and activities of governments or companies include campaigns, boycotts and protests, as well as constructive dialogue and partnerships. Collaborative forums can assist companies in addressing issues of environmental responsibility (for example, the Energy and Biodiversity Initiative) and engagement could be sought with the Central, North, East, South and West African Regional IUCN (World Conservation Union) Species Survival Commission (SSC) Sustainable Use Specialist Groups (SUSG) whose members are 'thinking practitioners' in the field of natural resource management. NGOs also create important business enterprises that are environmentally sound and demonstrate best practice in sustainable resource use. One example is Fauna & Flora International's Flower Valley project in the South African Cape where wild fynbos is sustainably, commercially harvested by the local community and marketed worldwide by partner corporations.

Millennium Development Goals (MDGs)

The MDGs set 48 targets for the alleviation of poverty by 2015. The MDGs have surprisingly little direct reference to business given the far-reaching impact of the private sector in terms of development, social equity and environmental impacts—leaving the whole MDG process rather obscure to business. However, businesses that intend to demonstrate a leadership role and credible commitment to poverty reduction should consider how best their corporate responsibility strategy can contribute to the MDGs. Goal 7: Ensuring Environmental Sustainability, has particular relevance in considering a strategy for corporate environmental responsibility (Roe 2005: xv). *Africa Investor* magazine provides an annual award for Best Initiative in Support of the Millennium Development Goals.

G8 (2005) Gleneagles Plan of Action

In Scotland in July 2005, the representatives of the world's eight wealthiest nations made commitments to environmental responsibility and security, which will be effective only if their implementation is supported, monitored and enforced. Every section of the global society has a role to play in this, including the African private sector. The commitments made were to:

- Transform the way we use energy
- Power a cleaner future
- Promote research and development
- Finance the transition to cleaner energy

- Manage the impact of climate change
- Tackle illegal logging

Corporate environmental responsibility strategies should reference, remind and reinforce these commitments as well as finding ways to achieve complementarity, co-financing, leverage or publicity.

In conclusion

Environmental responsibility underpins effective corporate responsibility in Africa. It is not an external agenda—in some ways it is a critically African concern. Nor can it be selectively relegated to a token project within a corporate responsibility programme that ostensibly prioritises poverty or health. Good environmental stewardship and sustainable use of natural resources are intrinsic to addressing human needs and ensuring the future of the people, ecosystems and businesses of Africa.

References

Business Respect (2003) 'Malawi: Vice President launches Global Compact', *Business Respect: CSR Dispatches* 68:21 (December 2003, www.mallenbaker.net/csr, accessed 20 July 2005).

De Villiers, L. (2003) *Africa 2004* (New Canaan, CT: The Corporate Council of Africa and Business Books International).

Ford, N. (2005) 'UN Throws Weight Behind Grand Inga', *African Business*, June 2005: 28-29.

G8 (Group of 8) (2005) 'Climate Change, Clean Energy and Sustainable Development: Text of the G8 Climate Change, Clean Energy and Sustainable Development Agreement and the Gleneagles Plan of Action', www.wbcsd.org, 30 July 2005.

Gruner, T. (2002) 'Corporate and Social Responsibility in Africa', *Environmental Leadership News*, Summer 2002: 19.

Hamann, R., and P. Kapelus (2004) 'Corporate Social Responsibility in Mining in Southern Africa: Fair Accountability or just Greenwash?', *Development* 47.3: 85-92.

Hansen, M. (2002) 'Environmental Regulation of Transnational Corporations', in P. Utting (ed.), *The Greening of Business in Developing Countries* (London: Zed Books): 159-84.

PEI (Poverty and Environment Initiative) (United Nations Development Programme and European Commission) (1999) *Attacking Poverty while Improving the Environment: Towards Win–Win Policy Options* (New York: UNDP).

Roe, D. (2005) *The Millennium Development Goals and Conservation: Managing Nature's Wealth for Society's Health* (London: International Institute of Environment and Development).

Trialogue (2003) *The CSI Handbook* (Cape Town, South Africa: Trialogue, 6th edn).

—— and AICC (African Institute of Corporate Citizenship) (2004) *The Good Corporate Citizen: Pursuing Sustainable Business in South Africa* (Cape Town, South Africa: Trialogue).

UNDP (United Nations Development Programme) (2004) *Human Development Report 2004: Cultural Liberty in Today's Diverse World* (New York: UNDP).

UNEPFI (United Nations Environment Programme Finance Initiative) (2004) *CEO Briefing: Sustainability Banking in Africa* (Johannesburg: UNEP FI African Task Force and African Institute for Corporate Citizenship.

WCED (World Commission on Environment and Development) (1987) *Our Common Future* ('The Brundtland Report'; Oxford, UK: Oxford University Press).

WGCCD (Working Group on Climate Change and Development) (2005) *Africa: Up In Smoke?* (London: New Economics Foundation).

World Bank (2002) *Building a Sustainable Future: The African Region Environment Strategy* (Washington, DC: World Bank).

—— (2005) 'Regional Brief', www.worldbank.org, 1 July 2005.

9

Voluntary initiatives and the path to corporate citizenship

STRUGGLES AT THE ENERGY–ENVIRONMENT INTERFACE IN SOUTH AFRICA

Geoff Stiles, assisted by Pierre Chantraine

Marbek Resource Consultants (Pty) Ltd, South Africa

This chapter focuses on a relatively new area of corporate activity in South Africa: the formation of so-called **voluntary initiatives** in the field of energy and environment. Although part of a worldwide trend towards corporate responsibility and environmental sustainability, voluntary initiatives have only recently become a significant factor in South African business. We believe this relatively slow beginning can be attributed at least partly to the nature of the business–government and business–community discourse in the immediate post-apartheid era.

To understand this discourse and its impact on the adoption of voluntary initiatives, we first examine the conflicting needs of, and confrontations between, industry and the 'environment community' in South Africa. We then review the difficulties experienced by one government-based voluntary initiative in South Africa, and then examine some more recent and successful examples which serve to illustrate the nature of this discourse and suggest a possible way forward.

Particular attention is given to the efforts of a local sectoral association to engage its members in reporting voluntarily on a wide range of safety, health and environmental activities. We also examine the initial success of a more recent voluntary initiative, which appears to have achieved an extremely broad consensus within the business community: the development of a **National Energy Efficiency Accord**, involving a wide range of actors from the business community and national government.

We argue that the latter initiative, despite some weaknesses and persistent uncertainties, provides the best available example of how the historical antipathies between government and business, and between business and the environmental community, can be overcome.

Background

As Africa's largest and most diversified economy, South Africa is uniquely positioned to play a leading role in developing responsible corporate governance. Nowhere is this more evident than in the areas of **energy** and **environment**, where the country is facing a number of major and potentially divisive issues.

Having inherited an economy based on cheap, locally resourced energy—primarily in the form of massive coal deposits—South Africa's post-apartheid government is now embarking on a path towards less energy-intensive, 'cleaner' production, while also dealing with the need to achieve sufficient economic growth to address the impoverishment of the growing black majority. Coal continues to be the major source of electricity for the country, accounting for over 95% of current use, but this is expected to change gradually over the next 10–15 years as government deregulates electricity supply, encourages independent power production using a great diversity of sources, and reorganises the distribution network.[1]

The recent arrival of natural gas from Mozambique[2] also promises to change the basic energy equation in South Africa, as local municipal networks replace coal-derived gas with higher-energy natural gas, and a number of industries contemplate shifting from coal to gas for their boilers. Finally, the country's major utility, Eskom, has embarked controversially on an aggressive programme to develop a new form of nuclear power plant, which it sees as both a means to reduce dependence on coal and as a potential export market.[3]

Although a gradual transition from coal to cleaner forms of energy is supported by the national government, the transition has been slowed considerably by the huge price differentials between coal and natural gas, the price of the latter having been set fairly high to reflect the initial cost of infrastructure and the perceived readiness of consumers to convert. Similarly, high prices combined with continuing technical uncertainties have hampered the adoption of wind and solar.

The role of national government in South Africa's energy transformation has been significant. Rather than intervene in the pricing of energy, as have many other African countries, they have offered other incentives and used regulatory instruments as a

1 The South African government is presently working on several fronts to reform and revitalise energy production and distribution, including creation of regional distributors, asking for proposals for independent power production from both renewable and non-renewable sources, and encouraging pilot projects using solar and wind energy.

2 The pipeline from coastal Mozambique is owned and operated by SASOL, the large South African multinational energy company which has also been responsible for production of liquid fuels and chemicals from coal.

3 For more on the Pebble Bed Modular Reactor programme, see www.pbmr.co.za.

means of encouraging the switch to more efficient and cleaner energy sources. For example, the national government is strengthening regulation of local atmospheric pollutants through a new Air Quality Act and improving its global carbon emissions footprint by encouraging Clean Development Mechanism (CDM) projects. It is also promoting both renewable energy and energy efficiency alternatives through various donor-funded programmes and through support for private initiatives in the power sector particularly.[4]

Government's involvement in such energy and environmental initiatives is paralleled by its pursuit of 'empowerment' for previously disadvantaged groups. To encourage more corporate involvement in the empowerment project, it has encouraged different business sectors to develop voluntary 'empowerment charters' which set targets for black employment and black business involvement. This specifically includes the energy and environment sectors, where substantial inroads have been made by black enterprises. The country's dominant power utility, Eskom, has been particularly active in this sphere, encouraging the formation of black-empowered energy service companies (ESCOs) as part of its mandate to deliver demand-side management.[5]

At the same time, government has been introducing powerful policy initiatives to encourage rapid industrial development, expected to benefit disadvantaged groups directly through job creation and indirectly through greater equity participation and various empowerment instruments. This policy has resulted in the establishment by the Department of Trade and Industry of a number of new 'industrial development zones' and many supportive programmes such as a National Empowerment Fund and an Innovations Fund, together with a range of soft loans and various forms of marketing and technical assistance.

The discourse

The pursuit of such complex and challenging goals—achieving rapid yet equitable economic growth on the one hand, while promoting a cleaner environment on the other—could never be easy or dispassionate, but in South Africa's case it has in fact been relatively constructive and peaceful. South African business, for example, has made a substantial effort to work with both government and labour on a wide range of initiatives, signified in part by their involvement in a major policy review institution, NEDLAC.[6] Business has generally chosen to voice any concerns it may have over government policy through recognised and legitimate institutions such as Business Unity South Africa (BUSA), preferring this route to more direct or unilateral interventions. Recently, BUSA

4 The main support for energy efficiency programming has been through Danish government sponsorship of the Capacity Building for Energy Efficiency and Renewables Programme, or CABEERE.

5 ESKOM's demand-side management (DSM) programme is funded through a levy on the electricity tariff, and is mandated by the National Electricity Regulator. The programme provides support for both load reduction and efficiency projects.

6 NEDLAC is the National Economic Development and Labour Council, developed to provide government, organised business, organised labour and organised community groupings with a forum to discuss and try to reach consensus on issues of social and economic policy.

has played a key role in co-ordinating business responses to such key environmental and energy policy initiatives as the draft National Energy Efficiency Strategy, the National Air Quality Act and the Renewable Energy white paper.

Non-government environmental organisations have also been active in the policy discourse and, with some exceptions, have supported government's efforts to strengthen environmental legislation but have taken a more sceptical view of industrial development goals and of business's sincerity in supporting these goals. Strong environmental movements have arisen within previously disadvantaged communities adjacent to major industrial developments, such as the Durban South Industrial Basin in the eThekwini municipality and the Vaal Triangle area bridging Gauteng and the Free State. These locally based movements have generally been anti-business and they have fought strongly and often effectively against development projects which appear to threaten the local environment or to ignore local community development goals. Among other achievements, they have forced government to deal harshly with polluters, have often undertaken independent monitoring of atmospheric emissions through activities such as the so-called 'bucket brigade', and have been responsible for well-organised interventions to many projects: for example, the recent efforts to defeat the use of a multi-fuel boiler by a large pulp and paper company in the South Durban Basin. They have also been instrumental as watchdogs during the government's implementation of procedures for approving CDM projects, ensuring that these meet national environmental sustainability goals and deliver benefits to local communities as well.

As one would expect, critical interventions by environment and community groups have resulted in a heightened discourse over the country's energy and environmental goals. In the most extreme cases (e.g. Durban South) this discourse has been characterised by a nearly complete failure of dialogue.[7] In others, the dialogue has been more temperate and pragmatic. Overall, South African business has come to accept that they must engage with both government and NGOs (non-governmental organisations) before projects can advance: a stark contrast with the situation under the previous government, where considerations of national security and in particular energy security were given precedence over local concerns, and certainly over concerns of black communities or organisations.[8]

Viewed historically, the confrontational character of this discourse is quite predictable, since it is in part a function of the increased voice given to traditionally disadvantaged groups by South Africa's new political dispensation, and of the historic dominance of the white minority in South Africa's industrial sector. Recognising the potential for such confrontation, the African National Congress (ANC)-led government has made deliberate efforts to encourage constructive community participation in key investment decisions, notably through the use of a public review process in environ-

7 The Durban South Industrial Basin has a long history of political confrontation, stemming from its earlier creation as a segregated living area providing cheap labour to one of the country's largest industrial complexes. It remains a 'hotbed' of community activism, particularly in regard to the health impacts of industrial pollution on the surrounding community.

8 In a striking recent instance of this, the country's largest energy and chemical company, SASOL, seeking approval for a large CDM project involving conversion of its production facilities from coal to natural gas, has asked key environmental NGOs to meet independently before the project design document is completed, to address their concerns prior to the period of public consultation. The NGOs have politely declined.

mental impact assessments under the National Environmental Management Act (NEMA) and more recently by applying stringent sustainability criteria to CDM projects. It has also embarked on a number of collaborative ventures to restore local confidence in industrial development: for example, the South Durban Basin Multi-Point Plan (MPP), which has established a programme to facilitate local monitoring of atmospheric emissions.[9]

In an environment of increasing vigilance by both government and the environment community, industry often feels that it is being treated unfairly: torn between pressure to increase employment through promoting new industrial developments on the one hand, and pressure to meet new environmental standards on the other—the latter in turn reducing (in industry's view) the options available for the former!

Viewed internationally, conflict between developmental and environmental policies and goals is of course nothing new, though in the context of South Africa's special history of racial and political confrontation it has attained a much more complex and perhaps more challenging character. Nevertheless, we believe it is useful to examine the experience of business communities elsewhere in confronting the development–environment discourse, and in particular to discuss one specific experience: the pursuit of **voluntary initiatives** to improve environmental performance. In the following section, we discuss this concept in the context of international experience, as a basis for examining its current and potential future application in South Africa.

Voluntary initiatives

The concept of voluntary initiatives is not new, but until now such responses have been more characteristic of North America and certain European countries than of Africa or Asia. There is also considerable variation in what is meant by a voluntary initiative. In some counties, such initiatives are highly formalised and even involve direct linkages to government; while in others, they are entirely separate from government and may involve independent action, which is contrary to government regulation. In this regard, it is important to note that the term 'voluntary' does not imply a lack of regulation, and can either combine aspects of regulation or, more often, provide a legitimate alternative to regulation.

The International Energy Agency (IEA)[10] produces reports regarding the status of government policies for energy efficiency on a regular basis, and these reports also include references to voluntary initiatives in this very important area.[11] A review by the authors of 18 developed countries, based on the IEA reports, showed that four have essentially no industrial voluntary energy efficiency initiatives, while five others have

9 This has enabled government as well as the local community to pinpoint key sources of toxic emissions and focus their efforts on these polluters rather than on the industrial community as a whole.

10 The IEA is an organisation providing energy information and support services primarily for the industrial countries of Europe and North America plus Japan. South Africa is not an IEA member, but subscribes to its services.

11 International Energy Agency website: www.iea.org/Textbase/publications/free_new_Desc.asp?PUBS_ID=1098.

legislation and regulations in place to levy taxes based on energy use or carbon released. Fourteen countries indicate that they operate some form of voluntary energy efficiency programme, although these programmes take on many different attributes or structures.

The spectrum of these programmes ranges from very loosely organised and structured to highly regulated and quasi-compulsory; from non-controlled participation to legal agreements and covenants; from no targets or planned actions to highly specific and enforceable targets; from no incentives to grants and tax reductions.

Figure 9.1 provides a summary of these programmes, based on a personal interpretation of the IEA data developed by P. Chantraine.

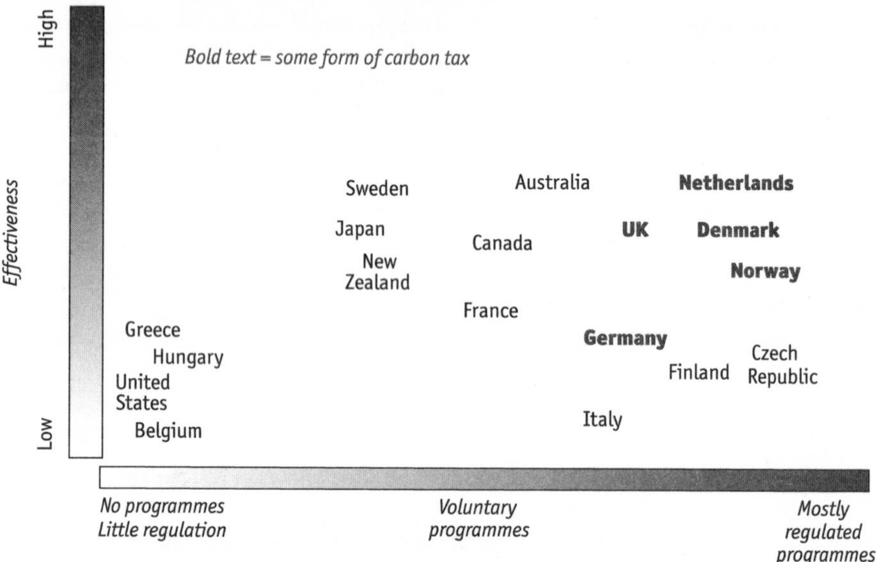

FIGURE 9.1 Personal view of international voluntary programmes

Source: based on information from the International Energy Agency, energy efficiency updates by country

As Figure 9.1 confirms, the term 'voluntary' need not imply a lack of regulation; on the contrary, many voluntary programmes operate within the bounds of regulatory systems that prescribe minimal standards for energy efficiency or environmental impact. Similarly, a lack of regulation does not necessarily lead to the creation of voluntary programmes to fill the void.

Even if based on reasonably common or similar principles and concepts, it is logical to expect that voluntary programmes in different countries will be designed and implemented differently considering the specific policy, political, economic and social needs of individual situations and their stakeholders. However, some common elements can be identified at a high level and are seen as critical to the very existence of an effective voluntary programme.

The critical 'must have' elements in most voluntary initiatives are (Chantraine 2005):

- An overall purpose for the existence of the programme; a statement of direction, of strategy, an overriding goal. This can take many forms and assume many names, but the overall process and its need or aim must be identified by some authority
- An entity or a number of entities which will manage the details of the programme, including general information, registration, data collection, filing and analysis of reports, statistics and recognition
- A commitment or sign-up process
- A set of procedural rules for participants and a set of tools or general guidance for implementation of the programme by participants

The effectiveness of most such programmes is dependent in part on how well many less critical elements are incorporated, including among others and where conditions warrant, some regulatory elements.

Voluntary programmes in South Africa

Voluntary reporting and targeting initiatives, though relatively new to South Africa, already have an established history. The national government initiated a compromise approach—intended to be 'regulated' but still essentially voluntary—through the Environmental Management Co-operative Agreements (EMCAs) launched by DEAT in 1998.[12] At the time of writing, EMCAs have failed to achieve broad-based acceptance, apparently because they satisfied neither industry's need for a flexible mechanism to improve environmental performance cost-effectively, nor the environment community's need for enforceable standards of environmental performance. Indeed, the major criticism of EMCAs from the NGO side has been that they permit industry to establish its own standards, and to be accountable only to these standards rather than to standards acceptable to government or the community. To quote from an editorial in the newsletter of Groundworks, a major environmental NGO commenting on a landfill site in Durban, 'If government cannot enforce and manage sites through permits, how is it going to enforce and manage industries through voluntary, self-regulatory tools such as Environmental Management Cooperation Agreements . . . ?' (Groundwork 2002).

Because of these and other objections to such non-regulatory processes, only a small number of EMCAs have actually been implemented by government in the seven years since the initial implementation of the concept.

Nevertheless, the concept of EMCAs is certainly worth further consideration, and in fact is similar to the concept of 'covenants' used by the Netherlands government, in which companies voluntarily agree to meet or exceed the high standards of environ-

12 Section 35 of the National Environmental Management Act (Act 107 of 1998; NEMA) (Government of South Africa 1998) provides specifically for the establishment of EMCAs as a management tool, and prescribes the legal frameworks within which these agreements must be accomplished.

mental (and energy efficiency) performance which the Netherlands government itself has mandated. In this context, the agreement is 'voluntary' only insofar as the industry or business signing the covenant can set realistic schedules and mechanisms for achieving the standards; it cannot be used to set different or lower standards from those of government.

In addition to EMCAs, and perhaps in an effort to move past the opposition to them, a number of companies and industry groups have developed voluntary programmes, including:

- The Chemical and Allied Industries Association (CAIA)'s Responsible Care programme, part of an international voluntary initiative of the chemical industries addressing health, safety and environmental issues, and, more recently, energy efficiency
- The Johannesburg Securities Exchange (JSE)'s new Sustainability Index, which requires participant companies to voluntarily complete an annual report on their environmental achievements, including energy efficiency, and which now covers 49 major South African companies
- The Global Reporting Initiative (GRI), which has been formally adopted by 25 South African companies to date but with a much larger number following the guidelines[13]
- The Greenhouse Gas Reporting Protocol developed by the World Business Council for Sustainable Development (WBCSD) and World Resources Institute (WRI), which has been trialled extensively in South Africa and adopted by several South African companies[14]
- Annual sustainability reports issued by companies such as Anglo Platinum, many of which are influenced by JSE or GRI reporting requirements

While all of these initiatives are voluntary, they are also extremely varied and not necessarily comparable. They range from basic reporting protocols, which either focus on particular areas (GHG) or provide a menu of possible reporting targets (JSE, GRI), to comprehensive programmes, which stipulate the actual standards to be achieved (Responsible Care). There is also considerable variation in the way in which 'voluntarism' is handled: for example, CAIA makes participation in Responsible Care voluntary within its membership, but requires adherence to certain reporting protocols once a company agrees to participate (though the 'management standards' underlying the protocols are not enforceable), whereas the JSE's index is ostensibly voluntary but its very public nature puts strong pressure on companies to participate if they wish to 'keep up' with their competition.

13 'As of 9 September 2004, there were only 24 South African companies listed on the Global Reporting Initiative's (GRI) website as having declared their use of their Sustainability Reporting Guidelines. However . . . [research] among the top 200 companies in 2004 shows that more than 40% claim to already be using the Guidelines (with almost 15% claiming full use/participation and nearly 30% partial use/participation), while a further 50% claim that they intend to use them in future' (Visser 2004).

14 The GHG Protocol now appears likely to be adopted widely by South African businesses under a programme sponsored by WWF, WRI and BUSA.

It must be said that the recent rush to embrace voluntary initiatives in South Africa has been fostered in part by international factors; those companies that are traded on international stock exchanges such as the London or New York Stock Exchanges are the ones most likely to adopt an internationally accepted reporting protocol such as the GRI. In the case of greenhouse gas emissions, there are often pressures from international head or branch offices to meet compliance standards in other countries, and these have been passed down to their South African operations.

At the same time, this rush has been greeted with considerable scepticism by the environmental community in particular and the NGO community generally—a reflection of the same concerns voiced around EMCAs. This suggests that the fraught discourse on developmental versus environmental issues has not been resolved simply because companies are becoming more proactive in addressing their environmental problems.

A good example of this attitude is the following quote, taken from the international 'Girona Declaration' of 2002 (Rio +10), but widely accepted by South African NGOs such as the South African Regional Poverty Network (from whose website it has been taken):

> In an attempt to pre-empt moves towards binding regulations, corporations are skillfully engineering the debate about 'corporate accountability' down to the narrowest of definitions. High profile voluntary reporting standards such as the Global Reporting Initiative are being sold as the answer to civil society demands for corporate accountability. Corporate groups such as Business Action for Sustainable Development (BASD) are actively redefining the language of corporate regulation to mean corporate-friendly regulation such as market-based 'solutions' to problems and intellectual property rights for corporations . . . By engaging in 'dialogues' with critics, incorporating the language of NGO criticisms into their rhetoric (such as 'corporate accountability'), publishing glossy reports, and demonstrating isolated examples of good 'corporate citizenship', they are succeeding in blurring the lines between business and NGOs, and deflecting pressure for fundamental change.[15]

One of the most common criticisms heard from these groups is that reporting on environmental (or energy) performance does not in itself eliminate substandard performance. Much as with its critique of EMCAs, the environmental/NGO community argues that companies must also set *goals* for improvement which can then be measured by their reporting systems. Simply reporting on improvements, or using reports to justify the lack of improvement, is not good enough; companies must first state their goals or targets clearly and, in a public forum, explain their variance (if any) from national or community standards, and then report on progress against these goals regularly and systematically.

15 Girona Declaration: From Rio to Johannesburg 2002.

The Energy Efficiency Accord

Perhaps the most recent and interesting example of a voluntary initiative in South Africa is the **Energy Efficiency Accord**, which was developed in the first half of 2005 in response to suggestions first proposed in the National Energy Efficiency Strategy (NEES). The Accord was developed initially through a joint effort of the National Business Initiative (NBI)—a voluntary business association with a strong sustainability programme—and a Canadian-funded project on greenhouse gas mitigation through energy efficiency.[16] After reviewing a range of possibilities co-developed with the Canadian project, the NBI decided to proceed with a fairly basic document which would be acceptable to both industry in particular and the business community in general, and this document—the Accord—was then signed by 32 industries and industry associations prior to its formal launch in May 2005.

The NBI worked intensively with its membership—as well as with government, in the form of the Department of Minerals and Energy—to find a version of the Accord that would gain the widest acceptance. It quickly became apparent that there was resistance to the idea of stipulating a single target for energy efficiency improvement for all companies and sectors—as the NEES in fact did—and that any such target would have to be consistent with the South African government's goal of increasing the rate of growth of the economy in general and industry in particular.

Initial drafts of the Accord were thus rejected because they appeared to be advocating efficiency improvements that would impede growth, and several signatories argued strongly for alternative measures of improvement: for example, using improvements in energy intensity as the key measure instead of reductions in 'final energy demand', which had been the government's expectation. Business representatives argued convincingly that it made no sense to set a single goal for a very diverse economy. Should the same 15% target be applied to mining companies, some of whose energy costs are fixed regardless of declines in ore grade, as for food or beverage producers, whose energy costs are generally directly proportional to production costs?

In fact, government's own targets, as spelled out in the NEES, were based on a 'business-as-usual' scenario of 2.4% annual 'real' growth (i.e. net of inflation). So the Strategy's goal of, for example, a 15% decrease in final demand for the industrial sector by 2015, was actually quite modest since it encompassed a relatively strong rate of growth in production. Based on experience in the industrial countries, efficiency improvements of this rather small magnitude can often be achieved with minimal capital investment, requiring instead that companies focus on no-cost/low-cost maintenance and operational improvements. In short, the stated goals of the Strategy required little more than better 'energy management'.

Nevertheless, getting agreement on the final form of the Accord was a difficult and complex exercise, in which the NBI's management played a key role. The absence of a final draft of the NEES was the major stumbling block in this regard, but that objection was quickly resolved when government published the 'final' Strategy in April 2005.

16 The CBLA (Capacity Building, Leadership and Action) project focused on using energy efficiency improvements to reduce greenhouse gas emissions in South African industry; it was funded by the Canadian Climate Change Development Fund and supported by several partner organisations in South Africa, including CAIA, Chamber of Mines and NBI.

Because of these and other concerns, the final version of the Accord was relatively modest and did not set specific targets for companies or sectors, although it confirmed that signatories would view the 15% target for industry as a basic goal. More crucially, the Accord provided no specific mechanism for *reporting* on targets, leaving this to later discussion and development, as follows:

> [The signatories agree] . . . to develop common reporting requirements for energy usage from all energy sources, taking into account, where possible, existing internationally recognised protocols for reporting such as those developed by the Global Reporting Initiative . . . [and also to] establish methodologies that will allow the baseline quantification for energy use/intensity (consumption per unit of production or any other relevant denominator) in various subsectors, and to take into account the need to measure specific energy intensity (providing for the differing subsectors) rather than absolute energy use in order to promote industrial growth whilst achieving energy efficiency and recognising the energy conservation measures already in use in some subsectors.

This rather lengthy statement—the last part particularly—is a clear reflection of industry's concerns over the direction of the NEES, and its fundamental disagreement with government over the idea of restricting growth in energy demand. Rather than simply accept government's interest in lowering 'final demand', the Accord in effect offers an alternative strategy: namely, using *energy intensity* as the key indicator for measuring improved energy efficiency. This would allow industries to grow, but would ensure that energy use was decoupled from growth in production.

As this chapter is being written, the final decisions regarding monitoring and reporting of efficiency improvements, and of the precise indicators to be used for this purpose, have yet to be made, although a technical committee has been established by NBI to address these issues. The Accord does provide a clear and concise basis for implementation and compliance, including both the use of existing initiatives such as GRI and the preference for using energy intensity as the key measure; but implementing these ideas is not as easy as it might seem, given the present lack of baseline data and of accurate benchmarking within the various industry sectors of South Africa. Nevertheless, business now recognises that there is a clear need for a more intensive analysis of this issue, before they commit themselves to a structured programme which may result in (as they see it) unnecessary and unreasonable constraints on economic growth.

An equally significant but less obvious omission in the Accord is that it fails to provide a clear distinction between 'soft' energy management goals and 'hard' energy reduction/efficiency goals. This last discrepancy demonstrates the need for a better understanding of the *process* that underlies energy efficiency improvements in the business world. Most successful energy efficiency programmes around the world—including voluntary initiatives such as we have discussed here—pay at least equal attention to the management systems that underlie improved efficiency as to the technological solutions which in the end produce the tangible efficiency benefits. Better 'management' of energy is, in short, the real key to successfully improving energy efficiency and/or intensity, and substantial international experience is already being brought to bear on this problem in South Africa, including the introduction of 'best practice' programmes, certification of energy managers, development of improved energy efficiency standards for equipment and buildings, and many others.[17] Ideally, the implementation of the Accord should provide for ongoing measurement of these 'soft' factors as well.

It may seem that the concern of NGOs and the environmental community generally over the effectiveness of voluntary initiatives, and their particular criticisms of corporate sustainability reporting, have not really been satisfied by the Accord. However, the Accord itself is only a first step in this direction and, as noted above, requires several additional measures. For example:

- Adopting a transparent and accessible reporting programme that meets international standards and practices
- Development of a 'culture' of energy management within corporations, as opposed to an approach relying exclusively on flagship or mega-projects to reduce energy use

If adopted, these two measures would demonstrate clearly that the business community intends to sustain these activities over time, and will go a long way towards satisfying the concerns and criticisms of the environmental community.

Next steps

The role of voluntary initiatives in South Africa has advanced significantly in the past five years, as institutions ranging from government through industry associations to individual businesses have adopted a wide range of international programmes promoting corporate sustainability reporting in general and reporting on energy/environmental performance in particular. The role of EMCAs—the earlier, government-driven concept for voluntary initiatives—has gradually been subsumed by this new trend, and most voluntary initiatives implemented to date are in fact based on the actions of individual companies or associations, rather than company-to-government agreements or covenants.

In this context, the Energy Efficiency Accord is really the first example of a locally developed voluntary initiative resulting in a 'covenant' between business and government. Although it is clearly based on international examples and seeks to incorporate internationally recognised procedures and standards already used by some of the signatories, it is also a reaction to the specific discourse that has characterised business–government relations over the first ten years since the fall of apartheid. Indeed, the Accord itself is very much a *symbol* of this discourse, having been created as part of an intensive debate within the business community over the contradictions inherent in the sustainability 'project'.

17 The Department of Minerals and Energy has funded several consulting studies at present, one of which includes examining the role of best practice programmes and energy management certification, and two others which involve development of energy efficiency standards for new commercial buildings and some industrial equipment.

Achieving rapid industrial growth as a principal means of alleviating poverty, while also ensuring that this growth is environmentally sustainable—as South Africa's government hopes to do—is an inherently difficult task which will doubtless take decades to achieve. Nevertheless, voluntary initiatives such as the Accord may provide an early example of how to achieve these goals within a framework of collaboration and open dialogue, effectively mitigating the confrontations that characterised business–government discourse in the past.

References

Chantraine, P. (2005) 'A Framework and Roadmap Study For Implementing a Voluntary Energy Efficiency Initiative For South African Businesses', Report to the National Business Initiative, unpublished.

Government of South Africa (1998) *National Environmental Management Act* (Act 107 of 1998; Pretoria: Department of Environment and Tourism).

Groundwork (2002) *Quarterly Newsletter* 4.1 (March 2002).

National Energy Efficiency Strategy (2005) *National Energy Efficiency Strategy* (final version; Pretoria: Department of Minerals and Energy).

Visser, W. (2004) *Corporate Sustainability in South Africa: A Ten Year Review* (Johannesburg: KPMG).

Part IV
Health and HIV/Aids

10
The ethical governance of health
A CASE STUDY OF WORKER HEALTH IN KENYAN FLORICULTURE

Julia Kilbourne and John Porter

London School of Hygiene and Tropical Medicine, UK

> It is but a sad profit which is achieved at the cost of the health of workers (Bernardino Ramazzini, 1633–1714).

The recent phenomenon of corporate social responsibility—in particular, the activity of 'ethical sourcing'—is an approach under way promoting decent working standards within globalised systems of production. The term **ethical sourcing** refers to the application of criteria influencing purchasing decisions usually made by Western consumers of products made in the developing world.[1] Its approach in informing the buyer about what he or she is purchasing or consuming is to apply ethical criteria throughout the entire system of production so that producers, those at the cradle end of production, benefit through decent working conditions and fair pay.[2] Yet, as production globalises and relocates across national boundaries, determining whether ethical standards are applied becomes a far more complex endeavour.

1 For background information on ethical sourcing, see www.ethicaltrade.org, www.impacttlimited.com, www.laborrights.org and www.sa-intl.org.

2 The underlying description of *ethical* in this paper includes a composite of professional skill and social responsibility. Thus, ethical business practice refers to a company's responsibility for operational, personnel and human rights practices in its supply chain. Specifically, it is how a business is judged by the ways in which it *makes* its money (see Gardner *et al.* 2001).

Nevertheless, businesses are being called to account in terms of upholding ethical principles throughout their globalised production networks while others—including sectors from supplier countries—have even seen an advantage in marketing an 'ethically produced' product.[3] And, increasingly, core human rights principles are being used to describe and determine ethical conditions at these cradle points of production.[4] Such scrutiny is usually applied to working conditions (e.g. union rights, fair pay, health and safety, child labour). The reason for this scrutiny is the recognition, among both business and civil society, that, in light of their scope and influence, transnational business networks have a greater unfulfilled potential for improving the context in which they operate (or from where they source) than any other sector, including government.

Ethical sourcing from Kenya

One country and sector of export production where there has been considerable ethical sourcing activity is the cut flower industry, where workers are often found in the most insecure forms of work with little protection. Kenya is one country renowned for its export horticultural production (e.g. fruits, vegetables, cut flowers) and is one of the top four producers of cut flowers for the European market.[5] The larger-scale cut flower producers in Kenya often have direct supply links with European retail chains, particularly UK supermarkets.[6] It is these key businesses—large-scale export growers and importing supermarkets—that are developing ethical practices to meet these demands since they source a variety of products from a myriad of countries and regions. Subsequently, a plethora of codes of conduct,[7] including health and safety standards, have been adopted both by the Kenyan export horticulture industry and their by UK and other European customers.

Quality assurance, product safety and environmental protection codes and testing have also arisen as a response to European regulations. Furthermore, the larger growers in Kenya have established their own codes as a means to promote their 'socially responsible' label.[8] The smaller-scale cut flower producers also participate in the production of export crops either directly through global markets (usually via the Dutch

3 For information on businesses and countries adopting marketing strategies based on quality and ethical criteria, see Anholt 2005.

4 See the Ethical Trading Initiative's Base Code at www.ethicaltrade.org; SA 8000 code at www.sa-intl.org; www.iblf.org; and the 'Decent Work' programme at www.ilo.org.

5 ILO Sector Publications 1999.

6 Although the trade distribution of flowers to the Dutch flower auction remains a substantial part of the intricate trading network, retailers are playing an active and increasing role in shaping the character of the international cut flower trade. Moreover, UK supermarkets are playing a powerful role in influencing the nature of the production of flowers in Kenya (see Barrett *et al.* 1999; Hughes 2001).

7 The term 'code of conduct' refers to a set of general, core principles that describe ethical behaviour. Such codes often refer to professional (e.g. medicine) or sectoral (business, industry) protocols through which to be both professionally excellent and socially responsible.

8 www.kenyaflowers.co.ke

flower auction) or through subcontracting to the larger cut flower producers in Kenya. The backdrop to all this ethical sourcing activity is a context characterised by increasing land poverty and unemployment (Government of Kenya 2000; McCulloch and Ota 2002). Yet the cut flower industry has been cited as one way in which to generate income for land-poor people since they employ substantial numbers of workers on their production sites (Barrett and Browne 1996; McCulloch and Ota 2002; *FAO Newsletter* 2002). Moreover, the majority of these workers are 'unskilled' and 'semi-skilled' women who are employed on a casual basis or on short-season contracts (Kilbourne 2005). These workers are also more likely to come from other rural parts of the country.

Globalisation and worker health

As developing countries industrialise, there will often be the lack of capacity or disregard in dealing with the steady increase in occupationally associated health problems. Yet occupational safety and health (OSH) is an instrumental component to public health and in ensuring the basic right to health and safety for working populations. Furthermore, occupational health has been utilised to protect surrounding communities and the environment, and contribute to safeguarding natural resources and improving production, thus linking work, health, environment and development aspects. It is, therefore, a key public health profession, needed wherever there is a workplace.

Ethical sourcing has been used as a strategy in which to address the far-reaching concerns of promoting and protecting the health status of populations linked to global networks and chains. Health status is inextricably linked to the well-being of working populations especially for those in emerging and developing economies around the globe with few, if any, adequate state-sponsored safety nets. Often workers in global supply chains serve as key providers for their families, and significant populations depend on the good health of workers and their ability to persevere in their income-earning capabilities (Kilbourne 2005). Additionally, the increasing feminisation of the global labour force—in both formal and informal economies—has meant that women are often these key providers (Benería 1989; Standing 1999) and their particular (or perceived) health and safety status contributes to the overall picture when raising worker health concerns.

Some of the codes of conduct for the Kenyan floriculture sector represent an awareness of the need to promote worker health and welfare within the industry. Yet the differences between the codes, their omissions and the lack of distinction or connection to proper mechanisms can result in low levels of compliance and understanding of the key requirements to establish sound worker health and well-being policies (Kilbourne 2005).

Although many of these codes include adherence to both international conventions and national legislation as a condition of compliance, Kenya has significant limitations in its legislation and participation in promoting health and well-being for workers (Kilbourne 2005). Subsequently, industry standards and international labour conventions can play an important role in highlighting the need to develop national and local instruments and actors with which to promote these standards.

Ethical sourcing approaches to worker health in Kenyan floriculture

In order to chronicle the ways in which worker health and well-being are interpreted and prioritised, qualitative research (Jorgensen 1989; Patton 1990) and a stakeholder analysis[9] were selected as the most suitable methods with which to analyse and describe (Glaser and Strauss 1968) the process at hand. To focus further on these key issues concerning worker health and ethical sourcing on a specific, more practical level, a case study of the Kenyan export floriculture market was chosen as a context for examination. This sector was selected as a result of timing, in that the Kenyan cut flower industry is an emerging and successful sector, which, in the late 1990s, was in the early stages of developing ethical codes of practice for its producers. Moreover, Kenyan floriculture employs a largely female semi-casual workforce that is representative of workforces linked to transnational supply chains around the globe. The following is a summary of the study's findings.

Results

Some of the key findings from the case study included the following:

- There is variety and variability to the Kenyan horticulture-sector codes. Most sets of codes refer to OSH provision as an extension of existing management, production and environmental standards
- Considerable concern has been expressed over the risks associated with agrochemicals in this sector. Concerns raised by campaigners and academics have focused mainly on the risk of exposure to the worker as well as surrounding communities. And those within the export horticulture sector have considered biological monitoring as a means to manage worker health status. The larger growers provide their own health services in which provision mainly focuses on agrochemical exposure, pregnancy and infectious diseases
- There was no evidence of OSH training for most company medical staff and there was no evidence of an occupational disease and accident monitoring and reporting system within the public sector. Nevertheless, among some horticulture producers, there was a stated awareness or suspicion of OSH-related maladies by certain staff members. Yet no mechanisms were in place for OSH-related staff to investigate these patterns further

9 The stakeholder analysis research findings describe: (1) the actors involved in (or linked to) the Kenyan floriculture industry and a description of their codes (if any); (2) their scope and involvement in the design and application of the codes; (3) the underpinning priorities and interpretations reflected in the design and application of the codes; and (4) the role of international and national frameworks in the design and application of the codes.

- Larger-scale growers provide health facilities for their workers, and in some places these facilities offered services and treatment that surpass what is available locally through the public sector. A few of these growers provide, for instance, screening, antenatal care, birthing facilities and counselling (including HIV), as well as consultation and medicine. Some of their well-established screening services, however, place more of an emphasis on controlling for food safety—known as 'traceability'—within the supply chain (Dolan *et al.* 2000)
- Advocates have raised concerns over the particular risks that women in this sector are encountering (Benería 1989; Barrientos *et al.* 1999; Barrientos 2000). A significant aspect of the Kenyan cut flower sector is that it depends highly on the employment of women, who constitute approximately 75% of the workforce in the labour-intensive tasks of planting, grading and harvesting. While the cut flower industry has increased the quantity of female waged employment, there is growing concern that women's economic participation is not being matched by qualitative improvements in their working environment (Smith *et al.* 2004)
- Maternity leave is in accordance with Kenyan law and is mentioned in the codes of the larger export growers. However, concerns were raised that pregnancy testing was used as a method with which to vet prospective employees for some of the farms. Among the large producers, strict policies were in place barring female employment from the more lucrative jobs of agrochemical handling and spraying as a measure to protect reproductive and foetal health

Core challenges

Even though Kenyan floriculture ethical sourcing activities provide an important basis for establishing minimum OSH and well-being conditions of workers, there are some limitations.

Problems in interpreting and addressing worker health needs

Although health services other than traceability testing may be provided at the on-site clinics, including testing for sexually transmitted infections such as HIV/Aids, no confidentiality and anti-discriminatory procedures were in place to protect and help those affected. Since it is standard procedure for most of the floriculture workers to be on temporary or seasonal contracts, companies employ workers principally on the basis that they are well enough to do their job. Other actors, including the public sector, could sponsor insurance and health schemes as part of their remit in supporting specific health issues for workers. Yet this study found that Kenya's health services are not equipped to treat HIV/Aids patients, neither are its insurance schemes able to accommodate these patients' disability and long-term needs.

Women workers' health needs were also envisaged, by the large growers, to be addressed through a foetal protection policy (FPP), disallowing women from jobs involving handling and mixing agrochemicals. This protective measure, however, has meant that women's employment in the more lucrative jobs of agrochemical handling and spraying is being prevented. Furthermore, no consideration is being made of the agrochemical effects on male health and fertility.

The governance of codes-based initiatives

There needs to be greater harmonisation of and consistency within the plethora of codes facing Kenyan floriculture producers, particularly when ethical codes are considered in the context of the many management, production and environmental standards they are also required to meet. Key issues remain concerning: (1) scope in terms of developing comprehensive coverage of worker health and well-being standards; and (2) actor remit in the way worker health standards are governed. These key issues influence the extent to which codes, even when combined with national legislation and public-sector capacity, can address worker health conditions across the sector. Although requiring compliance with national legislation can provide codes with an important additional strength in terms of their relevance on the ground and their scope across the sector, there is often variability between them in terms of an acceptable level of standard and in their strength of application.

Furthermore, the study's stakeholder analysis revealed participation in the formulation and application of codes to be imbalanced, especially in terms of worker involvement. There was also low capacity or inclusion by some government and civil-society actors in the design and application of these codes. Since the degree of actor participation largely depends on the number and capacity of stakeholders in existence at a local level, there was little or no means for government and civil-society involvement in the monitoring and verification of codes that articulate workers' health and well-being in Kenyan floriculture.

Asymmetrical ethics

Initially, supermarkets, retailers, importers and some international health and consumer groups have been instrumental in instigating decent standards for the horticulture sector, including cut flowers. One of the results, however, is that the *inclusion* of key rights principles has been ignored or skewed by policies based on traceability—those management and medical actions discussed above that cater to consumer concerns and health through product and worker testing and risk management. And these imbalanced policies have been ratified and adopted by Kenyan producers and exporters reflecting a global trend throughout the agricultural industries (Kaferstein *et al.* 1997; Lopez-Valcarcel 2001). Traceability policies, in turn, have impelled export companies to adopt mandatory testing procedures for both their products and their workers. Subsequently, company health services have been designed according to the objectives of these traceability guidelines rather than any OSH protocol linked to the public sector. Although these procedures can cater to the health needs of *some* of the workers (e.g. agrochemical exposure and gastrointestinal diseases) their intent, rather, is to treat the worker more in terms of product safety than as a complete human being. Indeed, there are benefits to pursuing exposure reducing strategies by requiring that workers receive OSH-related training and equipment to enable them to perform their work safely, but often the 'H' is missing from OSH training and information given to workers. Furthermore, those procedures that focus on the 'sick worker' rather than the 'sick environment' can also become discriminatory in that they are used to identify fault principally with the worker over other, and possibly more direct, determinants involving exposure to disease and agrochemicals.

Ethical sourcing, OSH and worker health: long-lost relatives

Health status is inextricably linked to the well-being of working populations especially for those in emerging and developing economies around the globe, with few, if any, adequate state-sponsored safety nets. Factory floors and production sites often represent a microcosm of larger, existing issues and conditions at play within a society or state. Thus, more consideration should be given not only to the methods of ethical sourcing in promoting 'safety' standards within the work sphere, but also to its role in multi-sectoral efforts to instil a broader comprehensive strategy in addressing conditions linked to health status. This is a form of governance requiring the inclusion of many sectors (e.g. civil society, government, business) in which sets of codes and their monitoring and verification arrangements adhering to international conventions and national legislation are a part.

Kenya has significant limitations in its legislation and public sector participation in promoting health and well-being for workers. Subsequently, the role of industry standards and international labour standards can play an important role in highlighting the need to develop national and local instruments and services with which to promote these standards. Local civil society plays a critical role in ensuring that worker health rights, especially for the most vulnerable groups, are instilled in the process.

If worker health is to be addressed coherently, reflecting a comprehensive set of health needs, partnership building and co-ordination is necessary in order to start fulfilling this goal. As explained above, the business sector is a crucial actor in facilitating the achievement of this goal but it is not entirely—or solely—responsible, especially for activities that extend beyond the remit of managing OSH risk. Civil society has a part to play in organising those workers who are the most under-represented and vulnerable so that they can start to take an active part in meeting and shaping the kinds of policy that aim to address their own health needs. Moreover, government's role is critical in legitimising rights-based standards in terms of worker friendly laws and codes, regulation and inspection, and supporting OSH and other relevant health services that meet workers' and their families' needs.

As a result, health codes of practice reflecting worker health needs for the sake of their *own* lives and not just for the sake of the consumer will be essential when considering the *purpose* and not just the methods of ethical sourcing activities. Ethical labour initiatives will also need to apply to 'flexible' and informal workers including seasonal, temporary, casual or part-time workers, subcontractors and homeworkers. Furthermore, ethical asymmetries created when too much focus is placed on how suppliers treat their workers in lieu of how buyers treat their suppliers can create problems between finding realistic and sustainable solutions that make business sense and fostering decent working conditions. In a larger context, the impact and scope of ethical sourcing will be curtailed if ethical initiatives are driven from the top down and by a single actor or a few stakeholders. The challenge is for the business, local civil society and government sectors to integrate their own ethical *modus operandi* into a co-ordinated effort that stimulates and facilitates more widespread change, beyond promoting ethical islands among a vast sea of unjust production. Additionally, the appropriate kind of balance of actor engagement needs to be explored so that (1) the responsibility of the state is not undermined; (2) core rights-based principles are instilled for all and not just an enclave of workers; and (3) a sustainable plan is crafted in which responsibility and cost are shared.

Moving forward

Despite the recent emergence of a plethora of 'codes of conduct' developed by the business world in which to promote, in part, the health and well-being of workers, many companies rely on schemes in which the management details and targets vary significantly in terms of scope and issues covered. This is because the codes state general values about health and safety rather than clear, more specific descriptions of worker health and well-being standards (Ferguson 1998). For example, company OSH approaches and policies are often interpreted or designed according to consumer or product, rather than worker, priorities (e.g. product safety). Yet, as stated above, *worker health* (i.e. the 'H' in OSH) is often not fully considered in training and worker health services which, although they may help workers perform their work safely, do not address a set of comprehensive and contextual issues including long-term health costs (Kilbourne 2005). And often in cases when an occupational health understanding is applied, it is left to the remit of the clinic or medical workers to apply a 'preventive' approach that relies solely on medical surveillance—including biological monitoring, early detection, or diagnosis of occupational diseases.[10] These may be indispensable approaches to primary prevention, but they can never replace it since they can only confirm exposure or disease. 'Early' is already too late for the detection of many irreversible impairments. The understanding that prevention should start at the workplace, and not the clinic, in order to eliminate or control hazards before health impairment occurs is what links public health with occupational health and requires a shift in focus from the worker to the environment (Kilbourne 2005).

10 Biological monitoring often includes the routine testing of workers for traces of harmful substances that may be passed on to the consumer. For example, in horticulture, workers may be tested for agrochemicals and bacteria as a means to assess exposure levels.

From good intentions to good governance

There is a gathering recognition that ethical sourcing contributes rather than adequately replaces the public sector when upholding worker health standards (BSR and PwC 2004). Moreover, even if ethical sourcing standards are relevant to international agencies and trade blocs, further efforts are needed to integrate them into regional and other sub-national agencies of economic co-ordination and regulation. Thus, the application of these standards requires political will and action from diverse sectors and partners, especially locally. Global instruments, therefore, need to be interpreted according to the practical realities within specific societies and governments, not so that these principles are diminished but rather to enable an active citizenry and government to uphold them. In light of these redefinitions of responsibilities, an expansion of an *ethical space* is needed in which to involve more and different actors. Moreover, new approaches are needed by policy advisers and donors promoting social, political and economic development on a national level that encourage the building of government capacity and public governance plans that incorporate universal core labour standards.[11] From this approach to governance, a basis can be established in which a nation's sovereignty, and thus ethical *modus operandi*, is underpinned.

Yet, as discussed above, the nation-state increasingly is not alone in influencing a process that assures the dignity and well-being of all parties. As a result, ethical sourcing schemes require the involvement of local and different *actors*:[12] (1) to promote responsible business behaviour; (2) to strengthen existing laws and guidelines; and (3) to enhance local capacity of the civil society, private and public sectors.

Conclusion

Considerable resources are being devoted to tracking an exponential increase in the number of corporate social responsibility (CSR) initiatives promoting decent working practices within global supply chains.[13] The emphasis has been more on which principles are endorsed and on arrangements for verification of application. This includes statements on occupational safety and health (OSH). Most of these statements, how-

11 One of the results of this approach could be for developing-country governments to create the conditions for responsible business behaviour, through strengthening the implementation of existing laws and guidelines: that is, by helping governments to translate international principles into national legislation. Furthermore, strengthening the capacity of the local private-sector, labour and civil-society organisations, who can act as intermediaries, advocates, technical advisers, whistle-blowers and pressure groups would be another approach with which to develop a series of sustainable governance strategies (see Moser and Norton 2001; Sengenberger 2002; Elliot and Freeman 2003; Fox and Prescott 2004).

12 Actors in this context are representatives from state or society who have varying degrees of involvement in a policy process.

13 The term 'supply chain' describes the complete business network of inputs that go into the production of a product. Thus, a supply chain includes retailers, distributors, transporters, storage facilities and suppliers (including a composite of subcontractors, outsourcers, smallholders and homeworkers) who participate in the sale, delivery and production of a product.

ever, remain general and refer to industry codes of practice in which engineered or 'scientific' monitoring systems are used to emphasise and verify the 'S' in OSH. Moreover, such practices and systems often focus on the safety of the product rather than including efforts to promote a safe and healthy work environment and worker, respectively. Few statements address how such standards are governed, whether they extend beyond the remit of the factory floor, or how they address workers' own short- and long-term health concerns. Even less is known about the extent to which the scope of OSH applications is being enlarged to include appropriate and relevant worker health issues. These include specific and contextual health and well-being issues affecting working populations, their families and communities and whether relevant actors, including government bodies, services and institutions, are fulfilling their own remit in addressing them. Finally, knowledge is especially scant about the way in which actors, particularly in developing countries, prioritise, implement and govern these worker health and safety standards and how relevant in context or beneficial they are to worker welfare.

In light of the emerging recognition of the need to develop and apply ethical forms of conduct to business practices, new forms of analysis are needed in order to view OSH problems not just in terms of managing occupational risk (e.g. chemical exposure, fire safety, machinery safeguards). More consideration actually needs to be given to the access and quality of worker health service provision, health education, and safety net policies and programmes (e.g. comprehensive occupational hygiene expertise and surveillance, reproductive health, HIV/Aids awareness and prevention, insurance schemes).

And, even though CSR activities have influenced traditional thinking about global governance and regulation to include, or focus on, the business sector's role and influence on global and local development matters, most of the emphasis has been placed on intersecting with actors beyond nation-state borders rather than sectors and infrastructure within the nation-state. Thus, in order to establish a symmetrical and sustainable *ethical* form of governance, in which all actors have rights as well as responsibilities, each actor relevant to the process needs to establish a normative framework to facilitate their participation and remit. Such a framework should be based on partnership building, through which trust and local democratic associations, institutions and the public sector can be developed and supported.

In recent years, progress has been made in engaging a wider circle of stakeholders in the process of considering decent working standards for Kenyan floriculture workers (ETI 2005). This can also be said for numerous other cases around the globe as new combinations of partnerships and methods are established to address ethical sourcing and larger socioeconomic and development concerns. As mentioned above, factory floors and production sites often represent a microcosm of larger, existing issues and conditions at play within a society or state. Thus, what was once just a primary concern over articulating *methods* (i.e. codes of practice and their monitoring and verification) with which to promote decent standards within the work sphere, has led to more consideration and questions about the *purpose* of ethical sourcing. The questions now being asked are how or whether ethical sourcing can improve standards for enough people, particularly the most vulnerable, and what role it has to play in a more comprehensive strategy to reduce poverty and strengthen corporate citizenship.

References

Anholt, S. (2003) *Brand New Justice* (Oxford, UK: Butterworth-Heinemann/Elsevier).

Barrett, H.R., and A.W. Browne (1996) 'Export Horticultural Production in Sub-Saharan Africa: The Incorporation on The Gambia', *Geography* 81.1: 47-56.

——, B.W. Ilbery, A.W. Browne and T. Brinn (1999) 'Globalization and the Changing Networks of Food Supply: The Importation of Fresh Horticulture Produce from Kenya into the UK', *Transactions of the Institute for British Geographers* 24: 159-74.

Barrientos, S. (2000) 'Globalization and Ethical Trade: Assessing the Implications for Development', *Journal of International Development* 12: 559-70.

——, S. McClenaghan and L. Orton (1999) *Gender and Codes of Conduct: A Case Study from Horticulture in South Africa* (London: Christian Aid)

Benería, L. (1989) 'Gender and the Global Economy', in A. MacEwan and W. Tabb (eds.), *Instability and Change in the Global Economy* (New York: New York Monthly Review Press): 241-59.

BSR (Business for Social Responsibility) and PwC (PricewaterhouseCoopers) Denmark (2004) *Public Sector Support for the Implementation of Corporate Social Responsibility (CSR) in Global Supply Chains: Conclusions from Practical Experience* (report for the World Bank; BSR and PwC).

Dolan, C., and J. Humphrey (2000) 'Governance and Trade in Fresh Vegetables: The Impact of UK Supermarkets on the African Horticulture Industry', *Journal of Development Studies* 37.2: 147-76.

Elliot, K.A., and R. Freeman (2003) *Can Labour Standards Improve under Globalisation?* (Washington, DC: Institute for International Economics).

ETI (Ethical Trading Initiative) (2005) *Addressing Labour Practices on Kenyan Flower Farms: Report of ETI Involvement 2002–2004* (London: ETI; www.ethicaltrade.org/Z/lib/2005/02/rept-kenyaflwrs/index.shtml).

FAO Newsletter (2002) 'A Thorn on Every Rose for Kenya's Flower Industry', *FAO Newsletter*, 18 April 2002.

Ferguson, C. (1998) *A Review of Company Codes of Conduct* (DfID Report; London: DfID).

Fox, T., and D. Prescott (2004) 'Exploring the Role of Development Cooperation Agencies in Corporate Responsibility', paper presented at the *Development Cooperation and Corporate Social Responsibility Conference*, Stockholm, Sweden, 22–23 March 2004.

Gardner, H., M. Csikszentmihalyi and W. Damon (2001) *Good Work: When Excellence and Ethics Meet* (New York: Basic Books).

Glaser, B.G., and A.L. Strauss (1968) *The Discovery of Grounded Theory: Strategies for Qualitative Research* (London: Weidenfeld & Nicolson).

Government of Kenya (2000) *Second Report on Poverty in Kenya. I. Incidence and Depth of Poverty* (Nairobi: Government of Kenya, Ministry of Finance and Planning).

Hughes, A. (2001) 'Global Commodity Networks, Ethical Trade and Governmentality: Organising Business Responsibility in the Kenyan Cut Flower Industry', *Transactions of the Institute of British Geographers* 26.4: 390-406.

Jorgensen, D. (1989) *Participant Observation: A Methodology for Human Studies* (London: Sage): 23.

Kaferstein, F.K., Y. Motarjemi and D.W. Bettcher (1997) 'Foodborne Disease Control: A Transnational Challenge', *Emerging Infectious Diseases* 3.4: 503-10.

Kilbourne, J. (2005) *Promoting Worker Health Rights within Global Supply Chains and Beyond: A Case Study of the Kenyan Export Floriculture Business*, unpublished thesis, London School of Hygiene and Tropical Medicine.

Lopez-Valcarcel, A. (2001) 'New Challenges and Opportunities for Occupational Safety and Health (OSH) in a Globalised World', *African Newsletter on Occupational Health and Safety* 11.3: 60-63.

McCulloch, N., and M. Ota (2002) *Export Horticulture and Poverty in Kenya* (IDS Working Paper 174; Brighton, UK: Institute of Development Studies [IDS], December 2002).

Moser, C., and A. Norton (2001) *To Claim Our Rights: Livelihood Security, Human Rights and Sustainable Development* (London: Overseas Development Institute).

Orton, L. (1997) *Change at the Check-out? Supermarkets and Ethical Business* (London: Christian Aid).

Patton, M.Q. (1990) *Qualitative Evaluation and Research Methods* (London: Sage): 169-86.

Sengenberger, W. (2002) *Globalisation and Social Progress: The Role and Impact of International Labour Standards* (Bonn, Germany: Frederich Ebert Stiftung).

Smith, S. (2003) 'Watch what you put in your vase', *The Guardian*, 6 August 2003.

——, D. Auret, S. Barrientos, C. Dolan, K. Kleinbooi, C. Njobvu, M. Opondo and A. Tallontire (2004) *Ethical Trade in African Horticulture: Gender, Rights and Participation* (IDS Working Paper 223; Brighton, UK: Institute of Development Studies).

Standing, G. (1999) 'Global Feminization through Flexible Labor: A Theme Revisited', *World Development* 27.3: 583-602.

11

Corporate citizenship, Aids and Africa

LESSONS FROM BRISTOL-MYERS SQUIBB COMPANY'S SECURE THE FUTURE™

Kari A. Hartwig, Alana Rosenberg and Michael Merson

Yale University School of Public Health, Center for Interdisciplinary Research on Aids, USA

The title of Alan Paton's South African novel, *Ah, But Your Land is Beautiful*, reflects the common impression of most visitors and residents as they travel across the widely differing terrains of sub-Saharan Africa. As the story tells, however, the beauty is often eclipsed by the evidence of human suffering, social injustices, environmental degradation and exploitation of resources exerted by ever-changing political elites. Today's South Africa and its neighbouring states are living on the foundations of this history, some with constitutions barely ten years old. Infrastructure and economic development were fostered within the urban and suburban centres allowing the rural areas with the majority of the population to remain in living conditions of decades past. The economic and human resources in southern Africa remain strong, but generating future economic development that will correct some of the current human and ecological imbalances will require new social contracts with businesses and corporations. Historically in this region, governments and corporations have often worked against the civil, social and political rights of the majority of its citizens, and worker–corporate relations have been tense, leaving the majority of the population suspicious of corporations and their motives (Bauer and Taylor 2005).

In the past two decades, the idea of corporate citizenship has moved from a peripheral activity in many corporations to one of strategic positioning, necessary to maintain a 'social contract' with the communities in which corporations do business (Matten and Crane 2005). In the context of globalisation, with greater civil-society monitoring of their actions, corporations are extending their roles in the provision of services and protections that are reshaping the requirements of corporate citizenship. These new definitions of corporate citizenship (Matten *et al.* 2003), and their consequent accountability requirements, place further responsibilities and expectations on corporations that initiate high-profile philanthropic initiatives.

In 1999, the Bristol-Myers Squibb Foundation (BMSF), together with its parent company, pledged US$100 million over five years to help South Africa, Botswana, Namibia, Lesotho and Swaziland find sustainable solutions for women, children and communities affected by the HIV/Aids epidemic in their countries. In early 2001, BMSF committed an additional US$15 million to support similar activities in four western African countries (Senegal, Burkina Faso, Mali and Côte d'Ivoire). This initiative, termed Secure the Future™, is intended to complement the broader efforts of governments to identify relevant and sustainable programmes for treatment, care and prevention of HIV/Aids.

BMSF has implemented Secure the Future (STF) in a way that diverges from traditional models of corporate philanthropic programmes. In this chapter, we use Matten and Crane's definition of extended corporate citizenship to analyse STF and offer lessons learned about the challenges and opportunities of corporate philanthropy in mitigating HIV/Aids in Africa. Specifically, we consider BMSF's approach in five domains: its grant-making procedure; human resource decisions; monitoring and evaluation activities; capacity-building initiatives; and approach towards ensuring sustainability.

In presenting this case study, we recognise the limits of the analysis within a framework of corporate citizenship. Questions go unanswered such as: why didn't this initiative begin four or eight years earlier? What motivated its entry? Would BMS have launched this initiative if it had continued in its lawsuit with the South African government about intellectual property rights regarding patents on its drugs? As Matten and Crane (2005: 175) note, 'regardless of motivation, corporations enter the arena of citizenship on a discretionary basis. There is no specific political or legal framework that institutionalizes a corporate responsibility for administering citizenship rights.' This allows corporations great flexibility in their process of prioritising and goal setting. For a company with net sales in 2004 of US$19.4 billion and total assets before taxes of US$30.4 billion, is a philanthropic initiative of US$150 million enough?[1] Working within the definition of corporate citizenship, can any company measure poorly if it is at least doing something? Does hiring a prestigious university to conduct its evaluation work assure objectivity? We have no benchmarks to provide answers to these questions.

This analysis draws on our experience as the independent Monitoring and Evaluation Unit for STF. In 2001, Yale University's Center for Interdisciplinary Research on Aids (CIRA) received a contract from BMSF to provide monitoring and evaluation oversight to STF. Our activities have included conducting process evaluations of community outreach grants and capacity-building initiatives, advising on medical research grants, and participating in various advisory group meetings, training sessions on monitoring and evaluation for STF funding recipients and BMSF-sponsored Learning and Sharing Conferences. Due to our late entry, we were unable to establish baseline indicators for

1 Bristol-Myers Squibb Company 2004 Annual Report.

impact assessment. Most of the analysis presented here focuses on STF activities in southern Africa.

Corporate social responsibility and corporate citizenship

Corporate citizenship has taken on greater prominence in recent years with the growth of public–private partnerships and the expectation by civil society and governments that corporations share in the responsibilities that merge with their increased governance role. Matten and Crane (2005) note that, typically when discussing corporate social responsibilities, four types of corporate responsibility are highlighted: economic, legal, ethical and philanthropic. Corporate success is no longer being judged solely on characteristics such as profit margins and market share, but also by its 'service to international stakeholders' and its standing as 'corporate citizens' (Wagner 2001). In decades past, corporations' social responsibility typically focused only on occupational benefits to their employees, grants to local community organisations, and donations directly related to their product area (Brummer 1991). Now, corporations are reaching out to provide grants and services that are not directly related to their organisations in order to respond to stakeholder expectations that they share in the power and resources under their control (Newell 2002; Collier and Wanderley 2005).

An ongoing concern, however, is how the term 'citizenship' is defined and whether systems to measure its accountability are appropriate (Newell 2002; Matten *et al.* 2003; Caldwell 2004; Matten and Crane 2005). Although some have equated corporations with 'citizens', Matten and Crane suggest that corporations should be seen as parallel partners with the state (Matten *et al.* 2003; Matten and Crane 2005). Typically, a state is responsible to its citizens and a corporation is accountable to its shareholders, but as corporations expand their role their responsibilities increase as well. This requires them to acknowledge a heavier responsibility to 'confer citizenship' and protect the rights of citizens in the areas of social, civil and political rights (Matten and Crane 2005). Administering citizenship rights according to this definition requires corporations to play a 'providing role' in the area of social services; an 'enabling' role for civil rights; and a 'channelling role' for individuals to express their political rights. After we review the structure of STF, we will assess how well it has implemented these roles.

Business responses to the pandemic

The global business response to the Aids pandemic has been slow and speculative, both in terms of grant-making and in instituting workplace policies. A 2005 report (World Economic Forum 2005) noted that, globally, 71% of businesses surveyed have no formal or informal policy regarding HIV. Only in countries where HIV prevalence is greater than 20% does one see a shift to the majority of firms with an HIV policy. Where such policies exist, they are largely oriented towards prevention.

In the area of philanthropy, corporate foundations are gradually beginning to play a larger role. In a 2002 report on the top 50 US HIV/Aids grant-makers, BMSF appeared sixth on the list in 2001 and second in 2002 with grant commitments of US$14.5 million and US$16.9 million, respectively (Funders Concerned About Aids 2003), representing the highest financial commitment among US-based companies including pharmaceutical companies. In 2005, the Global Business Coalition on Aids gave BMS one of six Business Excellence awards in the 'Community Award' category.

Southern Africa has some of the highest HIV prevalence rates in the world, ranging from 25 to 40% of the reproductive age population (UNAIDS 2004). Given the epidemic and BMS's recent lawsuit on patent rights, STF launched its initiative in a region of great need and high levels of distrust.

Secure the Future

Description of the programme

Planning for STF began in January 1998, and a meeting with UN Secretary-General Kofi Annan in late 1998 cemented the commitment of BMS to lead a new private-sector HIV/Aids initiative in Africa. By May 1999, STF was launched.

STF is part of BMSF, whose mission is to 'create meaningful and sustainable improvements in health and education of people around the world, through partnerships and innovations that actively fulfill the Bristol-Myers Squibb Company mission to extend and enhance human life' (BMS and BMSF 2004: 7). Philanthropic programmes are aligned with BMS's drug development areas, and its experience in developing HIV/Aids medicines was a motivation for STF's development. While STF was consistent with the Foundation's mission, it was much larger than previous foundation initiatives and required a new system of management.

With a working group of largely US scientists (IAPAC 2001), BMS identified the following priority areas for STF: (1) to prevent new infections; (2) to reduce the impact of HIV/Aids by assisting affected women and children; and (3) to expand access to treatment by informing public health policy. In order to accomplish these objectives, STF created three initial focus areas: Community Outreach and Education, Medical Research and Care, and Capacity Building. The first two of these became STF's main grant-giving categories.

Organisational structure

STF is managed through two local offices: six full-time professional and support staff are based at the BMS 'South Africa' Company Headquarters in Johannesburg and four full-time professional and support staff are based at a STF office in Bamako, Mali. In New York City at the company's headquarters, oversight for the initiative is provided by the BMSF President and one BMS financial accountant. Salaries for staff, as well as the administrative and infrastructure costs of STF, are borne directly by the company and are additional to the US$150 million, which is used solely for the grants and their evaluation. What remain unknown and unaccounted for are these complementary costs of salaries, infrastructure and marketing, and how decisions are made in balancing these expenses.

Two technical advisory committees (TACs) were formed in 1999, one for the review of medical research projects, and the second for community outreach and education (COE) projects. The TACs included both local and international HIV/Aids experts from ministries of health and other government offices, universities, and NGOs with participation from all five southern African countries. A parallel structure was established in West Africa. The TACs were charged with the task of reviewing grants received through a 'request for proposal' (RFP) mechanism and making funding recommendations based on set criteria. While ultimate funding decisions were made by BMS, the STF grant approval process included TAC review followed by Ministry of Health (MOH) endorsement for all recommended applications, to ensure that proposed activities were in line with MOH priorities.

Programme components

The COE component supports community-based programmes that provide education and outreach to women and children, as well as public health training fellowships (BMS and BMSF 2004). Key criteria for project selection included the degree of collaboration, significance of expected outcomes, consistency with government approaches, and capacity to develop a replicable model. General areas of focus are counselling (6), home-based care (17), capacity building (10), education and communication (18), and care and support for orphans and vulnerable children (18). The distribution of these grants by country and programme area can be seen in Table 11.1. The largest COE grant (US$2,482,982) was provided to the National School of Public Health at the Medical University of Southern Africa to provide training in public health to over 200 fellows. In West Africa, a grant to the University Cheikh Anta Diop in Dakar, Senegal, is currently providing public health training to professionals in the region. A community-based organisation (CBO), Bambisanani, received the second largest grant (US$605,847) to enable rural communities in the Eastern Cape of South Africa to conduct community mobilisation, and provide home-based care and income-generating activities.

The medical research (MR) component sponsored research focusing on women and children that would 'expand investigational research' and 'build health research capacity' (BMS and BMSF 2004: 16). The MR grants included a variety of clinical trials related to ARTs (anti-retroviral therapy) (5), trials focused on opportunistic infections including tuberculosis (TB) (11), trials in self-care and mother-to-child transmission (6), training and education (10), and laboratory and psychosocial studies (15). The largest MR grant (US$17,100,000) was given to the Botswana–Harvard Partnership for the Tshepo study on adult ART treatment and resistance. Baylor College of Medicine received the second largest MR grant (US$2,560,966) to establish a bi-directional physician exchange programme between southern Africa and Houston, Texas, for short-term training.

In 2002, STF created a third programme component called the legacy programme, which emerged from both the COE and MR programmes. This component, which is ongoing, consists of two major initiatives: an NGO Institute and the community-based

	Community outreach and education (no. of grants)	Medical research (no. of grants)
Botswana	8	6
Lesotho	7	0
Namibia	8	0
Swaziland	10	0
South Africa	33	37
Multiple countries	3	4
No. of projects funded	69	47
Largest grant (US$)	$2,482,982	$17,100,000
Smallest grant (US$)	$12,455	$2,507
Total funding (US$)	$14,370,467	$39,705,370

TABLE 11.1 **Distribution of grants for community outreach and medical research**

treatment support programme. The goal of the NGO Institute is to 'develop, build, and enhance management, good governance, and leadership capacity among the NGOs and CBOs working in HIV/Aids in STF countries' (BMS and BMSF 2004: 39). The NGO Institute was piloted between 2003 and 2004 and the Institute itself was launched in July 2005 with a three-year funding commitment.

The community-based treatment support programme aims to demonstrate that ART treatment can be delivered in resource-constrained environments. In consultation with Ministries of Health, one hospital has been identified in each of the five southern African countries to provide ART treatment according to government guidelines. A sixth site in Mali follows the same model. In some cases, BMS built facilities to assure delivery of the drugs. In addition to clinical services, the unique characteristic of this programme is the complementary funding of NGOs and CBOs in the communities to provide counselling, patient support, nutritional guidance, home-based care, community outreach and buddies for people living with Aids.

STF's newest initiative was announced in June 2005. It provides a US$22 million grant to Baylor College of Medicine to send 250 doctors to Africa to treat approximately 80,000 HIV-infected children and train local healthcare professionals (Williams 2005). The new commitment also includes an additional US$8 million to fund four new children's centres of excellence, bringing STF commitments since inception to US$150 million.

Corporate citizenship in action

How then has STF performed in its role of providing, enabling and channelling services and citizenship rights in these selected countries in Africa? In this section, we address this question by focusing on the areas of grant-making, human resource infrastructure, monitoring and evaluation, capacity building and sustainability. We use the concepts that Matten and Crane have set forth for the corporation as provider, enabler and channeller of services and rights, and extend these to both individuals and organisations, as STF's impact can be seen at both levels.

Grant-making

While STF represented one of the 'largest and most complex public–private partnerships focusing holistically on HIV/Aids in Africa' (IAPAC 2001), its reception within the region was met initially with suspicion from local governments, civil-society actors and the media. As noted above, the launch of the initiative coincided with pharmaceutical companies' lawsuit against South Africa. Some believed that STF was a tactic to develop a market for BMS's ARTs. Other criticisms were directed at the inclusion of clinical trials in STF despite the high cost of Aids drugs for governments in the region. Further, there were critiques that too many of the early medical research grants went to US universities that had representatives on the medical research TAC. In response to some of this criticism, STF formed TACs with government and local university representatives and created an objective criteria system for ranking proposals that came in response to the RFPs.

In its self-critique, BMSF noted that in its efforts to move quickly it did not initially spend enough time with local governments to work through their concerns and suspicions (BMS and BMSF 2004). In an HIV/Aids funding environment that often dodges infrastructure costs, STF has built clinics and related facilities, trained staff and worked with government to take over these facilities once STF ends. The role of governments and local researchers on the TACs can be seen as enabling citizen rights. In this process, STF ensured that programmes would be aligned with and supported by national governments, a necessary support for ensuring the sustainability of the community and clinical work being undertaken. To assist potential grantees, grant-writing workshops were offered and BMSF contracted with PricewaterhouseCoopers to conduct pre-award surveys and capacity building in the area of financial management. Despite this assistance, many of the COE grantees experienced gaps without funding due to lags in financial reimbursement and processing.

STF also contributed to the provision of services and programmes to local agencies, medical institutions and individuals that otherwise would not have been provided by the state. In some cases, BMS was able to leverage donations of drugs from other pharmaceutical companies for some of the clinical research programmes by virtue of its own involvement. The projects' quality varied depending on the skills and capacity of the organisations implementing the research or interventions, and the skill set and available time of the limited STF staff to provide technical assistance in a timely, ongoing manner.

The grant-making process had some limits to the extension of 'citizenship rights' that are perhaps inherent in a multiple-country, private-funding initiative. For example, as seen in Table 11.1, the distribution of programme grants across the five countries in southern Africa was very unequal.[2] South Africa received more project funding by far

2 The Namibian government chose not to participate in the MR grants.

than the other countries; this in part reflects its population size, but also its greater number of universities and higher percentage of the population to have completed secondary school and university training. Just as South Africa's institutions surpassed those of its neighbouring states in the quality of its proposals, so too did the US medical research proposals tend to outscore projects by local researchers; and in fact the largest grants went to US institutions. Certainly, the funding of these US universities reduced STF's 'providing' role to local institutions. Another critique of the proposal review process was that, although they recused themselves from review of their own institutional proposals, many of the US university recipients were represented on the TAC. Nevertheless, there are enabling benefits that derived from these projects, both in the significance of research outcomes and in skills transfer.

The RFP model itself had benefits and drawbacks that had major implications for STF's direction. It transferred decision-making power to a larger body of stakeholders, encouraged innovation and took advantage of local expertise. However, it limited STF's ability to be directive and engage in larger outcome-focused initiatives. STF's evolution takes into account these limits, and as time went on larger, more focused and strategic interventions were conceived and funded.

Human resources

As described earlier, the majority of STF employees were hired locally, sometimes from within the company. Hiring locally made use of regional expertise and skills and ensured that any human resources capacity built remained within the region. The associated administrative and salary costs of employees paid by the company rather than the foundation are an additional financial commitment by BMS; yet this funding mechanism acts as a double-edged sword. The justification for staff size was constantly being questioned by the company, since these salaries were derived from profits. The ratio of six professional staff to more than 125 projects in the southern Africa region was insufficient to provide adequate managerial and technical support to projects. In addition to these functions, staff were also meeting regularly with government officials, organising annual conferences and conducting a variety of training events. Although some of the organisational, training, evaluation and marketing functions were subcontracted, these services had to be managed and monitored. These constraints limited the 'enabling' benefits of the grants.

Monitoring and evaluation

The corporate citizenship literature points to the increasing responsibility that society confers to corporations in the absence of accountability structures (Newell 2002; Collier and Wanderley 2005). To what extent does STF achieve accountability for its actions? Demonstrating the impact of programmes has proved a challenge as there were no set benchmarks or baseline standards at the outset of the initiative. Contracting an external evaluator (Yale University) two years into STF was certainly commendable. Most evaluation efforts have focused on formative evaluation—informing the implementation and design of projects rather than evaluating their impact. These evaluations (primarily among the COE grants) have played an enabling role for the implementing agencies, which used mid-term evaluation reports to strengthen their programmes. STF also invested funds in evaluating its NGO Institute initiative and community-based treatment programme using local and international evaluators. As regards the latter, STF has contracted Family Health International to conduct an impact of the programme.

One apparent conflict of interest is the fact that BMSF funded both individual projects and the Yale team that evaluated them, although such funding scenarios are fairly normative. In our relationship with BMSF as the monitoring and evaluation unit, BMSF repeatedly encouraged our independence in both conducting evaluations and in disseminating the findings of evaluations.

An important accountability criterion for STF is its transparency. Through its years of experience in implementing STF, BMSF learned to negotiate new initiatives such as the community-based treatment programme with government, university and NGO stakeholders before launching them. Furthermore, they have listed on their website the names of people on their TACs, the agencies funded and the amount of funding each receives. In doing this, they have appropriately shared responsibility for their actions with local citizens and government agencies. Accountability and transparency may have been increased further if the proportion of funds spent on evaluation, management, grants, marketing and conferences was public so that a cost–benefit and cost-effectiveness analysis could be undertaken.

Capacity building

Throughout the life of STF, multiple investments were made in both individual and institutional capacity building, which served an enabling and channelling role in conferring citizenship rights. These efforts included training opportunities in financial management, clinical and laboratory skills building, public health education, and evaluation. In addition, using company funds, BMS hosted regional conferences for grant recipients, sponsored participation in international conferences, supported on-site mentoring, and eventually formed the NGO Institute. These achievements in local capacity building serve as markers for how STF has extended access to citizenship rights such as access to basic HIV information and services. When STF exaggerates these achievements in its own reporting, however, are citizenship rights being harmed? In its 2004 Corporate Responsibility Report (BMS 2005: 30) BMS indicated that: 'A Yale evaluation team in late 2004 called the NGO Institute the best and most successful African model of capacity building for HIV/Aids organisations.' In fact, as a pilot initiative, we declared it innovative, and potentially an African model, but not the 'best and most successful'.

Sustainability

Finally, we come to the question of sustainability. Through its two legacy initiatives—the NGO Institute and the community-based treatment programme—STF has worked closely with government and local institutions to help ensure that protocols are aligned with government priorities and that recurring costs can be covered by government and/or local funding sources. Governments, not BMS, chose which type of drug to use based on national protocols. In addition, BMS made the commitment to assure ARV drug treatment to all patients initiated under STF throughout their lifespan. However, most programmes funded through the COE component will probably not be sustained without identification of new donors. Many of the home-based care and orphans projects provide support that most local governments cannot afford, such as stipends for caregivers or school fees for orphans. These are recurring costs that few governments can adequately cover; thus, finding new donors becomes the recurring theme as with all other donor projects with time-limited funding. However, individual and institutional changes can be considered sustainable when individuals and organisations learn new skills that will increase their likelihood of future funding as some STF funded projects have demonstrated.

Implications for future work in Aids, Africa and corporate citizenship

Secure the Future serves as a model of corporate citizenship in Africa, but it also highlights the limits of corporate citizenship in conferring citizenship rights. Through STF, BMS invited and challenged other corporations—and particularly pharmaceutical companies—to take a much more personal and direct role in mitigating the impact of Aids in Africa. It began as an unprecedented financial commitment—to date, no other pharmaceutical company has matched its size or breadth. In 2000, Merck along with the Bill and Melinda Gates Foundation committed US$50 million to the African Comprehensive HIV/Aids Partnerships in Botswana; and in 2005, Merck announced a new US$30 million HIV/Aids initiative in China. These projects too are important; however, in dollar amounts, they are significantly less than the BMS commitment. In addition, other pharmaceutical companies such as Pfizer and Abbott have launched HIV/Aids initiatives in recent years. These programmes suggest that BMS's actions may have encouraged the active participation of other pharmaceutical companies in this new model of corporate citizenship.

STF began under a cloud of suspicion and criticism and made some mistakes early in its implementation; yet five years later it has succeeded in developing trust and confidence with many of its government and NGO partners. It has played a provider, enabler and channelling role to governments, universities, medical institutions, NGOs and local citizens through HIV/Aids prevention and care programmes and services. Two of the most important lessons learned have been the importance of early and continued stakeholder consultation with government officials and other local stakeholders, and the value of transparency of goals and processes. The expectation of sustainability for all programme efforts remains unrealistic, but the energy, time and resources devoted to organisational capacity building have much potential for bearing fruit.

One must also consider, however, the limits of corporate citizenship and its operational framework for assuring citizenship rights that go beyond the example of STF illustrated here. A company could be engaged in corporate philanthropy while simultaneously challenging a host country's patent rights, taxation or trade policies in an effort to promote greater financial profits for the company; if successful, this would probably increase costs and/or reduce income for the state. Such activities are legal and acceptable within the corporate citizenship definition. A reduced state budget, however, is likely to affect the quantity and quality of services it can offer its citizens. Further, the benefits and rights conferred through corporations are limited to a subsample of the population and remain time-bound. This illustrates the power exerted by corporations to enter and exit when they choose and to provide benefits on the one hand while possibly trying to diminish them with another.

As we grapple with the definitions of corporate citizenship and the responsibilities they confer to corporations, we need to determine common benchmarks for measuring these characteristics. Should full budgets for corporate philanthropy be made transparent so that management–programme ratios and cost–benefit analyses can be performed? Can we quantify extended 'citizen benefits' received under a corporate philanthropic programme which individuals receive in the absence of or in addition to government benefits? Can we identify benchmarks for low to high performance in the areas of enabling, providing and channelling roles as well as parallel actions by companies outside their philanthropic programmes that may be acting contrary to these roles? Active corporate citizenship that extends the state's role in providing citizenship rights and services is greatly needed in Africa whose history runs more often to tragedy than to triumph. STF's change and growth since its inception reflects an evolving sense of corporate citizenship: one that is laudable and by its actions has challenged other corporations to question whether they are themselves doing enough.

We must not forget Matten and Crane's observation that corporations participate in actions of corporate citizenship at their own discretion. Given that reality, and the growing role of public–private partnerships in the health of communities around the globe, we hope that corporations will see initiatives such as STF not as a one-time, short-term funding commitment, but as part of an ongoing sustained partnership to prevent and mitigate the impact of Aids throughout Africa.

References

Bauer, G., and S.D. Taylor (2005) *Politics in Southern Africa: State and Society in Transition* (Boulder, CO: Reinner).

BMS (Bristol Myers-Squibb Company) (2004) *Sustainability through Innovation: 2004–2005 Corporate Social Responsibility* (New York: BMS).

—— and BMSF (Bristol Myers-Squibb Foundation) (2004) *Our Story: Secure the Future* (New York: BMS and BMSF).

Brummer, J.J. (1991) *Corporate Responsibility and Legitimacy: An Interdisciplinary Analysis* (Westport, CT: Greenwood Press).

Caldwell, C. (2004) 'Examining Corporate Citizenship: Balancing Duties and Opportunities in the Modern Organization', *Business Ethics Quarterly* 14.4: 775-80.

Collier, J., and L. Wanderley (2005) 'Thinking for the Future: Global Corporate Responsibility in the Twenty-first Century', *Futures* 37: 169-82.

Funders Concerned About AIDS (2003) *Report on HIV/AIDS Grant Making by US Philanthropy* (New York: Funders Concerned About AIDS).

IAPAC (International Association of Physicians in AIDS Care) (2001) *Secure the Future: Evaluation Report* (Chicago: IAPAC).

Matten, D., and A. Crane (2005) 'Corporate Citizenship: Toward an Extended Theoretical Conceptualization', *Academy of Management Review* 30.1: 166-79.

——, —— and W. Chapple (2003) 'Behind the Mask: Revealing the True Face of Corporate Citizenship', *Journal of Business Ethics* 45: 109-20.

Newell, P. (2002) 'From Responsibility to Citizenship?', *IDS Bulletin* 33.2: 91-100.

UNAIDS (2004) *2004 Report on the Global AIDS Epidemic* (Geneva: UNAIDS).

Wagner, C.G. (2001) 'Evaluating Good Corporate Citizenship', *The Futurist*, July/August 2001: 16.

Williams, L. (2005) 'Bristol-Myers Squibb, Baylor College of Medicine establish pediatric AIDS Corps for Africa', www.bcm.edu/news/item.cfm?newsID=425, accessed 18 August 2005.

World Economic Forum (2005) *Business and HIV/AIDS: Commitment and Action?* (Geneva: World Economic Forum, Global Health Initiative in co-operation with UNAIDS).

12

De Beers

MANAGING HIV/AIDS IN THE WORKPLACE AND BEYOND

Tracey Peterson

De Beers Consolidated Mines Limited

Julie Shaw

Consultant

The De Beers HIV/Aids Programme includes treatment for employees and spouses—a fairly unique design in the broader mining industry. HIV/Aids threatens diamond industry employees, communities and countries. The epidemic presents a complex global challenge. The De Beers HIV/Aids programme is not only an investment in people but is also a clear corporate response to the economic impact of HIV/Aids on the company.

De Beers firmly believes that the challenges of HIV/Aids must be addressed collaboratively with key stakeholders such as government, NGOs (non-governmental organisations) and CBOs (community-based organisations). The company complements this with the work of The De Beers Fund, which directs De Beers' corporate social investment spending in South Africa.

Stories of the baobab tree

There are many symbols of Africa, some beautiful and some not; some true and some a blend of fact and fiction. Among these, the baobab leaves a lasting impression of versatility, tenacity, durability and longevity. It has none of the traditional beauty of a tree, with its upside-down appearance, bulbous smooth branches and pink-grey or copper-colour trunk, yet it leaves an indelible impression of majesty and magic with all who behold it. Such is Africa.

To be sustainable in an African climate, a sound HIV/Aids management programme requires a similar level of versatility, tenacity and durability to recoup the years of life that too many of Africa's people stand to lose. To those who work in HIV/Aids management, and to those who don't, it also demands a firm focus on the majestic qualities that each person brings to the human experience, the courage to question accepted truths, and an unwavering ability to keep going, even when there's no end in sight.

Whose problem is it anyway?

The expanding HIV/Aids epidemic has brought forth debates far more profound than the need for a disease management programme to tackle some new scourge. It was common in the early days to hear raging debates around fault, cause and blame. But perhaps the most profound debate of all is the emerging one of connection, something the ecologists have been talking about for decades—and then there was Aids . . .

As barren as an African landscape can look to the untrained eye, with a baobab standing sentinel, an old baobab tree can, in fact, create its own ecosystem. Countless lizards, snakes, spiders and insects live in its crevices and a variety of birds make their homes in its branches. Great furry fruits thud to the ground to be eaten by a variety of animals, carrying the seeds far and wide. An HIV/Aids programme should be similarly embedded in the landscape, with sensitivity to the broader ecosystem it serves. It needs to hear and respond to tough questions such as: 'why are you so focused on Aids when there are other challenges to face?', 'what about cancer and other diseases?', 'is this the best use of resources?' and so on.

Company profile in brief

De Beers was 'born' in South Africa and has responsibilities to around 22,000 employees in 19 countries, of whom roughly 13,000 are based in southern Africa. It is the largest diamond mining company in the world—long-standing and durable (not unlike its product).

De Beers encompasses global diamond exploration, mining, sales and marketing. In 2004, the De Beers Group generated US$5.7 billion in revenue and US$498 million in net earnings. The company is privately owned by DB Investments, which comprises Anglo American (45%), Central Holdings Group (40%) and the Government of Botswana (15%).

Aids profile

In 2003, it was estimated that almost 5 million people became newly infected with HIV globally, the greatest number in any one year since the beginning of the epidemic. This brings the total number of people living with HIV in 2003 to 38 million. In the same year, almost 3 million people were killed by Aids, and over 20 million have died since the first cases of Aids were identified in 1981 (UNAIDS 2004).

While HIV prevalence appears to be stabilising in sub-Saharan Africa, home to 10% of the world's population, the picture is still bleak. In 2003, an estimated 3 million people in sub-Saharan Africa became newly infected, while 2.2 million people died of Aids—75% of Aids deaths globally. The HIV epidemic continues to gain momentum in South Africa. Data from the 2003 national antenatal sero-prevalence survey showed an average incidence of 27.9% (Makubalo *et al.* 2003).

These figures have serious implications not only for De Beers and its employees, but also for their families and communities. De Beers has many employees in sub-Saharan Africa and business interests in a number of the countries threatened by the next wave of HIV infection. De Beers' strategic approach to HIV/Aids reflects both care and concern for people *and* sound commercial considerations. Indeed, it is this commercial viability that makes it possible to provide resources, opportunities and support to employees.

In a June 2005 speech at London's International Institute for Strategic Studies, De Beers chairman Nicky Oppenheimer noted that many African countries are poorer now than they were 50 years ago, despite sub-Saharan Africa having received more than US$1 trillion (thousand million)-worth of aid during those 50 years. He questions both the accuracy of the West's view of Africa, and the efficacy of their efforts to 'help'. While such questioning may be controversial, it is essential not only in the search for efficient solutions to complex HIV/Aids management questions on this most-affected continent of the world but also in the search for answers to systemically related questions of poverty, employment, wealth creation and healthcare solutions.

What is the business of a business?

The short answer is that it depends who you ask, where they are in the world, and to what economic model they subscribe. Perhaps a common answer is that the business of business is to make a profit, but this begs the question of how profit is achieved and what it contributes in the process to the economy and to the lives of the people it touches. De Beers firmly subscribes to Sir Ernest Oppenheimer's assertion that the aim of the Group is to make profits while making a real and lasting contribution to the communities in which it operates.

The company has 'a good track record' in corporate citizenship. But what constitutes a good track record? What could have been done better, differently, quicker? In the face of the challenges that HIV/Aids presents globally, answers to these and other questions are imperative if the future is indeed to be better than the past.

The De Beers HIV/Aids programme

Strategic intent

With a view to minimising the impact of HIV/Aids on the organisation and its people, and the vision of being a key partner in broader HIV/Aids solutions, the De Beers HIV/Aids strategy has four objectives:

1. **Saving lives**: preventing new infections by motivating employees to change their behaviour
2. **Living with HIV/Aids**: providing treatment, care and support for employees and life partners who are infected with, or affected by, HIV to enable them to continue to live productive lives
3. **Minimising the economic impact of HIV/Aids**: developing an effective, integrated management control system to measure the economic impact of HIV/Aids on the organisation and enable timely responses
4. **Communications and stakeholder engagement**: establishing mutually beneficial relationships with key stakeholders in HIV/Aids management to support the achievement of the above objectives

Policy considerations

Policy creates a guiding framework for HIV/Aids management

To create workplace acceptance of people living with HIV/Aids, De Beers focuses strongly on the advancement of best-practice policies, procedures and guidelines that meet legislative requirements, and on commitment to human dignity, human rights and non-discrimination. It is a proactive policy rather than simply a responsive one.

A global policy

Crossing boundaries to safeguard people and business

Globally, De Beers faces challenges such as treating people sensitively in different and diverse countries, economies and cultures, not imposing an unduly Western approach on developing countries and allowing the customisation of policies and approach to meet local requirements. Accordingly, the De Beers global corporate HIV/Aids workplace policy reflects the common principles of the De Beers Group for its operations: honouring the rights of all employees; minimising the spread and impact of HIV infection; and facilitating access to treatment, care and support for both infected and affected employees.

A South African policy

In South Africa, the joint HIV/Aids Workplace Policy,[1] co-signed by De Beers and the National Union of Mineworkers, formalises a shared commitment to protect employees.

1 The joint HIV/Aids Workplace Policy is available at www.debeersgroup.com.

Key aspects of the programme

Operations emphasise issues of local importance, but are required to implement all aspects of the broad-based HIV/Aids strategy itself.

Prevention

Education and training are vital

With the aim of educating and empowering people, De Beers delivers training interventions at all levels of the organisation and strives to facilitate the sharing of experiences through discussion and debate. Peer educators, sharing a common cultural and communal background, play an important role as HIV/Aids communicators, and KAP (knowledge, attitude and practice) studies monitor progress to shape subsequent responses.

Knowing your status is the first step

Voluntary counselling and testing (VCT) is recognised as the single most important intervention for both prevention and treatment. VCT uptake is stimulated through easy access to services and clear communication of the benefits of knowing your status.

All employees have access to health programmes

A health programme for employees includes the physical and psychological[2] components of well-being and is supported by targeted initiatives that include:

- Regular medical surveillance as part of occupational health
- Access to specialist physicians where necessary and possible
- Counselling support for employees and their families
- Access to free VCT
- HIV/Aids education and awareness programmes
- Access to general information on healthy living
- Disease surveillance and management programmes (e.g. TB, sexually transmitted infections)

No glove, no love

De Beers provides its employees with condoms and femidoms, and promotes their use through various educational initiatives.

Spreading the awareness message

A variety of media campaigns communicate De Beers' vision, principles and messages.

2 Key psychological components to health and quality of life are detailed in the publication *Icebergs in Africa: A Wellness Journey through the Visible and the Invisible* (Shaw 2004), many of which are applicable to HIV/Aids workplace programmes.

Educating our children through art

The De Beers Children's Aids Awareness Art Competition increases HIV/Aids awareness and stimulates discussion between employees and their children on sensitive issues such as sex, drug usage, death and discrimination.

Sero-prevalence and KAP studies

De Beers shares the results of sero-prevalence and KAP studies on its sites to stimulate discussion, raise awareness and reduce risk. In the process, all employees are equipped to 'talk HIV/Aids' in their home and community settings.

Sexually transmitted infections as an indicator of risky behaviour

Employees presenting with STIs offer an opportunity to influence risky behaviour. De Beers provides for the management of STIs, including testing, treatment and monitoring at its healthcare facilities.

Post-exposure prophylaxis and preventing mother-to-child transmission

Medical and first-aid standards for HIV risk situations such as blood-spills are in place. PEP (or post-exposure prophylaxis) is offered as part of the comprehensive treatment programme, for exposure through incidents such as work-related accidents or rape. The company's anti-retroviral treatment programme also offers treatment to prevent mother-to-child transmission (MTCT) of HIV.

Care, support and treatment

De Beers' employees are supported through general wellness initiatives, and those infected with and affected by HIV/Aids also receive treatment, care and support through the comprehensive HIV/Aids management programme.

Baseline and ongoing assessments

All HIV-positive employees and partners who join the treatment programme undergo an initial baseline physical and laboratory assessment.

Proactive interventions save lives

As part of the company's anti-retroviral treatment (ART) programme, HIV-positive employees and life partners receive:

- Immunisations and vaccinations for pneumococcus and influenza
- Prophylactic drugs, including bactrim and INH (isoniazid), to prevent opportunistic infections
- Dietary supplements such as plant sterols and vitamins
- Dietary counselling

Active monitoring of opportunistic infections

Opportunistic infections, often associated with a compromised immune system, are prevented through the use of prophylactics. For example, all sites minimise the spread of TB in the workforce through education and early detection programmes and effective case monitoring.

Support through assistance programmes

The company provides support structures such as employee assistance programmes (EAP) to help address issues that may cause physical and emotional stress for employees and their families. This includes positive-living programmes for those infected with and affected by HIV/Aids. Access to home-based care (HBC) structures is facilitated for employees who are medically retired, wherever possible.

The De Beers anti-retroviral treatment (ART) programme

With an initial focus on southern Africa, the De Beers anti-retroviral treatment programme was launched in South Africa in July 2003. Partner companies Debswana in Botswana and Namdeb in Namibia also provide access to anti-retrovirals for their employees through their own treatment programmes.

ART not only increases the productive lives of HIV-positive employees but also enhances quality of life for them and their families, within a holistic HIV/Aids programme in which individuals take responsibility for their own health and well-being.

The treatment programme is fully subsidised and is available to all De Beers employees and a spouse or life partner where this can be provided in a responsible and sustainable manner. It covers access to consultations with doctors, regular pathology testing, nutritional supplements, counselling, support and medication.

A network of medical professionals, including mine doctors and general practitioners across the country, means that spouses or life partners not staying near the mine can be treated, as well as retrenched and retired employees who leave the workplace. A third-party disease management service provider (DMSP) is employed to confidentially administer the programme and provide the clinical expertise to effectively treat HIV/Aids. The treatment protocols designed by the DMSP, in consultation with leading experts in HIV/Aids treatment, dictate the clinical criteria for the treatment of programme participants.

The company encourages HIV-positive employees and their spouses to join the programme as soon as they know their status, rather than waiting until they are ill. The wellness advice and emotional support offered by the programme contributes to better immune system management in the period between diagnosis and start of ART. Early enrolment also enables ongoing monitoring of the viral load and CD4 count (a measure of the strength of the immune system) to ensure that treatment begins at the appropriate time. It is heartening to see that, to date, there has consistently been an early uptake: more than 50% of those registered on the programme are not yet taking ART medication.

Programme uptake steady

The uptake rate on the De Beers ART programme is in line with similar corporate and medical scheme programmes. Employees need to know their status before they can make a decision to join the treatment programme, so voluntary counselling and testing is strongly promoted to all employees and partners.

The way forward

The programme is monitored against developments in the economic, legislative and healthcare environments in South Africa. In other countries in which the company operates, there is a commitment to finding equitable solutions that consider the impact of the epidemic, the available infrastructure to support the provision of ART and the feasibility of treatment in relation to business intentions in those areas.

The financial impact of HIV/Aids on De Beers operations

The most recent actuarial analysis, using company-specific sero-prevalence information and employee demographics, reveals a cost to the company per HIV-positive employee of R8,000–20,000 per year over the next 10–14 years (when the full impact of the disease will be realised). This includes direct employment-related costs such as absenteeism, lost productivity, medical costs, training and replacement costs, and the cost of HIV/Aids management interventions. The indirect costs often associated with HIV/Aids are harder to measure, but include the impact on safety, low morale, and the risk of business partners being unable to fulfil their obligations because of the impact of HIV/Aids on their businesses.

The cost of providing ART to employees and a spouse or life partner

De Beers knows that the cost of inaction will ultimately far exceed the cost of treatment and, in Debswana, where the treatment programme has been running for some time, the introduction of a disease management programme and ART has reduced the predicted mortality rate.

ART currently costs about R8,000 per person per year. The cost, however, is a function of the number of people who join the ART programme and when they join. The cost of health management in the early stages of the disease is lower than it is at later stages.

Integrated programme management

The effectiveness of the HIV/Aids workplace programme relies on integration with broader frameworks such as occupational health and safety requirements and practices, international codes of good practice and country-specific legislation.

In addition, support is generated through policies such as the Diamond Best Practice Principles, corporate governance requirements, and mechanisms to drive strategy through to individual performance objectives. Collectively, this ensures that HIV/Aids management receives strategic attention and the personal attention of employees.

Rigorous measurement

Regular measurement in KAP studies, sero-prevalence surveys and actuarial analyses informs planning and indicates the likely current and future impact of HIV/Aids on the organisation. The measurement and monitoring of appropriate key performance indicators highlights areas to address and enables the company to update actuarial models to more accurately reflect potential future costs.

Succession and manpower planning strategies are reviewed and refined according to estimated prevalence figures and business objectives. Trends in different environments are monitored and interpreted to ensure that De Beers is managing the disease in line with internationally accepted best practice.

Corporate social responsibility alignment

By assisting those who work to transform society for the better, the De Beers Fund[3] helps to build citizens with the skills, confidence, determination and resources to play their part in the well-being of the nation. The proportion of social investment budget directed at HIV/Aids initiatives is increasing. In 2004 alone, over R2.5 million was invested in 28 projects such as training for home-based care and prevention projects aimed at young people. De Beers invests more than just financial aid: time is spent with funding applicants to help develop sustainable projects.

De Beers does not think of this as philanthropy, but as a strategically informed approach for aligning social investment with business interests. Expenditure primarily goes to regions where employees live or return to, or on projects that have an impact on the lives of employees. It is a fine balance between acting strategically overall and responding flexibly at a local level.

Accolades based on partnerships

De Beers continues to receive recognition for its achievements in HIV/Aids management:

- The De Beers HIV/Aids programme was commended in the category 'Workplace Programmes' in the Global Business Coalition (GBC) awards for Business Excellence in 2004
- De Beers was one of only ten companies to receive global recognition from the International Chamber of Commerce (ICC) in 2004 for the role of its HIV/Aids programme in supporting the Millennium Development Goals
- In 2005, De Beers was recognised by the GBC for its voluntary counselling and testing programme

Lessons learned and a path to the future

Some early interventions failed

HIV/Aids was recognised as a business and social threat by the southern African De Beers operations as early as the mid-1980s, and a number of awareness and prevention programmes were initiated. However, new infections continued to rise as:

3 De Beers' social investment vehicle in South Africa.

- Early interventions were targeted largely at awareness rather than behaviour change
- There was a lack of collaboration with key stakeholders
- Almost no company-specific information was available to direct the interventions

Review of the approach

HIV/Aids management was elevated to a strategic company consideration in 2000 and a co-ordinated approach to the epidemic was created, along with a dedicated central platform of expertise. HIV professionals across the operations work together to limit the impact of the epidemic on the business, its employees and the communities in which it operates.

Many hard-learned lessons and paths to the future

The importance of involving and equipping managers

Each manager has HIV/Aids management responsibilities and, with hindsight, they should have been equipped far earlier to manage their people and plan their business effectively in the midst of the epidemic.

De Beers developed an HIV/Aids training programme to enable managers and supervisors to:

- Competently deal with employees who disclose that they are HIV-positive
- Answer employee questions confidently and accurately
- Know where to refer employees for assistance or additional information
- Be able to reinforce the company position on HIV/Aids
- Respond appropriately and compassionately
- Deal with issues such as discrimination, productivity, discipline and employee relations
- Know the legislation that affects HIV/Aids in the workplace
- Proactively develop solutions that serve business and employees

Peer educator programmes are a critical component of a sound HIV/Aids management programme, yet they are a mixture of failure and success. Managerial support is critical to success and, again, more upfront managerial involvement would have been valuable. In particular, peer educators need direction, support (including debriefing) and acknowledgement, and without managerial support these needs may well be disregarded.

The importance of a representative peer educator population

A representative profile of peer educator volunteers across different levels of the organisation is ideal, yet most come from junior levels. This limits and frustrates peer educators and gives mixed messages about the real worth of peer education. Resolution of this issue, coupled with proper management of peer educators, will result in greater successes and enhanced return on investment.

Linked to this, corporate head office-type environments seem to be more problematic than industrial plants or rural mines when it comes to effective peer educator programmes. Possibly, the more educated employees typical of a knowledge-worker environment believe that HIV/Aids is not their problem, or that, armed with the facts, protection is guaranteed (even though KAP studies show serious vulnerabilities in this population).

The need to critically evaluate treatment support

In the De Beers treatment programme, where employees and spouses elect to use the services of a *private* doctor, there is little *ongoing* support for the patient unless HIV status is voluntarily disclosed to individuals in the workplace who could provide support. If, on the other hand, the patient uses the mine clinic, or reaches the doctor through an Employee Assistance Programme counsellor trained in HIV/Aids, the opportunity to provide support is far greater. This support is critical to long-term compliance, which, if not achieved, could ultimately lead to drug resistance and the creation of multiple strains of the virus.

The importance of defined deliverables

An effective HIV/Aids workplace programme needs to progressively ensure that managers, HR managers, HIV/Aids managers, peer educators and employees have clearly delineated performance objectives in HIV/Aids management and that these objectives are seen to be legitimate.

If targets are set, success needs to be measured. The importance of measurable goals and information systems to support monitoring, reporting and decision-making cannot be underestimated. This is often interpreted to mean quantifiable measures, but qualitative measurements in HIV/Aids management should be explored further—particularly where success is based on perceptions. Certainly, the combination of defined deliverables and measurable goals helps to maintain impetus in HIV/Aids management, when it is often difficult to see the end result.

A key area of impact, in terms of whether defined deliverables are in fact met, is that of organisational culture. The daily issues of workload, deadlines and perceived priorities—the informal 'what's important around here?'—should be actively influenced to support the achievement of HIV/Aids management goals.

Linked to this, greater integration across the various functions of organisational life is seen to be key, not only between HIV, EAP, SHE (safety, health and environment) and medical services but also in the areas of human resources that shape and define culture, values, work design, workflow and beyond.

The importance of focusing on what really is important, rather than what is seen to be important

The urgency of the Aids epidemic has sometimes prompted problem-solving at one level of logic that creates bigger problems at a higher level of logic. Protecting unborn children through MTCT prophylaxis without considering the full impact of untreated mothers and Aids orphans is a case in point. In a rush for solutions, there is a need to critically evaluate one's own thinking.

This includes evaluating the balance in any HIV/Aids management programme. In De Beers' case, it was realised that, in emphasising treatment, it is important to keep sight of the social issues around Aids management and to work just as emphatically in the area of prevention.

The role of culture

Africa is a multiplicity of cultures that meet in their fullest diversity at work. With this in mind, the 'plugging-in' of Western solutions is not always appropriate and, more importantly, does not always work. A case in point is the provision of written HIV/Aids 'facts' with the belief that people will then, by osmosis, understand the issues and change their behaviour. Culture, personal priorities, and vastly differing life experiences influence propensity for behaviour change. Understanding such 'entry points' is key to a meaningful HIV/Aids programme, which should be situated in a broader context of better use of life opportunities through knowledge and sound decisions. The efficacy of pushing information towards people is debatable simply because people process it through their perceptual filters. It is through true dialogue, story-telling, industrial theatre and other interactive processes that HIV/Aids messages are more likely to be heard. If Africa holds 'sense of community' dear, how could this be defined? Koka (cited in Shaw 2004: 106) describes the African concept of *uBuntu* as: 'the Divine spark of life that weaves the fabric of all humanity together, determines our relationships, and reflects the quality and dignity of the human personality'. Just as the baobab tree is often a meeting place to exchange stories, news and views, so HIV/Aids programmes in Africa should create similar spaces for human interactive learning.

It is important to understand that HIV/Aids in an African context is far broader than healthcare—pointing to issues such as food security, poverty alleviation, and the importance of addressing 'mindstate' in a continent damaged by its past. It is naive to arm people with facts with the belief that they will then be equipped to avoid risk. For example, it is important to acknowledge that material poverty creates human conditions such as hopelessness, in the context of which risk-taking behaviour is far more likely to occur. It is also important to acknowledge that psychological coping skills can play an instrumental role in risk avoidance, and in the longevity, quality of life, and productive capacity of *all* people, whether they are HIV-positive or HIV-negative, healthy or ill.

Using the lessons learned from HIV/Aids management

While HIV/Aids programmes around the world are receiving significant funding and attention, we should be smart in applying lessons learned to the management of other chronic diseases. HIV/Aids has required policy and strategy design, educator training, counsellor skills building and creative communications that interrogate attitudes, beliefs and practices—all skills that can be more actively positioned in broader disease and health management programmes. Working with HIV/Aids gives people knowledge and understanding that will build compassion, and this is valuable way beyond the management of this epidemic.

Strengthening the broader community

With the recognition that the boundary between company and community is a tenuous distinction when combating disease and building health, De Beers has committed R10 million over the next three years to extending the HIV/Aids programmes existent in the workplace to the communities around its operations. These programmes will seek to reduce HIV infection by building the coping skills that enable people to make healthy, informed, low-risk decisions, and to empower communities to best support people living with HIV and Aids.

In conclusion . . .

Although HIV/Aids management has come a long way since the 1980s, many challenges remain. When it all seems too much, it helps to remember an African proverb that says: 'Knowledge is like a baobab tree—one person's arms are not enough to encompass it.' It is important to learn from others—different countries and approaches have excelled in unique ways, and each provides a crucial learning opportunity. De Beers does its best to work first and foremost as a willing *community* encompassing the challenges, forging partnerships and drawing on the qualities of the tree itself—tenacity, versatility and durability—to build longevity.

References

Makubalo, L., P. Netshidzivhami, L. Mahlasela and R. du Plessis (2003) *Report National HIV and Syphilis Antenatal Sero-prevalence Survey in South Africa 2003* (Pretoria: Department of Health).

Shaw, J. (2004) *Icebergs in Africa: A Wellness Journey through the Visible and the Invisible* (Cape Town, South Africa: Kima Global).

UNAIDS (2004) *2004 Report on the Global AIDS Epidemic* (Geneva: UNAIDS).

Part V
Industries and sectors

13

Can oil corporations positively transform Angola and Equatorial Guinea?

Jose A. Puppim de Oliveira

Brazilian School of Public and Business Administration

Saleem H. Ali

Rubenstein School of Environment and Natural Resources, University of Vermont, USA

Oil production has been a major source of export revenues for many African countries, and yet has played a questionable role in the development of sub-Saharan Africa. Multinational companies in the oil sector have had established operations in the continent for several decades, despite many operational difficulties. In some countries, they endured an institutional environment that was not particularly attractive to business, such as civil wars, famine, lack of safety, disease and widespread corruption. On the other hand, once they were established, they could operate with limited government regulation or social control from civil society, especially with respect to environmental and social standards. Allegations of bribery, environmental degradation, social conflict and lack of integration with the local economy have historically plagued the behaviour of corporations in Africa (Bayart *et al.* 1999). Recently, however, there appears to be some positive movement towards responsible management of African oil revenues that is gaining attention (Katz *et al.* 2004). How companies and governments leverage these opportunity costs is particularly important to understand in the context of African development.

Background on oil in Africa

Oil has become one of the main sources of revenue for countries in sub-Saharan Africa (Table 13.1). Several countries have turned into oil exporters since the 1970s: Nigeria, Angola, Congo-Brazzaville, Gabon, Equatorial Guinea, Cameroon, Chad, the Democratic Republic of Congo and Sudan. Many others are exploring their subsoil in search of the 'black gold', such as Sierra Leone, Mauritania, Niger and Uganda.

Country	% of GDP	% of exports	% of government revenue
Nigeria	40	95	83
Angola	45	90	90
Congo-Brazzaville	67	94	80
Equatorial Guinea	86	90	61
Gabon	73	81	60
Cameroon	4.9	60	20

TABLE 13.1 Weight of oil in some African economies (2002 estimates)

Source: CRS 2003

The estimates for sub-Saharan Africa run at around 7% of the world's reserves of oil. Fields in the Gulf of Guinea alone contain an estimate of 24 billion barrels. There is a trend of increase in these values, as most of the new discoveries of oil reserves happen in the region. In 2001, the fields of West and Central Africa's Atlantic coast accounted for 7 billion out of 8 billion barrels of new crude oil reserves found around the world (CRS 2003).

Sub-Saharan oil is attractive to the main oil markets of the United States and European Union (EU) because of several technical factors, such as its high-quality crude (low sulphur content) and the proximity to the main markets. However, the region's sociopolitical factors are even more appealing compared with other regions. Nigeria is the only country affiliated with the Organisation of Petroleum Exporting Countries (OPEC). Moreover, sub-Saharan countries are more open to foreign companies than countries in the Middle East or Latin America, whose oil reserves are mostly in the hands of state companies. The recent instability in the Middle East due to Islamic terrorism and the Chavez factor in Venezuela makes Africa even more attractive to oil development.

Case overviews

We follow a comparative case research methodology to understand the patterns of corporate influence on development trajectories in Angola and Equatorial Guinea. This study is not meant to be a detailed ethnography of the cases and instead uses a prospective methodology. Our aim is to develop an argument with stipulated assumptions that could potentially be considered in policy formulation.

The Angolan case

Since its independence in 1975 from Portugal until 2002, the established Angolan government and the rebel group UNITA fought a ruthless war that killed thousands and left more than 4 million displaced, out of a total population of approximately 11 million (estimated in 2004 according to EIA 2005).

Angola is the largest oil producer in southern Africa, and second in sub-Saharan Africa, only behind Nigeria. Crude oil production reached over 900,000 barrels per day in 2003 (see Fig. 13.1). More than half of the oil is found in the Cabinda province, an enclave north of the country and separated from the rest of Angola by 60 km of Congolese (Democratic Republic of Congo) territory. In 2008, it is estimated that Angolan production will exceed 2 billion barrels a day, as the new deep-water sites are expected to operate at full capacity. In Angola, oil accounts for 90% of total exports, more than 90% of government revenues and 45% of the country's GDP (Table 13.1).

The low operating costs and large reserves attract most of the large oil companies to the country, including ChevronTexaco, ExxonMobil and Occidental (Angola Embassy in the UK 2004). Chevron (now ChevronTexaco) has the largest operations in the country and a long history, with more than 40 years of operational experience. The company produces more than 500,000 barrels a day in Angola (Chevron 2005). In the 1990s, Chevron developed deep-water oil fields in the country, increasing its production capacity. It has also invested in the production of natural gas.

There are a series of issues involving the oil business and corporate social responsibility (CSR) in Angola.

First, oil production has always been linked to supporting conflicts in the country. Oil revenues, from the activities of multinational oil companies, undoubtedly helped the government war structure, while the diamonds, on the other hand, were helping the rebel group UNITA (Cilliers and Dietrich 2000). The war is over, but other conflicts remain, such as the separatist movement in Cabinda, Angola's prime oil production region. In production terms, Cabinda generates about 60% of the country's oil, but it has a tiny population (around 170,000, compared with the country's 15 million). Cabinda has had a separatist movement since independence, and claims oil money keeps the repression over their claims of freedom.

Second, there is a large financial imbalance between the huge oil companies and national governments of Africa, and Angola in particular. For example, ExxonMobil's profits of US$15 billion in 2001, are almost double Angola's GDP of US$8.8 billion (in 2000) and more than tenfold greater than the US$1.4 billion GDP of Chad in 2001 (CRS 2003). The differences in resources may lead to a huge asymmetry of power in negotiations with governments.

Third, there are claims that some of the government money from oil goes unaccounted for. For example, a total of US$4.22 billion (or approximately 9% of GDP) was unaccounted for between 1997 and 2002 from Angolan accounting books, according to an analysis by Human Rights Watch (HRW 2004). Suspicions of corruption were also

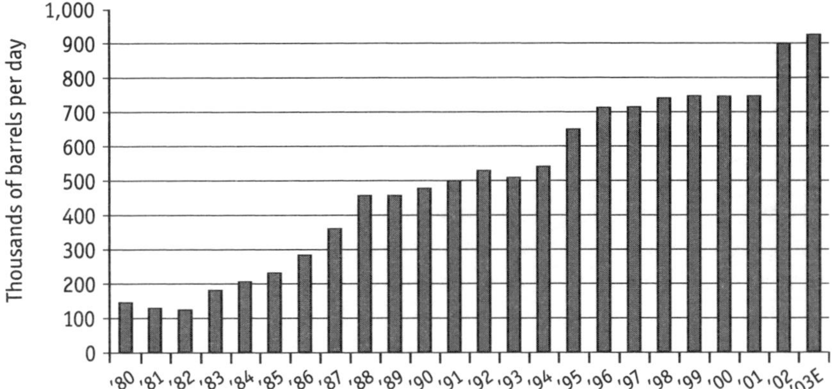

FIGURE 13.1 Oil production in Angola

Source: EIA 2005

raised when the International Monetary Fund (IMF) set up a Staff Monitored Program (SMP), which found that revenues from oil had been diverted to the presidency and the state company Sonangol. Moreover, Sonangol is pointed to by some authors as a distributor of benefits to the local elite, such as scholarships abroad and travel expenses (Hodges 2004). This bonanza from oil revenues has also led to over-borrowing by the government in the so-called oil-backed loans. The IMF calculated that the oil-backed debt has reached 33% of Angola's total external debt; thus a large part of the oil revenue has to be used to pay back loans.

Fourth, oil companies have been accused of many oil spills, which have affected the environment and the local population. There are many examples in Nigeria with Shell and Angola with Chevron (BBC News 2002).

Finally, revenues from the oil sector have abounded for the companies and governments, but the life of most Angolans has not changed much. An estimated 900,000 Angolans remain displaced from the civil war times. Many more have no access to basic needs and citizenship, such as education and healthcare. The United Nations cites that 67% of the urban population is poor in Angola (UNDP 2000). Part of the oil money could be used to remediate those problems, but not much is left at the local level. For example, Cabinda produces most of the Angolan oil, but gets only a small fraction of the revenues, equivalent to 10% of the tax paid by ChevronTexaco and partners in its operations in the province. Moreover, the oil boom and the liberalisation of the economy seem to have contributed to an increase in social inequality in the country. The Gini coefficient, a widely used measure of income inequality, increased from 0.45 in 1995 to 0.54 in 1999 (UNDP 1999).

However, there have been some positive developments in the last few years since the civil war ended and companies have reacted to the wave of corporate social responsibility and strengthening in regulation as discussed in Section 13.4.

The case of Equatorial Guinea

In many ways Equatorial Guinea has been an anomaly in African history. It is the only Spanish-speaking country on the continent. While the past decade has seen relative political stability in the country, it has been at the expense of democracy and human rights (Bolender 2003). The Equatorial Guinea government is considered by many commentators as one of the most notorious kleptocracies in Africa (Wood 2004), and has eluded accountability long before the advent of oil. The World Bank and IMF withdrew financial support from Equatorial Guinea in the late 1990s on account of corrupt governance but have initiated some limited assistance since 2003 as part of the Regional Integration Assistance Strategy (World Bank 2003a).

Though much of the literature on kleptocracies and their survival would lead us to believe that oil wealth might perpetuate the regime's strength (Acemoglu *et al.* 2004; Global Witness 2004), we would like to offer an alternative prospect, based on recent developments in corporate social responsibility (CSR). In contrast to Angola, we hypothesise that a smaller, more tightly dependent economy such as Equatorial Guinea might be more amenable to positive influences from CSR, even though the nature of kleptocratic governance is far more acute in Equatorial Guinea.

A detailed history of oil development in Equatorial Guinea has already been provided in very recent publications (Frynas 2004; Wood 2004), and our aim here is to focus instead on developments pertaining to corporate governance in Equatorial Guinea and its influence on the regime in terms of environmental and social responsibility.

It is important to note, however, that there appears to have been a noticeable improvement in the Human Development Index (HDI) of Equatorial Guinea since the oil industry began activities there in the last decade or so. Figure 13.2 shows this change in comparison with other countries in sub-Saharan Africa and the average global HDI. While there are methodological critiques that can be made of the HDI measure, it is a fairly useful composite measure of health, education and standard-of-living changes. Comparable data for Angola is unavailable; however, the HDI for Angola in the *2004 Human Development Report* is reported to be 0.381, which is well below Equatorial Guinea.

Some scholars have attributed the rapid development and investment in infrastructure as occurred in the Middle East oil states or indeed in African states such as Gabon to 'rentier theory' (Yates 1996). Thus the increase in HDI, according to this theory, is predictable but not sustainable, since the rentier economy considers development to be a commodity that can be purchased rather than a process. Based on this trajectory, rentier theorists contend that, while diversification may be the answer, oil economies are resistant to diversification because the structure of revenues encourages complacency. However, recent scholarship and indeed the economic performance of many Gulf States such as the United Arab Emirates are questioning the validity and universal applicability of rentier theory (Moore 2002).

Given the high level of publicity accorded to the role of oil companies in US politics, the US State Department decided to support precautionary measures against capital flight and corruption in the case of oil development in Equatorial Guinea.[1] A Social

1 The United States reopened its embassy in Malabo in 2003 and the State Department asserts that US 'intervention has resulted in positive developments, such as the release of a half dozen persons

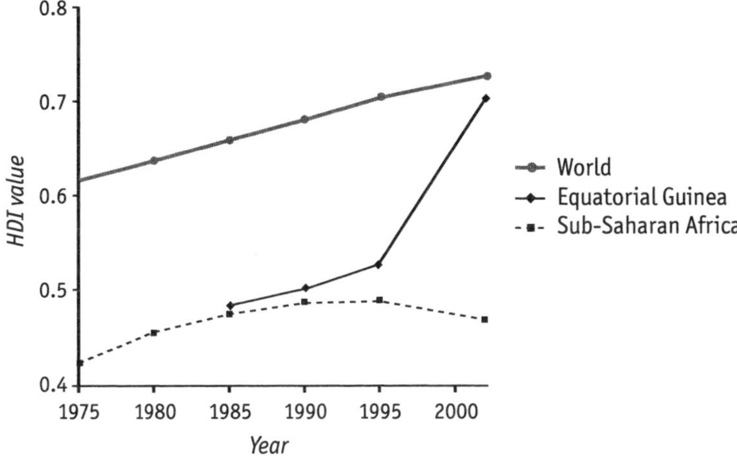

FIGURE 13.2 **Changes in Human Development Index for Equatorial Guinea (1975–2000)**

Needs Assessment was commissioned by the State Department which led to a comprehensive set of recommendations from Business for Social Responsibility (BSR), a non-profit group that works to improve social practices of companies. A detailed plan for setting up a Social Development Fund was also part of the project, completed in May 2005.

Analysis of the cases

While there is considerable literature on the adverse effects of oil development on developing economies through 'Dutch disease' or 'resource curse' mechanisms (Karl 1997; Ross 2001a, 2001b; Le-Billon 2001), studies have neglected to pose the question in terms of positive causal factors that certain kinds of oil development might bring about, especially with the recent changes mentioned above.

We do not dispute the potential for negative effects of certain kinds of oil development but rather propose that some of the negative causality can be managed and transformed to lead to positive outcomes. Thus we eschew the fatalistic tendency of resource

detained without charge. The position of "second vice prime minister over human rights and public administration" was created to improve and monitor the human rights situation in the country' (US Embassy in Equatorial Guinea 2005: malabo.usembassy.gov).

curse theorists and approach the issue from a prescriptive planning perspective using evidence from two recent cases of oil development in Africa, in Angola and Equatorial Guinea.

This study aims to provide analyses for understanding mechanisms by which the investment of multinational oil companies could potentially play a role in promoting more transparent and responsive states. Both countries being studied were in dire economic and political predicaments even before the advent of oil and hence provide a common baseline to look for any positive or negative trends since oil development began.

Our analysis harks back to the divergence of perspectives in the political economy of development literature. On the one hand a more negative view of dependence leading to 'peripheral states' has been offered, often through a Marxist critique (dos Santos 1970) or using rentier theory (Yates 1996). On the other hand, a relatively positive view of dependence on resources and external involvement from multinational corporations and international actors has been offered by some scholars working in Nigeria and Brazil (Evans 1979; Bierstecker 1987). These dependency theorists recognise that states such as Nigeria and Brazil are by no means role models of development but that they are probably better off than they might have been in the absence of resources and international involvement. The key failure has been in the accountability and enforcement means imposed on multinationals. Our research tries to understand and provide some alternatives to improve this point.

How companies and governments leverage these opportunities is particularly important to understand in the context of African development. Angola and Equatorial Guinea provide examples of how geographic differences in size, demographics, post-colonial linkages and alternative industrial sectors can lead to different development trajectories. This is not to say that those trajectories are immutable but rather that different regulatory mechanisms might be needed to bring about change.

Three trends seem to have influenced companies to change their behaviour regarding issues related to social responsibility: the global movement for CSR, the pressure from international organisations and the strengthening of the state's regulatory capacity. We discuss these trends below.

Rise of the CSR movement

Companies are increasingly worried about being considered socially and environmentally responsible by their peers, consumers and society in general. The World Business Council for Sustainable Development (WBCSD) and other industry organisations have played a fundamental role in organising business and spreading concepts and tools to deal with social and environmental issues, as well as particular government efforts such as the Extractive Industries Transparency Initiative.[2]

2 The Extractive Industries Transparency Initiative (EITI), launched by the British government in 2002, is an important step in this regard. Both Angola and Equatorial Guinea have officially endorsed the initiative and are exploring ways for implementation. Angola commissioned a diagnostic study of the oil sector's finances in 2004 by KPMG. Equatorial Guinea has procured technical assistance from the World Bank to implement the EITI, including a stakeholder meeting in March 2005.

Historically, CSR reputation has not affected the profitability of companies. However, there is growing evidence that this trend is changing (Schneitz and Epstein 2005). This is not due as much to consumer demand changes as it is to the growing threat of litigation costs that may result through civil-society action. In particular the oil industry is beginning to feel this impact as illustrated by a recent study by Gueterbock (2004) of the impact of the Greenpeace campaign against ExxonMobil.

Since most of the companies operating in Equatorial Guinea and Angola are American companies or have strong economic interests in America, there is also the possibility that US legal recourse would be more easily applicable to operations in these countries. Hence any potential violations of environmental and human rights might be litigated under the Alien Torts Statute of 1789 (ATS). While this law was originally enacted to combat piracy on the high seas, it has been applied in lower courts to violations of human and environmental rights by companies with American linkages. The recent US supreme court ruling on the applicability of the ATS in *Sosa* v. *Alvarez-Machain et al.* (2004), has limited the applicability of the ATS but has 'kept the door ajar' for some specific cases of violations in which corporations may be culpable.[3]

At the World Summit on Sustainable Development in Johannesburg in 2002, the International Association of Oil and Gas Producers presented a social report, which described their intentions and actions to be more socially and environmentally responsible in their operations. Those actions range from water provision projects and HIV/Aids programmes to the enormous revenues they have generated to local and central governments in Africa.

Social projects and philanthropy have been the chief CSR actions of oil companies in Africa. ChevronTexaco reports that it has invested heavily in all kinds of social project, such as construction of health centres and schools, technical training to local populations, funding of small business and Aids programmes. For example, it supports the development of the Futila Industrial Park in Angola. Although some organisations claim that many of those projects are useless or are not working anymore (CRS 2003), the attitude of investing more resources than before in the countries and communities in which they have operations is a significant change in the behaviour of oil companies.

Under pressure from NGOs and some governments in their own home countries, many companies have introduced codes of conduct to deal with governments in Africa. BP was the first to create an initiative of transparency in its contracts in Angola in 2001. The company promised to release all its payments to the government, including net production, aggregate payments, total taxes and signature bonus. However, in its first release of information,[4] the Angolan government through the state-controlled oil company (Sonangol) reacted firmly, saying that a confidentiality clause and legislation did not allow the disclosure of information (CRS 2003). Thus, a well-intentioned unilateral attitude of a company can provoke a backlash that hurts the company that tries to be responsible. In a competitive business environment, such as oil, and in a context such as parts of Africa with centralised governments with little accountability, companies

3 Additionally, action in state courts such as the recent ruling to move to trial in a case against the Californian gas company Unocal (*Doe et al*. v. *Unocal* 2004) for alleged complicity in human rights violations in Burma/Myanmar may also be an additional recourse for litigants. Ultimately, however, this case was settled out of court in March 2005.

4 BP said that it paid US$111 million signature bonus to the Government of Angola for a 26.7% operating share in Block 31 (CRS 2003).

cannot go against local authorities alone. The Publish What You Pay campaign led by NGOs can force more companies to act together and generate a more transparent contracting environment and make governments more accountable in the region.[5]

Influence of international issues: international financial institutions and globalisation of civil society

Empirical research is showing that International Financial Institutions (IFIs) and international networks of NGOs are important drivers of change worldwide (Vives 2004). Many countries depend significantly on the monies and expertise from international organisations to implement development programmes and projects. Groups of civil society and NGOs in Africa are still in a relatively weak position to influence change, but they are increasingly getting organised and connected with larger local and world networks of movements related to CSR. Moreover, NGOs in the Northern countries are progressively building institutional capacity to monitor multinational corporations in Africa, directly or with the help of local partners. The recent campaign led by Friends of the Earth against Shell in the UK is an example. Friends of the Earth published, in partnership with other organisations, its own social and environmental report of Shell activities around the world, denouncing many shortcomings (FoE 2003). There is also a group of NGOs that have specialised in being the watchdogs of multinationals, such as Corporate Watch, or even networks of NGOs that focus their activities on oil issues in Africa, such as Oilwatch Africa.

IFIs are particularly important in shaping African governments and companies in certain aspects. Besides direct finance of development projects, IFIs act as risk reducers for private investment, such as in the development of oil fields. The World Bank Group and export credit agencies (ECAs) work together with many oil companies in Africa. The latter give even more resources than the traditional multilateral organisations. In Angola, ECAs of nine countries funded US$3 billion in projects, or more than 25% of the estimated foreign direct investment that came to the country in the same period (Carbonell 2002 cited by CRS 2003). IFIs can attach conditions to finance projects or release credits, so they can be fundamental for improving legal and administrative systems. Even though ECAs generally do not require strict social or environmental safeguards, the World Bank has increasingly applied social and environmental conditions to its loans, as well as supporting innovative projects, such as the Chad–Cameroon pipeline (World Bank 2003b). This project is supported by the World Bank and introduced a series of innovative social and environmental guidelines. NGOs and local communities

5 The viability of corporate responsibility as a means of initiating change in Equatorial Guinea was tested by a recent scandal involving the alleged siphoning of funds from oil revenues to an account held by President Obiang's family at Riggs Bank in Washington, DC. There were direct linkages made to acquisition of property in Washington suburbs from these accounts (Global Witness 2004). This led to a senate hearing on the issue and an investigation by the Office of the Comptroller of Currency (OCC). However, the focus of the investigation has been more on the bank than on the oil companies or the Equatorial Guinea government. Even so, the Equatorial Guinea government has vehemently objected to this interference in its affairs since oil revenues and their use are considered a 'state secret' by the Equatorial Guinea authorities. Nevertheless, the government is obliged to co-operate with authorities in the investigation since US companies are bound by the Foreign Corrupt Practices Act.

have an important role in monitoring the project. Regrettably, violations of the agreement led the World Bank to temporarily stop support of the project in January 2006.

Regulatory capacity

The regulatory capacity of some African governments over oil activities has grown in recent years. Some governments have gained expertise in the technical matters of the oil business, improved their capacity to negotiate concession contracts and regulate social and environmental issues. For example, ChevronTexaco got a US$2 million fine from Angolan authorities because of an oil spill in the sea in 2002. Even though companies have a history of oil spills and pollution in the region, this was the first time an oil company was fined for environmental degradation in the gulf countries of Africa. ChevronTexaco also compensated local fishermen for losses in their incomes.

Another institutional improvement in government is the consolidation of Sonangol (the Angolan state oil company) in terms of technical and management capacity. Over the years, even during the civil war, Sonangol gained technical capacity in many aspects of the oil business including regulation, contracting, product distribution, industry support services and refinery, as well as in non-commercial areas such as education, training and health. It has also entered other areas of the economy such as insurance, the airlines and telecommunications. Sonangol has been almost a state within the state. The state company is a kind of role model to other countries in the region. It is using its experience to increase Angola's influence in southern Africa. Sonangol has passed technical expertise on to the governments of Congo-Brazzaville and São Tomé e Príncipe, a new entrant among oil-producing countries in the region.

In Angola, the partnership between the state and oil companies is done through Sonangol, the state oil company. There have been concession contracts (Contratos de Partilha) that specify the terms of division between Sonangol and the partner. They are very important because oil is the main economic activity and source of revenue for the state.

A new Petroleum Law was passed in 2004 (Law 10/04 of 12 November 2004). Under this law the powers of the Ministry of Petroleum increased, and new safeguards were introduced. While previously contracted concessions remain, the changes are valid for new contracts. Two basic principles permeate the law: oil reserves are a property of the state and Sonangol is the sole and exclusive concessionary of this property. The law tries to give more power to the Ministry of Petroleum, promotes local content and firms in the oil sector, requires the hiring of Angolan citizens wherever possible and forbids discrimination in terms of salary between local workers and expatriates (US–Angola Chamber of Commerce 2005).

In the concession contracts there are few safeguards for oil spills. However, there are general environmental laws and a specific environmental law for the oil sector, the Environmental Law for the Oil Sector (Lei do Ambiente do Sector Petrolífero). This law prescribes what companies should do to prevent pollution or accidents, determines contingency plans in case of accidents and prescribe fines for oil spills. At the national level, there has been some improvement in the enforcement of the environmental laws and strategic actions, such as the national plan for contingencies. The elaboration of this plan included the participation of the oil companies and two international organisations, the IMO (International Maritime Organisation) and IPIECA (International Petroleum Industry Environmental Conservation Association).

Equatorial Guinea's regulatory capacity is severely limited compared with Angola, but nevertheless improving. The level of dependence for technical expertise extends even to the regulatory arena. Much of the regulatory capacity is managed by a British consulting firm Exploration Consultants Limited (ECL). According to the Ministry's public website (www.equatorialoil.com), the current law concerning hydrocarbon exploration and production activities is Decree Law No. 7/1981 of June 1981 (the Hydrocarbons Law) as amended by further decree in November 1998. While the production-sharing contract legislation is under review, it contains provisions for a minimum royalty of 10%, escalating to a maximum of 16%. Environmental and social concerns are being addressed primarily through the impact assessment process rather than through regulatory compliance.

Conclusions

The argument has been made by resource curse theorists as well as social/environmental activists that good governance must be a prerequisite for oil development in Africa. The reasoning they present is that oil development once begun can perpetuate corruption, despotism and economic inequality because of the spatial and economic nature of oil operations and revenue management. However, instead of being trapped in the resource curse or the Dutch disease hypotheses, we have to move on and look at the changes that the region and the oil sector have undergone in the past few years. This allows us to make a more positive assessment and policy analysis of how further change can happen and how the different actors may influence those changes.

This chapter has attempted to provide a preliminary analysis of how negative presumptions might be reversed and oil development could potentially catalyse good governance in Africa. There are numerous cases of poor governance in Africa without any oil development. Hence a question that might be asked is would these countries be any better off with oil? While such a question is impossible to address empirically, what we have attempted to provide is a scenario analysis that lays out conditions under which a positive role for oil development in Africa could be considered in two African states of varying size. Our analysis recognises that the argument developed here is based on the hypothetical behaviour of certain organisations. However, the aim has been to present a positive scenario that could be used to guide policy choice by various stakeholders and provide a pragmatic development path for African oil states.

Bibliography

Acemoglu, D., J.A. Robinson and T. Verdier (2004) 'Kleptocracy and Divide-and-Rule: A Model of Personal Rule', *Journal of European Economic Association* 2.3: 162-92.

Angola Embassy in the UK (2004) www.angola.org.uk/facts_resources_invest.htm, 14 September 2004.

Bayart, J.-F., S. Ellis and B. Hibou (1999) *Criminalization of the State in Africa* (Bloomington, IN: Indiana University Press).

BBC News (2002) 'Angola fines Chevron for pollution', 1 July 2002, news.bbc.co.uk/1/hi/business/2077836.stm, 15 January 2004.

Bierstecker, T.J. (1987) *Multinationals, the State and Control of the Nigerian Economy* (Princeton, NJ: Princeton University Press).

Bolender, J. (2003) 'Blind eye on Africa: Human rights, Equatorial Guinea and oil', *Z-Net*, 16 August 2003.

Carbonell, T. (2002) *Export Credit Agency Activity in Angola 1980–2002* (unpublished paper; Washington, DC: Environmental Defense).

Chevron (2005) www.ChevronTexaco.com/operations/africa/angola.asp, 2 March 2005.

Cilliers, J., and C. Dietrich (eds.) (2000) *Angola's War Economy: The Role of Oil and Diamonds* (Johannesburg: Institute for Strategic Studies).

CRS (Catholic Relief Services) (2003) *Bottom of the Barrel* (London: CAFOD).

Culverwell, M., *et al.* (2003) *Towards an Improved Governance Agenda for Extractive Industries* (London: Royal Institute of International Affairs).

Cusack, I. (2001) 'Nation-builders at Work: The Equatoguinean "Myth" of Bantu Unity', *Nationalism and Ethnic Politics* 7.3: 77-97.

Dos Santos, T. (1970) 'The Structure of Dependence', *American Economic Review* 60.2: 231-36.

EIA (Energy Information Administration) (2005) www.eia.doe.gov/emeu/cabs/angola.html, 2 March 2005.

Equatorial Guinea, Ministry of Mines, Minerals and Energy (2004) www.equatorialoil.com, 5 November 2004.

Evans, P. (1979) *Dependent Development: The Alliance of Multinational, State and Local Capital in Brazil* (Princeton, NJ: Princeton University Press).

FoE (Friends of the Earth and other organisations) (2003) *Behind the Shine: The Other Shell Report 2003* (London: FoE).

Frynas, J.G. (2004) 'The Oil Boom in Equatorial Guinea', *African Affairs* 103.413: 527-46.

——, G. Wood and R.M.S. Soares de Olivera (2003) 'Business and Politics in São Tomé e Príncipe: From Cocoa Monoculture to Petrostate', *African Affairs* 102.1: 51-80.

Global Witness (2004) *A Time for Transparency* (London: Global Witness Publications).

Goldwyn, D.L. (2004) 'Extracting Transparency', *Georgetown Journal of International Affairs* 5.1: 5-12.

—— and J.S. Morrison (eds.) (2004) *Promoting Transparency in the African Oil Sector: A Report of the CSIS Task Force on Rising US Energy Stakes in Africa* (Washington, DC: Center for Strategic and International Studies).

Gueterbock, R. (2004) 'Greenpeace Campaign Case Study: StopEsso', *Journal of Consumer Behaviour* 3.3: 265-71.

Hodges, T. (2001) *Angola from Afro-Stalinism to Petro-diamond Capitalism* (Bloomington, IN: Indiana University Press).

—— (2004) *Angola: Anatomy of an Oil State* (Lysaker, Norway: Fridtjof Nansen Institute).

HRW (Human Rights Watch) (2004) 'Some Transparency, No Accountability: The Use of Oil Revenue in Angola and Its Impact on Human Rights', www.eia.doe.gov/emeu/cabs/angola.html, 2 March 2005.

IMF (International Monetary Fund) (2004) *Are Developing Countries Better Off Spending their Oil Wealth Upfront?* (Washington, DC: IMF Publications).

Karl, T.L. (1997) *The Paradox of Plenty: Oil Booms and Petro States* (Berkeley, CA: University of California Press).

Katz, M., *et al.* (2004) *Lifting the Oil Curse: Improving Petroleum Revenue Management in Sub-Saharan Africa* (Washington, DC: IMF).

Klitgard, R. (1991) *Tropical Gangsters: One Man's Experience with Development and Decadence in Deepest Africa* (New York: Basic Books).

Kofi, T.A. (1981) 'Prospects and Problems of the Transition from Agrarianism to Socialism: The Case of Angola, Guinea-Bissau and Mozambique', *World Development* 9.9: 851-70.

Kyle, S. (2002) *The Political Economy of Long-Run Growth in Angola: Everyone Wants Oil and Diamonds but They Can Make Life Difficult* (working paper; Ithaca, NY: Department of Applied Economics and Management, Cornell University).

Le Billon, P. (2001) 'The Political Ecology of War: Natural Resources and Armed Conflicts', *Political Geography* 20.5: 561-84.

Liniger-Goumaz, M. (1988) *Small is Not Always Beautiful: The Story of Equatorial Guinea* (London: C. Hurst).

Moore, P.W. (2002) 'Rentier Fiscal Crisis and Regime Stability: Business–State Relations in the Gulf', *Studies in Comparative International Development*, Spring 2002.

Ross, M. (2001a) *Extractive Industries and the Poor* (Boston, MA: Oxfam America).

—— (2001b) 'Does Oil Hinder Democracy?', *World Politics* 53 (April 2001): 325-61.

Schneitz, K., and M. Epstein (2005) 'Exploring the Financial Value of a Reputation for Corporate Social Responsibility during a Crisis', *Corporate Reputation Review* 7.4: 327-45.

Transparency International (2003) *Corruption Perceptions Index* (London: Transparency International).

—— (2004) *Global Corruption Report 2004* (London: Transparency International).

UNDP (United Nations Development Programme) (1999) *Human Development Report: Angola 1999* (Luanda, Angola: UNDP).

—— (2000) *Políticas de Redução da Pobreza, Procurando a Equidade e a Eficiência* (Luanda, Angola: UNDP).

US–Angola Chamber of Commerce (2005) 'Business Symposium in Angola, 4–5 May 2005', www.us-angola.org/2005business_sym1.htm, 14 June 2005.

US House of Representatives (2004) *United States Economic Assistance Conditionality Act of 2004*. 108th Congress, 2nd session, 13 May 2004.

Velloso, A. (2003) 'From Cocoa Fields to Oil in Equatorial Guinea', *Counter Punch*, November 2003.

Vives, A. (2004) 'The Role of Multilateral Development Institutions in Fostering Corporate Social Responsibility', *Development* 47.3: 45-52.

Wood, G. (2004) 'Business and Politics in a Criminal State: The Case of Equatorial Guinea', *African Affairs* 103.413: 547-67.

World Bank (2003a) 'Africa: World Bank Presents a Regional Integration Assistance Strategy for the Central African Economic and Monetary Union' (news release no. 2003/217/AFR; Washington, DC: World Bank).

—— (2003b) *The World Bank Group and Extractive Industries: The Final Report of the Extractive Industries Review* (Washington, DC: World Bank).

Yates, D.A. (1996) *The Rentier State in Africa: Oil Rent Dependency and Neocolonialism in the Republic of Gabon* (Trenton, NJ: Africa World Press).

14

Tracking sustainability performance through company reports

A CRITICAL REVIEW OF THE SOUTH AFRICAN MINING SECTOR

Markus Reichardt and Cathy Reichardt

University of the Witwatersrand, South Africa

Over the past decade South African resource companies have begun reporting on an increasing range of sustainability issues in their annual reports. Their activity in this area forms part of a wider trend among companies worldwide. In 1995/1996, less than a quarter of the top 100 companies listed on the Johannesburg Securities Exchange (JSE) provided some form of sustainability information within their public reports. By the 2003/2004 reporting cycle, 99 of the 154 companies listed on the JSE were found to be providing some level of sustainability information within their annual reports. Among these, the resource companies were disproportionately well represented (KPMG 2004: 1, 5).

However, the value of providing such information is rarely considered. This chapter argues that, in order for stakeholders to be able to compare and rank company performance via the annual or sustainability report, the reporting format and content needs to provide comparable information and data on issues identified as material to the company and/or relevant to stakeholders. By reviewing the reports of 12 major mining companies operating in South Africa in 2005, we found that, at present, only the larger multinational companies provide the consistency and level of detail that would allow third parties to track their sustainability performance through their reports. This suggests that most South African mining companies are still not using the annual or sustainability report as an effective tool to build stakeholder relationships and trust.

Company reports and their audiences

To the public eye, mining operations produce the most visible impact—both on the environment and society—of any business. Thus mining companies were among the first to be engaged by concerned stakeholders. Often seen as an inherently unsustainable business activity, the mining sector requires greater efforts to communicate its contribution to the economy as well as to sustainable development. As a result, mining companies tend to have more and longer experience in engaging and communicating with stakeholders, and often regard themselves as leaders in this field.

Despite greater activism and interest from stakeholders and the media—necessitating growing direct engagement on the part of the company and its officials—the overwhelming source of information on a company's activity remains the company itself.[1] And, despite the growing usage of company websites, the key document for the dissemination of this information remains the annual and/or sustainability report.[2]

From a corporate perspective, the annual sustainability report performs a variety of internal as well as external functions. Often its mere existence and the need to populate the report with information and/or data have acted as drivers for the development of internal sustainability capacity or management systems. For company employees, the report can also present an authoritative reference source on sustainability-related information that can be used as a context for their own line functions, or as the basis for informal information exchange with third parties.

Beyond these internal audiences, the annual sustainability report also represents a potentially standardised format for the company to demonstrate that its strategies, policies and activities in the various areas of sustainability are generating results or progress and are, hopefully, showing improved management of these issues that can be reported in a measurable format. In short, outside targeted public meetings that form part of an environmental impact assessment (EIA) approval process, the annual sustainability report is generally the only means for stakeholders to gain a broader, regular insight into the organisation's approach to, and progress on, sustainability challenges.

1 For example, the only source of information used for the assessment of a listed company for its inclusion in the Dow Jones Sustainability Index (DJSI) or the JSE SRI (Socially Responsible Investment) Index was company-supplied information. This holds true for most of the US-based ethical investment funds as well (e.g. Brill *et al.* 1999: 300-38).

2 For the purposes of this chapter the term 'annual sustainability report' is used generically and meant to cover corporate sustainability reports, corporate citizenship reports, corporate reports to society, as well as environment, health, safety and community reports—and also the sections of the annual report that address these issues.

Sustainability reporting coverage and level of detail in the mining sector

In order to track a company's progress in any given area, it is critical for stakeholders to access quantitative, comparable information over time. This review therefore considered the reports of the ten major South African-based gold[3] and platinum group metals (PGM)[4] miners with a view to determining the extent of their coverage, as well as the degree to which this coverage included some form of detail that could be deemed quantitative and was reported over time in a manner that allowed year-on-year comparison. The reports reviewed covered the 2001–2004 reporting cycles. The results of these ten South African-based miners were then compared with those of BHP Billiton (BHPB) and Anglo American (AA) plc, two of the largest mining multinationals with significant South African presence and recognised leaders in these fields, in terms of both sustainability performance and reporting.

Tables 14.1–14.3 provide a summary which illustrates the considerable divergence of topics covered by sustainability reporting and topics for which there are any comparable quantified data series. Table 14.1 depicts the extent of coverage for key sustainability topics. It thus reflects the topics for which mining companies have, for at least three out of four years, given regular feedback.

Table 14.2 depicts the extent to which this coverage is supported by any numerical detail. This gives an indication of those topics—again for at least three out of four years—for which companies have found themselves willing and able to provide some numerical yardstick for their performance in a given reporting cycle. Table 14.2 is significant because it suggests what, at present, is possible, should companies wish to report on such issues in a quantified manner.

Table 14.3 depicts the extent to which this reporting coverage is supported by comparable, quantified data series that would allow external parties to assess performance over time. Again, companies scored positively in this assessment if coverage, detail or data series were provided for at least three of the four reporting cycles reviewed.

Analysis of trends

The tables suggest that, while most company reports regularly cover a wide range of sustainability topics, less than half of this coverage (in terms of the number of topics covered) is supported by quantitative data whose year-on-year comparison would allow stakeholders to independently assess company progress. This suggests that the majority of sustainability reporting by South African mining companies is still not providing information that would empower their stakeholders to determine their performance in addressing more than a limited range of sustainability issues over time.

3 The gold mining companies were, in no particular order: AngloGold Ashanti Ltd, ARMgold Ltd (later African Rainbow Minerals Ltd), Durban Roodepoort Deep Ltd, Gold Fields Ltd and Harmony Gold Mining Company Ltd.

4 The platinum group metal miners were, in no particular order: Anglo American Platinum Corporation Ltd, Aquarius Platinum Ltd, Impala Platinum Holdings Ltd, Lonmin plc and Northam Platinum Ltd.

Topic	PGM1	PGM2	PGM3	PGM4	PGM5	G1	G2	G3	G4	G5	BHPB	AA plc
Assurance	X	X	X				X	X			X	X
Mining Charter	X	X	X				X	X		X	X	X
Corporate governance												
Legal compliance	X	X					X				X	X
Structures	X	X	X	X	X	X	X	X	X	X	X	X
Risk assessment		X	X	X	X	X	X	X	X	X	X	X
Economic impacts												
Value added	X	X	X	X			X	X			X	X
Beneficiation	X	X	X	X	X		X	X	X	X	X	X
Environmental impacts												
Policy	X	X	X		X		X	X	X	X	X	X
Incidents	X	X	X				X	X			X	X
Performance	X	X	X	X		X	X	X	X	X	X	X
Evaluation/audits	X	X	X	X		X	X	X		X	X	X
Stakeholder engagement		X	X				X	X		X	X	X
Labour												
Safety	X	X	X	X	X	X	X	X	X	X	X	X
Health	X	X	X	X	X	X	X	X	X	X	X	X
HIV/Aids	X	X	X	X	X	X	X	X	X	X	X	X
Housing and living conditions	X	X	X				X	X			X	X
Staff development/ employment equity		X	X	X	X	X	X	X			X	X
Society												
Corporate social responsibility/philanthropy	X	X	X	X			X	X		X	X	X
Black economic empowerment	X	X		X	X	X	X	X	X	X	X	X
Stakeholder engagement	X	X	X	X	X		X	X		X	X	X
Community development		X	X	X	X	X	X			X	X	X
Human rights	X	X	X				X	X			X	X
Global Reporting Initiative	X	X					X	X			X	X
Glossary	X	X					X				X	X
Reply form	X						X	X				X

TABLE 14.1 Coverage of sustainability topics for at least three out of four reporting cycles (2001–2004)

Sources: see References section on page 188

Topic	PGM1	PGM2	PGM3	PGM4	PGM5	G1	G2	G3	G4	G5	BHPB	AA plc
Assurance	X	X	X				X	X			X	X
Mining Charter	X	X	X				X	X		X	X	X
Corporate governance												
Legal compliance	X	X					X				X	X
Structures	X	X	X	X	X	X	X	X	X	X	X	X
Risk assessment		X	X	X	X	X	X	X	X	X	X	X
Economic impacts												
Value added	X	X					X	X			X	X
Beneficiation	X	X	X	X			X	X		X	X	X
Environmental impacts												
Policy	X	X	X				X	X		X	X	X
Incidents	X	X	X				X	X			X	X
Performance	X	X	X	X		X	X	X	X	X	X	X
Evaluation/audits	X	X					X	X		X	X	X
Stakeholder engagement	X	X	X				X	X		X	X	X
Labour												
Safety	X	X	X	X	X	X	X	X	X	X	X	X
Health	X	X	X	X	X	X	X	X	X	X	X	X
HIV/Aids	X	X	X	X	X	X	X	X	X	X	X	X
Housing and living conditions	X	X					X	X			X	X
Staff development/ employment equity		X	X	X		X	X	X			X	X
Society												
Corporate social responsibility/philanthropy	X	X	X	X			X	X		X	X	X
Black economic empowerment	X	X		X	X	X	X	X	X	X	X	X
Stakeholder engagement	X	X	X	X			X	X			X	X
Community development		X	X	X	X	X	X			X	X	X
Human rights	X	X	X				X	X			X	X
Global Reporting Initiative	X	X					X	X			X	X
Glossary	X	X					X				X	X
Reply form	X						X	X				X

TABLE 14.2 **Quantitative sustainability data provided (not necessarily consecutive or comparable) for at least three out of four reporting cycles (2001–2004)**

Sources: see References section on page 188

Topic	PGM1	PGM2	PGM3	PGM4	PGM5	G1	G2	G3	G4	G5	BHPB	AA plc
Assurance	X	X	X				X	X			X	X
Mining Charter	X	X	X				X	X		X	X	X
Corporate governance												
Legal compliance	X						X				X	X
Structures	X	X	X	X	X	X	X	X	X	X	X	X
Risk assessment		X					X				X	
Economic impacts												
Value added	X	X					X	X			X	X
Beneficiation	X	X	X				X	X		X	X	X
Environmental impacts												
Policy	X		X				X	X		X	X	X
Incidents	X	X					X				X	X
Performance	X	X					X				X	X
Evaluation/audits	X							X			X	X
Stakeholder engagement	X						X			X	X	X
Labour												
Safety	X	X	X	X	X	X	X	X	X	X	X	X
Health	X	X	X	X	X	X	X	X	X	X	X	X
HIV/Aids	X		X		X			X			X	X
Housing and living conditions	X	X					X					X
Staff development / employment equity		X	X					X			X	X
Society												
Corporate social responsibility/philanthropy	X	X	X	X			X	X		X	X	X
Black economic empowerment	X	X		X	X	X	X	X	X	X	X	X
Stakeholder engagement	X										X	X
Community development		X	X		X		X				X	X
Human rights	X	X	X				X	X			X	X
Global Reporting Initiative	X	X					X	X			X	X
Glossary	X	X					X				X	X
Reply form	X						X	X				X

TABLE 14.3 Consecutive comparable sustainability detail provided for at least two of the reporting cycles (2001–2004)

Sources: see References section on page 188

At the same time the tables suggest that in areas where disclosure of quantitative and comparable information is mandated by law—such as occupational health and safety issues—companies are able to provide relevant data in a consistent, comparable manner. Regulatory pressure has forced the mining sector to reach consensus on an industry-wide definition of mining-related health and safety incidents and it is notable that, even for more controversial data such as fatalities, companies appear to find no difficulty in reporting on the issues, once required to do so by law.

Similarly, corporate social investment (CSI) data is dominated by numerical disclosure as companies rely on the monetary value of their contributions as the only measurement of their performance. In contrast, no sector-wide consensus has been reached on the definition of, and reporting on, environmental incidents, and there is currently no statutory requirement for companies to report in a consistent and quantifiable manner on such aspects of their performance.

A trend noted across the board was that the introduction of the Broad-Based Socio-Economic Empowerment Charter for the South African Mining Industry in 2002 (which specified performance target categories) has markedly increased the reporting on certain aspects of environmental and especially social performance in a more comparable format. In contrast, in areas where such disclosure requirements do not exist (such as aspects of environmental performance) companies have been much slower to move towards disclosure of quantitative, comparable information. Therefore, while all companies consistently assert their full legal compliance, few provide stakeholders with the means of verifying this significant statement.

Compared with the overall performance of South African-based miners, the large multinationals surveyed appear to have little difficulty in providing data that allows readers of their annual reports to assess their non-financial performance. This observation could support the argument often made by smaller operators that detailed, extensive sustainability reporting is the preserve of big business because of the resources such activity requires. By contrast, smaller operators also tend to assert at a general level that their operations are in compliance with sustainability-related aspects of the legislation.

However, it must be assumed that, in order for such smaller operators to have comfort and certainty in their assertion of legal compliance, some form of data collection and analysis must be taking place to demonstrate such legal compliance, and stakeholders could legitimately query why such data, or parts of it, has not been released into the public domain. Similarly, stakeholders may query whether the reporting of data in a quantified, comparable format required for responsible management of non-financial risk is necessarily more resource-intensive than the publication of the aspirational and generic statements that tend to dominate the reports of smaller operators.

Far from being solely a resource issue, it could be argued that the large multinational mining companies, such as BHP Billiton and AA plc, are more likely to have developed their internal data-gathering to their current level in order to ensure and demonstrate legal compliance and good risk management. Hence, they have less need to rely on the sort of aspirational statements that dominate sustainability coverage in some of the less data-rich reports of other companies. Instead, in response to civil society's increasing demand to 'show' rather than just 'tell', these leading multinationals are able to report on non-financial issues in a manner that provides reassurance that non-financial risks are being responsibly managed by demonstrating measurable progress in their key risks areas.

Those organisations that remain wedded to the idea of aspirational, unquantified reporting appear to be motivated primarily by:

- A persistent unwillingness to communicate news that is not exclusively positive
- A tendency to treat the annual sustainability report as a one-off communications medium that is not linked to the management information of their operations
- The treatment of the annual sustainability report as a one-way communication

In contrast, the leading companies have identified the issues they deem material and have established visible stakeholder communication channels to facilitate feedback that can be used to adjust their reporting coverage where required. Whether these companies are reporting on the matters in the format and to a level of detail every stakeholder would like to see is a matter for subsequent debate. What is critical is that this more systematic approach suggests that their communication via the annual sustainability report is not the product of a once-a-year panic that involves a last-minute search for 'good news' stories and supporting ad hoc data.

By relying on internal data-gathering systems for risk management and reporting purposes, these companies have also established a means of providing data streams over time that allow analysts and others to assess performance, at least on a macro scale. From an internal perspective these data-gathering systems are critical to their ability to achieve and maintain legal compliance, thereby contributing to better non-financial risk management.

In summary, this survey suggests that, over the past five years, only a minority of the resource companies operating in South Africa have consistently provided the information required by empowered shareholders and other stakeholders to assess their corporate performance in various areas of sustainability. By contrast, for the majority, evidence to support corporate claims of ongoing legal compliance, improved performance and advancing standards across the range of sustainability-related activity, remains weak.

Reporting progress: case studies

While not every topic readily lends itself to comparable, quantified reporting, it is clear that there is still considerable scope for many of the companies reviewed to explore the development of quantifiable indicators. The section below outlines some case studies of best practice and poor practice in this respect, which demonstrate the pitfalls associated with non-comparable reporting. In essence, the absence of a systematic approach and consistent format can generate mixed messages that over time undermine stakeholder trust. Similarly, the continued tendency of some companies to repeat virtually unaltered statements year after year in the sustainability reports is highlighted as problematic.

Best practice

Consistent descriptions of progress in EMS implementation

The example in Case 1 shows a mining company returning over a period of six reporting cycles to the progress it has made against the commitment in its 1998 annual report to implement an environmental management system (EMS). While the reader would have had to have searched for this information in different parts of the environmental section, he or she would have been able, over time, to gain reassurance of progress from the various references made over the years (Amplats 1998: 56, 1999: 61, 2000: 57, 2001: 75, 2002: 37, 2003: 56, 2004: 57).

Annual Report	Extract
1998	'[the company] has committed itself to implementing the ISO 14001 environmental management system at its [. . .] mine. Other business units will be encouraged to implement the system over the longer term, as it complements the environmental policy and environmental management programmes already in place.'
1999	'the [. . .] mine will commence with ISO 14001 implementation during 2000.'
2000	'the [. . .] mine commenced with the implementation of the ISO 14001 Environmental Management System during the year. The final certification audit is planned for early 2002.'
2001	'[the company] has also committed itself to ISO 14001 certification by end-2004, key elements of which are pollution prevention and control of impacts. [. . .] mine is leading the way in this regard and will apply for certification early in 2002. All other business units have completed the initial review required by ISO 14001.'
2002	'[. . .] mine was the first business unit to achieve ISO 14001 certification. A Group Environmental Systems Manager was appointed during the year to oversee the implementation and standardisation of the environmental management systems based on ISO 14001 requirements throughout all operational units.'
2003	'Five business units have fully implemented the ISO 14001 standard and have been audited and certified by BSi, while one is close to certification. BSi conducts follow-up audits at certified business units on an agreed timetable to measure the required continual improvement aspect of ISO 14001. Three other business units are working towards certification.'
2004	'During 2002 the Group set itself a target to have all operations certified to ISO 14001 standard by end-2004. The Group achieved its target during 2004.'

CASE 1 **Best practice: consistent descriptions of progress in EMS implementation**

Source: Anglo American Platinum Corporation

Reporting progress against the Mining Charter Scorecard

The Mining Charter provides a format of targets against which to report. The example in Case 2 of tabulated performance reporting against the Charter's various categories comes from a so-called 'medium-cap' JSE-listed company, suggesting that the com-

The Mining Scoreboard	The progress SA Chrome has made towards targets	5-year target
HUMAN RESOURCE DEVELOPMENT		
Every employee to be offered the opportunity to be functionally literate and numerate by 2005	Only 8 out of 211 employees need literacy training—ABET programmes are being implemented, as is computer literacy and numeracy training	On the way to complying
Career paths and skills development plans implemented for all HDSA employees	Career path planning that will provide upward movement for all employees is in progress, and skills development plans are in place	On the way to complying
EMPLOYMENT EQUITY		
Has the company published its employment equity plan and reported on its annual progress in meeting that plan?	Yes	Yes
Has the company established a plan to achieve a target for HDSA participation in management of 40% within the five years and is it implementing the plan?	Yes—as set out in its Employment Equity Plan	Yes
Has the company identified a talent pool and is it fast-tracking it?	A talent pool has been identified in terms of our equal opportunities policy and it is being fast-tracked	Yes
Has the company established a plan to achieve the target for women participating in mining of 10% within the five years and is it implementing the plan?	Yes—we have already exceeded the scoreboard target of 10% participation of women in the mining industry (13% of our employees are women in operational positions)	Yes
MIGRANT LABOUR		
Has the company subscribed to government and industry agreements to ensure non-discrimination against foreign migrant labour?	Yes	Yes

CASE 2 Best practice: reporting progress against the Mining Charter Scorecard
(continued opposite)

Source: SR & I 2005

The Mining Scoreboard	The progress SA Chrome has made towards targets	5-year target
MINE COMMUNITY AND RURAL DEVELOPMENT		
Has the company co-operated in the formulation of integrated development plans and is the company co-operating with government in the implementation of these plans for communities where mining takes place and for major labour sending areas? Has there been effort on the side of the company to engage the local mine community and major labour sending area communities? (Companies will be required to cite a pattern of consultation, indicate money expenditures and show a plan)	Monthly meetings are held with the local mining communities. Workshops were held with the communities on the new legislation's implications. Now that the company is in production and the new mining legislation has been published, it is in the process of formulating a social plan which will include engaging the local communities before discussing its proposals with government so they can be included into an integrated development plan for these communities	On the way to complying
HOUSING AND LIVING CONDITIONS		
For company-provided housing has the mine, in consultation with stakeholders, established measures for improving the standard of housing, including the upgrading of the hostels, conversion of hostels to family units and promoted home ownership options for mine employees? Company will be required to indicate what they have done to improve housing and show a plan to progress the issue over time and that it is implementing the plan	No housing is provided for employees. Employees determine their own living arrangements	Not applicable
Has the company established measures for improving the nutrition of employees? Companies will be required to indicate what they have done to improve nutrition and show a plan to progress the issue over time and implementation of this plan	The company does not provide meals for its employees. It is preparing a health education programme, which will include nutritional training, to be implemented in the near future	On the way to complying

CASE 2 (from previous page; continued over)

The Mining Scoreboard	The progress SA Chrome has made towards targets	5-year target
PROCUREMENT		
Has the mining company given historically disadvantaged South Africans preferred supplier status?	HDSAs do have preferred suppliers status where commercially competitive. The company has in place a procurement committee, which is responsible for awarding tenders and supply contracts. All potential suppliers are required to provide us with details of HDSA shareholding/ participation in their business	On the way to complying
Has the mining company identified the current level of procurements from historically disadvantaged South African companies in terms of capital goods, consumables and services?	Yes—our current level of HDSA procurement is identified and recorded. During the construction phase of the plant approximately R318 million was allocated to subcontractors with local area and empowerment credentials	Yes
Has the mining company indicated a commitment to a progression of procurement from historically disadvantaged South African companies over a 3–5-year time-frame in terms of capital goods, consumables and services, and to what extent has the commitment been implemented?	SA Chrome has indicated its commitment to procuring capital goods, consumables and services from historically disadvantaged South African companies where and whenever possible and is implementing this commitment. We are hopeful of achieving our targets within the stipulated time-frame	On the way to complying
OWNERSHIP AND JOINT VENTURES		
Has the mining company achieved historically disadvantaged South African participation in terms of ownership for equity or attributable units of production of 15% in historically disadvantaged South African hands within five years and 26% in ten years?	The Royal Bafokeng Nation currently own a 35% shareholding in SA Chrome. In addition, the IDC owns a 24% shareholding	Yes—have already exceeded both the 5- and 10-year targets
BENEFICIATION		
Has the mining company identified its current level of beneficiation?	The main business of SA Chrome is the beneficiation of chromite at our Boshoek smelter	Yes
Has the mining company established its baseline level of beneficiation and indicated the extent that this will have to be grown in order to qualify for an offset?	Yes	Yes
REPORTING		
Has the company reported on an annual	This progress is reflected in the Corporate	Yes

CASE 2 (from previous page)

pany's relatively small size has not compromised its ability to standardise reporting on performance in this area (example taken from SR & I 2005: 22-23).

Poor practice

Repetitive or stasis reporting

The paragraph repeated in Case 3 was taken from three consecutive annual reports. The value of repeating this aspirational statement to the readers of this company's reports is questionable and begs the question of whether quoting this strategy in an unaltered form year on year reflects a lack of progress in addressing this issue (DRD 1999: 53, 2000: 34, 2001: 17).

Annual Report	Extract
1998, 2000 and 2001	'Future Strategy As embodied in its Environmental Policy, [the company] is committed to preserving the environment for posterity in a responsible manner. Current and future planning takes cognisance of environmental issues and liabilities with an emphasis maintained on the key sustainability issues discussed here. Financial provision will continue to be made in an environmentally responsible manner within an overall framework, which has been designed to integrate the best possible environmental practices with the economic realities of a marginal mining business.'

CASE 3 Poor practice: repetitive or stasis reporting

Source: Durban Roodepoort Deep

Getting things done?

The excerpts in Case 4 all individually suggest progress in the management of water issues on the part of this major mining company. However, when read consecutively, it would appear that the phrases describe essentially the same activity: namely, regulatory permitting. One must wonder how the permits were obtained if there were no monitoring programmes in place prior to 2001.

If an activity as critical as obtaining water permits genuinely took three years—as the reports would suggest—then the company should have considered flagging this as a business risk. At the very least, it should have highlighted at some stage that legal compliance had not been achieved for all operations and detailed what actions it was taking to resolve the outstanding matters, rather than presenting its apparent lack of success in resolving this matter as progress (AGA 1999: 28, 2000: 28, 2001: 21, 2002: 29).

Meaningful activity?

Another drawback of descriptive (as opposed to quantified) reporting is that activity—rather than outcome—is (sometimes misleadingly) reported as 'progress' and is presented as a meaningful end in itself, as illustrated by the statements in Case 5.

Annual Report	Extract
1999	'In response to the new National Water Act all the necessary water permits were granted.'
2000	'Water licenses were issued to all South African operations under the National Water Act'
2001	'All operations registered their water uses with the Department of Water Affairs in line with recent legislation governing water utilization. [the company's] program to decrease water utilization gained momentum during the year.'
2002	'Water monitoring programs and procedures were developed and implemented . . .'

CASE 4 Poor practice: getting things done?

Source: AngloGold Ashanti

The problem here is that, for the non-specialist, the mere demonstration of activity may appear reassuring, while in reality this may not necessarily be the case. Reading such statements from consecutive reports, it could also be interpreted that there is a significant time lag in addressing audit findings (AGA 2002: 29, 2003: 42, 2004: E12).

Annual Report	Extract
2002	'All our operations are audited annually for compliance.' [no comment about findings or remedial actions]
2003	'All our operations are audited annually for compliance.' [no comment about findings or remedial actions]
2004	'A total of 72 audits were performed . . . in 2003. Attention during 2004 was focused on addressing the findings of these audits.'

CASE 5 Poor practice: meaningful activity?

Source: AngloGold Ashanti

Inconsistent EMS implementation

A further weakness of using descriptive statements to demonstrate progress or ongoing risk management is that, when there is a change in wordsmith generating the prose, consistency may not be maintained. Note in Case 6 that from 1998 until 2003 'EMS implementation continued' across the various business units of this multinational miner, until in 2004 they 'realised' that implementation of the EMS was not driving environmental management. Such inconsistencies raise fundamental questions concerning the validity and purpose of past activities that have been highlighted, as well as reputational and ethical concerns (AGA 1998, 1999: 28, 2000: 28, 2001: 21, 2002: 29, 2003, 2004: E9).

Annual Report	Extract
1998	'EMS are being implemented across all business units'
1999	'EMS are being put in place for all business units'
2001	'In late 2001 an implementation guideline was developed to assist all operations establish their own EMS'
2002	'the region committed itself to the development of a web-based electronic Environmental Management System. The system is based on ISO 14000 principles. The first of four phases, involving policy, development and planning was completed in 2002.'
2003	'EMS continue to be implemented across all regions' Objectives for 2004: —'Fully implement EMS across the Group'
2004	'Environmental management systems form the backbone of environmental management at an operational level.' 'Environmental management is currently being driven, not through EMSs, but mainly through the implementation of DME-required EMPs and . . . a number of projects.'

CASE 6 Poor practice: inconsistent EMS implementation

Source: AngloGold Ashanti

Inconsistent standards for EMS

The example in Case 7 again highlights inconsistencies in the assertions regarding the company's EMS. By reading the reports consecutively one would be forgiven for assuming that this company had not yet determined to what standard its purported EMS, supposedly in place since 2001, actually conformed (Harmony 2000: 29, 2001: 21, 2003: 63, 2004: 41, 2005: 41).

The features of good reporting

Given its wide-ranging audience, the sustainability report by necessity has to cover diverse topics and seek to remain accessible to various groups of readers with differing ability to grasp technical issues. Nevertheless, these diverse demands do not alter the requirement that the information provided in these reports should—in order to be credible over the longer term—be provided in accordance with principles comparable to those governing statutory reporting. In other words readers should, over time, be able to compare year-on-year performance.

To communicate their sustainability performance to shareholders and other stakeholders, companies need to demonstrate through their reporting that they have the ability and capacity to identify, understand and manage the range of non-financial risks and opportunities relevant to their sectors. In the African context this also requires an

Annual Report	Extract
2000	'The company, its operations and associates work within the applicable regulatory requirements and are guided by the ISO 14004 in the establishment of environmental management systems.'
2001	'[The company], its operations and associates work within the applicable regulatory requirements and are guided by the ISO 14004 in the establishment of environmental management systems.'
2003	'We have integrated pollution control, waste management and rehabilitation activities into our operating procedures.'
2004	'The development of a proprietary Environmental Management System is nearing completion . . . which is currently being tested and rolled out to the various operations.'
2004	'Our Environmental Management System, which encompasses the principles of ISO 14000, is an electronic-based system.'
	'[The company] is considering the adoption of the international environmental standard ISO 14001. An external consultant has been engaged to assess the current degree of compliance by the operating units with the fundamental principles of ISO 14001.'

CASE 7 Poor practice: inconsistent standards for EMS

Source: Harmony Gold Mining Company

acknowledgement that not all stakeholders may have the technical capacity to engage at a technical or specialist level. The information should therefore demonstrate the features discussed in the following sections (the headings below are based on SR & I 2005: 2-3).

Relevant and timely

Reports should consistently provide information that communicates key issues based on company or sector risk/materiality profile. This could include explicit statements that certain issues—as a result of a review or audit—are not, or are no longer, relevant to a company's operation. Where reporting is done by exception, the context of data is critical to its relevance. Reports should also be tailored to user needs by reporting data in accordance with the reporting period.

Accessible

Reports should be written in non-technical language with the intent of being accessible to the lay person. The text should as far as possible, remain free of qualifiers, jargon, acronyms and lengthy aspirational statements. Quantitative information and technical data (especially when abbreviated) should be supported by a glossary, graphics or readily identifiable footnotes.

True, non-selective and fair

Balanced reporting is essential to building stakeholder trust. Reports should therefore avoid selective coverage or presentation of information, and rather strive to provide a balanced account of the organisation's overall performance by presenting both positive and negative information and stakeholder feedback.

Systematic and comparable

It is important that the reader is able to assess year-on-year changes using the presented data. Information presented in reports should therefore maintain consistency in its scope and calculation methods. Changes to data collection, sampling methods, measurement units or cycles should be highlighted and should preferably result in restating of previously reported data to ensure comparability.

Quantitative information with context

Data and information presented, especially where reporting is by highlight or exception, should be placed into the context of company performance, company or sector benchmarks, and preferably stated in the broader context of the company's risk profile. This is particularly important where reports may imply that all activities not explicitly covered are in legal compliance and/or policy compliance.

Sustainability reporting should, therefore, over time, aim to reassure both shareholders and other stakeholders that non-financial risks are being responsibly managed by demonstrating a company's progress in addressing these key principles. Companies also need to take a realistic view of the best practical means of getting the material information to its relevant, and often dispersed, stakeholders such as neighbouring communities.

Conclusion

The resources required for the generation of the annual sustainability report represent a considerable demand on the often-limited corporate capacity in this field. In purely financial terms such reports can consume budgets equivalent to those required to support major research projects.[5] It should therefore be in the interests of companies seeking to motivate such expenditure to focus on the benefits that the implementation of robust data collection and management systems offer for the effective and consistent management of non-financial risk. The gathering of quantified, comparable, non-selective data that can also be presented to external stakeholders to demonstrate legal compliance and proactive sustainability risk management is a key element of this approach.

5 The costs for the production of the annual sustainability report can vary from ZAR 0.25 million (ZAR = South African rand) to as much as ZAR 5 million for larger multinationals.

At present, however, it appears that only a limited number of South African companies feel comfortable in providing consistent resources to support the activities required to implement their sustainability policy objectives. As the case studies have shown, there is considerable room for non-comparable, more descriptive presentation of activities to convincingly demonstrate progress, at least at an aggregate company level. However, the case studies also suggest that, as issues become more complex or external interest in an issue becomes more acute, this form of communication can also lead to greater inconsistencies in corporate sustainability reporting which, over time, can undermine the trust of stakeholders.

Key conclusions that emerge are that:

- The large multinationals surveyed appear to have little difficulty in providing data that allows readers of their annual reports to assess non-financial performance
- In contrast, reporting by individual smaller miners demonstrates an ability to match the performance of their multinational peers when using the Mining Charter Scorecard format, weakening the argument that comparable, quantified reporting is more resource-intensive
- Reporting by most marginal and smaller South African-based miners retains an emphasis on aspirational statements as opposed to data disclosure
- Reporting without a consistent format is more likely to lead to material inconsistencies on key issues that have the potential to undermine stakeholder trust

What emerges from this analysis is that many companies in the South African mining sector at present are not realising the potential benefits that quantified, comparable reporting can bring to their stakeholder relationships owing to a continued unwillingness to utilise their annual sustainability reports for balanced, consistent reporting on performance. This suggests that disclosure for operators and sites beyond South Africa's northern borders may, except for leading multinationals, be very limited, and at this stage is unlikely to serve as a tool for the sector to demonstrate widespread progress in sustainability performance.

References

African Rainbow Minerals (formerly ARMgold) (2001–2004) *Annual Report*, available at www.arm.co.za.

AGA (AngloGold Ashanti Ltd) (formerly AngloGold) (1998–2004) *Annual Report*, available at www.anglogoldashanti.com.

Amplats (Anglo American Platinum Corporation Ltd) (1998–2004) *Annual Report, Business Report, Sustainable Development Report*, available at www.angloplatinum.com.

Aquarius Platinum Ltd (2004–2005) *Pre-listing Statement, Annual Report*, available at www.aquariusplatinum.com.

Brill, H., J.A. Brill and C. Feigenbaum (1999) *Investing with Your Values: Making Money and Making a Difference* (Princeton, NJ: Bloomberg Press).

DRD (Durban Roodepoort Deep Ltd) (1998–2004) *Annual Report*, available at www.drd.co.za.

Gold Fields Ltd (1999–2004) *Annual Report, Sustainable Development Report*, available at www.goldfields.co.za.

Harmony (Harmony Gold Mining Company Ltd) (2001–2004) *Annual Report*, available at www.harmony.co.za.

Impala Platinum Holdings Ltd (2001–2004) *Annual Report, Environmental, Health & Safety Report*, available at www.implats.co.za.

KPMG Sustainability Services (2004) *2004 Survey of Integrated Sustainability Reporting in South Africa* (Johannesburg: KPMG).

Lonmin plc (2000–2004) *Annual Report*, available at www.lonmin.com.

Northam Platinum Ltd (2000–2004) *Annual Report*, available at www.northam.co.za.

SR & I (2005) *Sustainability Reporting: Highlighting South African Examples* (Johannesburg: SR & I).

15

The *gift* of CSR

POWER AND THE PURSUIT OF RESPONSIBILITY IN THE MINING INDUSTRY

Dinah Rajak

University of Sussex, UK

An anthropological approach to CSR

> All gifts have an inevitable tendency to pauperise the recipients (Charles Dickens, *Hard Times*).

In August 2002, when Johannesburg played host to the WSSD (World Summit on Sustainable Development), a cartoon by the South African satirist Zapiro appeared in the *Mail and Guardian*. The cartoon is entitled *A Gift from the Corporate World!* It shows the doors of the summit opened wide to embrace a Trojan horse. On the outside of the horse is written 'sustainable development'. On the inside, Zapiro shows us cigar-smoking corporate fat cats holding a banner of 'profit, self-regulation and unfair trade' (Zapiro 2002). The Trojan horse of Homeric myth remains a potent image for the potential danger of the gift. The metaphor suggests that, like the Trojans, in receiving gifts we can unwittingly be embracing our own enslavement. The veiled power of the gift to empower the donor while oppressing the recipient is summed up most poignantly by a community worker from South Africa's platinum mines: 'As long as we're dependent on hand-outs from the mines, we'll be their slaves.'

This chapter is based on ethnographic research conducted at the headquarters of transnational mining corporations in London and Johannesburg, and at the platinum mines that surround the town of Rustenburg in South Africa's North West Province. By drawing on anthropological theory of the gift this chapter explores how the discourse of CSR, as practised by multinational mining corporations, creates categories of benefactor and recipient, on which structures of patronage and dependency are built. As Crewe and Harrison state, 'as in a relationship between landlord and tenant, at the centre of the donor–recipient relationship is an exchange of deference and compliance by the client in return for the patron's provision' (Crewe and Harrison 1998: 74).

In recent years CSR within South Africa's mining industry has been subsumed under the all-embracing mission of sustainable development (SD). The redefinition of CSR as SD suggests a radical paradigm shift from corporate philanthropy, to a progressive focus on 'transformation' and 'participatory development' aligned with the political agenda of the post-apartheid government.[1] Where mining companies once expressed their social responsibility through '*ad hoc* charitable donations to good causes' (Hamann 2004: 6), companies now have teams of CSR managers, finely worded policies, and annual sustainability reports.

However, I question whether the lines between CSR and philanthropy are not blurred, whether the notion of CSR is not profoundly bound up with the politics of the gift. In adopting the language of responsibility, are corporations speaking, in what Ferguson describes as the 'language of economic correctness' (Ferguson 1998: 11) according to which development agencies hide the power they exert over states behind the guise of benefactor or even partner? While the rhetoric and form of CSR have been transformed, this chapter challenges the assumption that these discursive developments represent a philosophical shift from philanthropy to responsibility.

Conventional models of modern capitalist economics have always claimed the independence of the market from other forms of social life and from the concerns of morality. Yet, *The Economist* tells us that: 'Greed is out. Corporate virtue, or the appearance of it, is in' (*Economist* 2004). This chapter is concerned with what might be called the moral underpinning of CSR. How can the CSR movement with its claims to 'compassionate capitalism' (*Economist* 2004) be reconciled with this conventional representation of the modern market economy? 'Corporate virtue'[2] is juxtaposed with that of 'corporate greed'. CSR seems at times to be held up to represent the triumph of selfless good over the selfish pursuit of profit. The widely used phrase 'compassionate capitalism' even seems suggestive of a merciful and beneficent ruler. Ultimately we must ask: **does the advent of CSR signify the reconnection of the market economy with the realm of morality?**

Writing on CSR often overlooks both the moral and the social dimensions of CSR which are veiled by the sanitised discourse of policy and corporate rhetoric. Such writing reduces corporations to the skeleton of their structural borders, neglecting the social relations created, shaped and sustained by the practice of CSR, and overlooking the less tangible shape of the corporation, extending its reach through its army of consultants, networks of partnerships, and subsidiaries. Equally, research often tends to view institutions as manifestations of singular sectional interests.

1 CSR within the mining industry is 'a special case' owing to the inevitable social and environmental footprint it leaves behind. Furthermore, 'in South Africa, such concerns are aggravated by mining companies' implication in South Africa's tortuous history' (Hamann 2004: 5).

2 The much-extolled ideal of 'corporate virtue' evokes visions of Victorian philanthropic industrialists, the John Cadburys and Joseph Rowntrees, who were openly motivated by religious principles.

By drawing on anthropological approaches to development, this chapter attempts to dismantle these essentialised visions of corporations; to trace what Quarles van Ufford refers to as the 'roots and routines of moral encounters' (Quarles van Ufford *et al.* 2003: 19) that are generated through the practice of CSR. In doing so, it aims to shed light on new regimes of power created by these encounters and the ways in which they are authenticated through an appeal to a moral narrative of *responsibility*.

Corporations are not 'monolithic machines' (Quarles van Ufford *et al.* 2003: 19). Despite the continuous production of mission statements and management systems, and the appeal to ideas such as 'core values' and 'intrinsic nature', behind the scenes 'actors are negotiating all the time at various intersections of development practices' (Quarles van Ufford 2003: 25). As the resident anthropologist of one mining company put it: 'we're always represented as a homogeneous organisation . . . you should see the way we go at each other in meetings'. The anthropological encounter with CSR explores what I refer to as the *Social Life* of CSR: investigating the informal alongside the formal, the individual alongside the institutional.

Between policy and practice

In recent years, significant attention has been devoted to developing effective, comprehensive CSR policy both within companies and in the national and international arenas concerned with the role of corporations as vehicles for SD.[3] Most companies mining in SA (South Africa) now have a package of policies covering various areas which fall under the broad spectrum of CSR which, within the SA mining industry, has become almost synonymous with socioeconomic development (SED).[4] These policies are supported by detailed implementation and reporting mechanisms, a formal corporate social investment (CSI) budget, often set at around 1.0% of pre-tax profits (Hamann 2004: 6), and teams of CSR or SED officers charged with the job of implementation.[5]

However, the emphasis on creating perfect policy has led to the neglect by researchers of the relationship between these frameworks and the practices that they are assumed to drive and legitimise (Mosse 2003: 2). Policy is all too often taken as statements not only of intentions, but also of activity. This chapter challenges the prevailing belief that the practice of CSR is driven by policy rather than by an intricate web of social relations, power dynamics and organisational culture interacting within constantly changing socioeconomic realities.[6] As Mosse suggests, 'the things that make for "good

3 Examples of such initiatives include the UN Global Compact, the International Council on Mining and Minerals (ICMM) and the World Business Council for Sustainable Development (WBCSD).

4 These commonly include HIV/Aids awareness and treatment, community engagement, education and infrastructure development.

5 Anglo Platinum, for example, a subsidiary of Anglo American plc, established a department dedicated to SED in 2002 and in 2005 created the post of SD manager at corporate level to sit alongside the already established SED and HIV/Aids managers.

6 This is highlighted in recent criticism of global CSR strategy and reporting mechanisms developed in the North and exported to the South, often with little regard for the historical, socioeconomic and political specificities of the regions in which they are to be implemented (see, for example, Hamann *et al.* 2005).

policy"—policy which legitimises and mobilises political support—in reality make it rather unimplementable within its chosen institutions and regions' (Mosse 2003: 1).

Policy claims to be, and is seen to be, concerned with apolitical and pragmatic goals such as efficiency and productivity. The formal framework of policy has the effect of isolating and institutionalising a particular belief or position as a collective good. CSR policy-making is framed in terms of an objectively identifiable societal or collective need and expressed through the language of scientific rationalism, masking the moral impetus behind a policy or decision under a veil of neutrality. As Bauman states, policies are the product of supposedly 'non-moral institutions which lend them their binding force' (Bauman 1989: 170). The effectiveness of power is seen to rest on this ability to 'hide its own mechanisms' (Foucault 1978: 86). Policy can thus be seen as part of the political technology used to remove the highly political issue of social responsibility from the realm of moral discourse, by translating it into a neutral language of science and pragmatism. The notion of responsibility is therefore stripped of its subjective nature and the discursive framework from which it derives.

Yet a disjuncture exists. On the one hand we have the ritualised frameworks of policy, SEIAs (social and environmental impact assessments) and codes of conduct in which CSR is represented as technical, neutral and rooted in efficient business practice, cleansed of awkward notions of morality, and reformulated as the latest orthodoxy, 'sustainable development'. On the other hand, a contradictory impulse exists in the reconnection of business with notions of virtue—an impulse that enshrouds CSR with the language of moral and, at times, almost spiritual duty. This moral discourse is manifest in the words and actions of individuals charged with conducting the 'ethical' work of the company—the front-line CSR agents so to speak. As one CSR manager put it: 'I am the conscience of the company.'

While the mechanical frameworks of policy and planning depersonalise and depoliticise CSR processes, CSR managers at the Rustenburg mines often present a vision of CSR in which it is tightly bound up with a sense of personal ethics and morality. The sense of moral mission is evoked by one such CSI manager: 'My passion is nutrition . . . I have visions of being a Mother Theresa in khaki pants and white shirt . . . I have visions of . . . taking hydroponics up and down Africa.'

At the same time internal corporate management systems, alongside external frameworks such as the GRI (Global Reporting Initiative), demand that the actors involved strive to 'maintain a coherent representation of their actions as instances of authorised policy' (Mosse 2003: 7). Thus the power of this moral discourse resides in its ability to mask itself behind the current orthodoxies of *sustainability, empowerment* and *participation* and the technology of policy and management systems.

The emotiveness and zeal of CSR rhetoric, like that of the broader development movement, endows it with the sense of a moral mission, projecting images of 'liberation', 'human fulfilment (and) . . . flourishing' (Gasper 1996: 643), as epitomised in the words of the CSI manager quoted above. Such statements express a grand modernising paradigm of development, underscored by the concept of *progress* towards a singular, technological concept of modernity. The language of CSR can therefore be viewed as part of the modernising discourse of development, as it espouses a universal vision of social improvement and elevates the corporation as both architect and agent of this vision. Thus the SD manager of a major mining house stated that: 'We've come up with a post-closure vision for Rustenburg . . . we must now take that vision to the municipality, because it must become a societal vision.'

As an ethical agenda, CSR implies 'an agenda of care of the other in a hegemonic manner where what is good for the other has already been defined by the benevolent self' (Giri and Quarles van Ufford 2003: 254). The company's vision of SD becomes a hegemonic vehicle through which its authority over the social, environmental and economic order is authenticated. The appeal to the concept of responsibility—and the agenda of care it implies—supports the role of transnational corporations (TNCs) as dominant institutions of governmentality, for, as Ferguson argues, claims to moral purpose have enormous power in their ability to naturalise authority (Ferguson 1998: 5). In this way, the beneficiaries of this ethical agenda—those commonly referred to as 'partners in development'—come under the authority of the company as they become subject to its notions of responsibility, and recipients of its paternalistic concerns.

CSR as a *gift*

In recent years, TNCs have moved away from the discourse of philanthropy towards that of capacity building and social investment allowing them, as Stirrat and Henkel write with respect to NGOs, 'to avoid the charge that they are patrons' (Stirrat and Henkel 1997: 73). Nevertheless, CSR within mining corporations takes on many of the forms of the anthropological concept of the gift. Personal and organisational relationships between the corporation and the community are both expressed and transformed by the process of giving. In his seminal essay of 1924, *Essai sur le Don*, Marcel Mauss identifies reciprocity as one of the distinguishing characteristics of the gift economy in so-called 'primitive' societies. The bonds created through the exchange of gift and counter-gift provided Mauss with a model of the social contract. The gift represented the perceived solidarity and cohesion of 'primitive' societies, which he juxtaposes with commodity exchange on which, according to Mauss, 'modern' societies are based (Mauss 1967: 13). Yet I argue that the Maussian dichotomy between 'primitive' and 'modern' forms of exchange—between gift exchange and market economy—is disrupted by the phenomenon of CSR which reconnects the 'modern' and depersonalised world of commerce with the moral discourse and social politics of giving.

Following Bourdieu, Stirrat and Henkel underline the ideological power of the distinction between commercial exchange and giving: 'By reducing the universe of exchanges to mercantile exchange which is obviously and subjectively orientated towards the maximisation of profit, i.e. (economically) self-interested, it has implicity defined . . . other forms of exchange as noneconomic and therefore disinterested' (Bourdieu 1986, quoted in Stirrat and Henkel 1997: 74).

However a gift is anything but disinterested. It always has an intention behind it. As Stirrat and Henkel have shown in their analysis of 'the development gift', 'what starts off as a counterpoint to the logic of the real world (gifts versus markets) ends up as part of the real world. The gift becomes . . . the currency of systems of patronage' (Stirrat and Henkel 1997: 72). Behind the rhetoric of partnership and the economistic language of 'social investment', the politics of the gift prevail, undermining Mauss's representation of the gift as the antithesis to the amorality of the market economy and 'the cold reasoning of the businessman, banker or capitalist' (Mauss 1967: 73). Indeed, the words of Ernest Oppenheimer, founder of Anglo American, continue to be invoked by the mining executives of today: the aim of the company is 'to make profits, but profits in such a way as to benefit the people and communities in which we operate'.

The interplay of gift and counter-gift creates a social bond between donor and recipient providing an essential method of forging diplomatic alliances. The exchange of gifts is thus seen to express both the co-operative and competitive values of society. Similarly, CSR performs the crucial cohesive function of building links, and avoiding conflict, acting as a form of consensus building in the communities around the mines. For example, bursaries awarded by companies as part of their education initiatives to students selected from mining areas create permeating ripples of loyalty to the mines. The obligation of reciprocity implicit in a gift is crucial for ensuring the continuation of these ties. The gift acts as a powerful mechanism for the company to generate 'social capital'. This is clear in the case of CSR as it is seen to lubricate the harsh realities of the mining business. Thus one CSR co-ordinator stated:

> A few years ago CSR . . . was just a 'nice-to-have', but now with the mining charter it's an imperative. We had a meeting with the mine manager, he said . . . 'in a rugby match the guy with the ball is being protected by all the other players from being attacked' and he sees CSR as protecting the guy with the ball, a buffer, keeping the community happy.

Through CSI, mining companies extend the hand of ownership over the community, which often becomes '*our* community' in company discourse. The claims to 'our community' express a sense of personal relationship between corporation and community, reflecting the way in which gift relationships are usually described in terms of 'the personal, rather than the institutional' (Eyben 2003: 9). Gifts wrapped up as CSI contain inescapable elements of power and morality which create a social bond between giver and receiver as the expectation of reciprocity inherent in the gift leaves the receiver in a position of indebtedness, vulnerable to the whims of the donor, so empowering the giver, while weakening the recipient. This is explicit in the words of the co-ordinator of a company-sponsored education programme at the mines:

> People around the mines feel an entitlement over and above the level of productivity they are willing to put in. Even my schoolchildren, who we've been giving a 40,000 Rand bursary . . . more than their parents will earn in a lifetime, . . . you know those are the kids who phone me the first night they're on the programme and tell me they don't like the food.

The recipients of the company's 40,000 Rand bursaries are placed in a position of indebtedness in which they are expected to receive the bursary with gratitude and not complain. The expectation of reciprocity-in-kind is implied as the co-ordinator criticises people for expecting more than they can give back in terms of productivity. Crucially, the 'gift' is juxtaposed with 'entitlement', so asserting the dominance of the company as a paternalistic institution. The gift appears as the antithesis to entitlement, which is 'alienable', defined in terms of the impersonal rather than the personal: 'once passed over to the other person the original owner no longer has any claims on it' (Eyben 2003: 10). In contrast, ownership of CSI projects around the mines tends to remain with the donor. As Eyben puts it, 'while *giving*, the owner is also *keeping* . . . if the donor maintains most of the decision-making powers he remains the owner although the recipient is in possession of the money' (Eyben 2003: 10).

No recipient wants to be dependent on a donor. Recently a paradigm shift is emerging as the CSR activities of mining companies are increasingly responding to a state-driven national agenda for black economic empowerment (BEE) and SD. The South African government's legislative transformation agenda, as articulated in the BEE Scorecard,[7] has gone some way towards translating responsibility into obligation. As stipulated by the MPRDA (Mineral and Petroleum Resources Development Act), companies are now required to convert their 'old order' mining rights into 'new-order rights'; in order to do so, and in competing for new exploration and mining rights, they must meet a number of social and labour targets. As one CSR co-ordinator put it: 'The mining charter means that we're changing from the attitude of just handing things out. The company can't try to be Father Christmas anymore'.

Partnership or patronage?

In recent years the concept of partnership has been invoked as a central strategy in the pursuit of corporate citizenship, linking TNCs with governments, NGOs and 'local communities'. The partnership paradigm has, to a large extent, supplanted the traditional notion of corporate philanthropy. Where once TNCs spoke loudly of their philanthropic gifts to society, they now speak in terms of partnerships with local communities or national governments in pursuit of the mutual goal of SD. This change seems to mirror similar shifts in the development industry from the language of charity and gifts to that of SD, capacity building and empowerment (Stirrat and Henkel 1997: 73) and is encapsulated in the words of an ex-chairman of one of the world's largest mining companies:

> I don't see it as my responsibility to spend shareholder money on grand philanthropic gestures, it's . . . how we build security for long-term business investment. It makes the company a much more attractive *partner* to a host government or . . . community.[8]

Under this new rhetoric, 'donor' and 'recipient' have been re-categorised as 'partners'. Eyben suggests that this change in terminology is 'symptomatic of the essential discomfort that those involved feel about the anomaly of a gift relationship' (Eyben 2003: 11). However, while donors might use the language of *partnership*, attempting to 'assert identity between the rich giver and the poor receiver, a gift in practice reinforces or even reinvents these differences' (Stirrat and Henkel 1997: 69).

Partnerships claim a common cause, that business interests can be pursued in parallel with those of other stakeholders. Government, business and civil society are brought together in what has become the new orthodoxy of the CSR world: tri-sector partner-

7 The scorecard rates corporate performance according to a set of CSR-related and BEE criteria. These include criteria such as 'community development [and] affirmative procurement' (Hamann 2004) as well as targets for HDSA (historically disadvantaged South Africans) quotas in management positions (Scorecard, Department of Minerals and Energy, SA 2004).

8 Interview with ex-chairman of a multinational mining corporation, 19 May 2004.

ships. Yet partnerships are as much a site of struggle as solidarity. The discursive power of partnership has been highlighted by anthropologists of development who have revealed dramatic inequalities of power and conflicting interests masked behind the veneer of equal collaboration (see, for example, Stirrat and Henkel 1997; Crewe and Harrison 1998: ch. 4). Following Stirrat and Henkel's analysis of the relationship between donors and NGOs in the delivery of development aid, I argue that, for corporations, the great benefit of the partnership paradigm is legitimation: 'it allows them to claim a certain authenticity: "we are of and for the people" ' (Stirrat and Henkel 1997: 75). This generates competition between companies operating in the same area to publicly claim partnership with the 'community' around the mines. In this way they co-opt local and national political support and 'reap the rewards of high-profile visibility and reputation' (Mosse 2003: 13). Thus the director of a local NGO in Rustenburg described how:

> One mining company gave us money to set up the foundation. They wanted us to put up a . . . billboard with their name on it. But we knew if we did then none of the other mines would touch us. So they put it up and we took it down . . . [it's] supposed to be about partnerships with the community, but when it comes down to it they just want their name on it and to say it's theirs.

Such relationships are at best precarious, at worst serve to increase the power of corporations to pursue their own interests at the expense of communities while blurring the lines of accountability between the company and the NGOs they work with. For, as Stirrat and Henkel point out, there is always an asymmetry between givers and receivers: 'he who pays the piper not only calls the tune but attempts to make sure that it is performed' (Stirrat and Henkel 1997: 75-76). This asymmetry of power is described by the director of an NGO contracted by a company to provide entrepreneurship training in the communities around the mines:

> When the mine opened . . . four years ago there was a lot of demonstrations . . . we were part of [their] attempt to please the community . . . They make use of us when they have to brag about their CSR, when they have important people they bring them to see us . . . we must give up whatever we've planned, so they can have their photos taken . . . and put it in the magazine . . . Maybe our view of partnership is different from theirs . . . They don't listen to our financial realities. We're constantly getting feedback from their . . . management that our statistics aren't good enough, but their expectations are unrealistic . . . They put in 500,000 Rand and want to see a major miracle . . . But they're giving it to us for free so what can we do.

By extending the hand of patronage to civil-society organisations—giving and taking away social investment where it sees fit—the practice of CSI further weakens the NGO sector as it strips NGOs of autonomy under the banner of empowerment.[9]

Front-line CSR practitioners often found themselves acting as local patrons: a role that at times inspired a sense of personal achievement; at others, discomfort. In this way responsibility is personalised and shifted from the corporation to an individual.

9 The weakness of the NGO sector in post-apartheid South Africa (Habib and Taylor 1999) has, arguably, contributed to the dominance of the corporate model of company and service provider.

The sense of personal honour derived from the role of patron is evident in the words of a CSR co-ordinator at the mines:

> You see this is how we empower the community—we needed some land clearing—so I got young people from around here who were unemployed to form a company and I contracted them to do the job . . . Now in the village they'll shout 'hey Mr Enele'.[10] This is the thing that Daniel has done . . . I can feel proud of that.

Conversely, the co-ordinator of the mining company's education programmes, when honoured at a function for one of the projects said:

> I don't like it when people give me things like this—because it's not me it's [the company]—I'm just a vehicle for [the company] to work through—so you must thank them—it's they who gave you all this, it's their money.

The sense of personal achievement expressed by local-level CSR employees was often balanced by a contrasting sense of impotence resulting from the individualisation of responsibility. While on the one hand they had become individual patrons driven by personal commitment, they remained, on the other hand, trapped under the weight of the company's rigid hierarchy and opaque bureaucracy. Many CSR officers spoke of budgets suddenly cut, projects prematurely curtailed, and having to creatively negotiate ways to fulfil commitments to their beneficiaries and sustain relationships they had personally built up.

The Rustenburg Municipality has a sophisticated Integrated Development Plan,[11] a strategy for multi-stakeholder partnership to which all parties claim to subscribe. CSR managers commonly referred to the IDP as the 'motherboard' or 'template' guiding the company's SED activities and stated their commitment to working with local government. A different picture emerges from the accounts of local government officers: a picture in which decision-making within the company appears to outsiders as opaque rather than transparent, and planning seems driven by company interests rather than local needs. As one local government officer stated:

> If they followed the IDP as they say they do, they would come to us to ask where is the need that we have identified through our . . . consultation process—but instead most companies send a junior manager with no power to the meetings; they send the photocopy boy.

Companies argue that lack of resources and capacity within local government has forced them to take on this responsibility. However, by adopting the position of guardian of the social as well as economic order, they are arguably complicit in the weakening of local government as they undermine it through the webs of patronage generated by CSI. This in turn 'reinforces the perception that the company, rather than the . . . government, is responsible for decision-making, benefits and change' (Sillitoe and Wilson 2003: 248). Ultimately, the accounts from the Platinum District seem to expose, rather than affirm, the myth of partnership.

10 For the purposes of anonymity all names have been changed.

11 The South African government demands that each municipality produce a comprehensive IDP every five years (reviewed annually) in consultation with local stakeholders.

Conclusion

The theory of the gift is a theory of 'human solidarity' (Douglas 1990: xiii). As such the gift has both a bright and a shady side: on the one hand, trust, personal commitment, and even affection; on the other, paternalism, patronage and control. The latent power of the gift to oppress the recipient is poignantly expressed in the words of the CSR director of a SA mining corporation:

> Many times we kill people with kindness . . . with the education programme we said that any student who is accepted must pay 600 Rand . . . it's not much, but . . . it makes people feel that they've earned it, . . . paid for it; it's not just given.

This chapter has argued that the politics of the gift are embedded in the practice of CSR. It has argued that CSR represents a powerful moral discourse, exposing the hegemonic myth that business is politically and morally neutral. The quest for responsibility generates categories of donor and recipient binding people in relationships of power and dependency. The precarious and personalised relationships created by this quest unsettle the confidence placed in the scientific rationality of policy and increasingly sophisticated management models.

In pursuit of the slippery notion of responsibility, mining corporations operating in SA, and the individuals within them, are demonstrating significant commitment to the national goals of transformation and empowerment, and the international targets for SD. Yet the very concept of *responsibility* is problematic. As a moral discourse, responsibility inspires a paternalistic duty of care on the part of the corporation, while placing the 'beneficiary' in a position of deference and subordination. In this way, CSR can serve to empower the corporation, rather than the supposed subjects of their empowerment and development initiatives. As long as the emphasis remains on voluntary initiatives—on responsibility rather than obligation, benefits rather than entitlement—the coercive properties of the gift will prevail in the practice of CSR.

References

Bauman, Z. (1989) *Modernity and the Holocaust* (Cambridge, UK: Polity Press).

Crewe, E., and E. Harrison (1998) *Whose Development? An Ethnography of Aid* (London: Zed Books).

Douglas, M. (1990) 'No Free Gifts', in M. Mauss (ed.), *The Gift* (London: Routledge): 9-23.

Economist (2004) 'Business: Two-faced capitalism', *The Economist* 370.8359 (24 January 2004): 59.

Eyben, R. (2003) 'Who Owns the Gift? Donor–Recipient Relations and the National Elections in Bolivia', *EIDOS Workshop*, SOAS, London, 26–28 September 2003.

Ferguson, J. (1998) 'Transnational Topographies of Power: Beyond "The State" and "Civil Society" in the Study of African Politics', in H.S. Manussen and S. Arnfred (eds.), *Concepts and Metaphors: Ideologies, Narratives and Myths in Development Discourse* (International Development Studies, Roskilde University, Occasional Paper No. 19).

Foucault, M. (1978) *The History of Sexuality* (Harmondsworth, UK: Penguin).

Gasper, D. (1996) 'Culture and Development Ethics: Needs, Women's Rights and Western Theories', *Development and Change* 27.4: 627-61.

Giri, A.K., and P. Quarles van Ufford (2003) 'Reconstituting Development as a Shared Responsibility: Ethics, Aesthetics and a Creative Shaping of Human Possibilities', in P. Quarles van Ufford and A. Kumar Giri (eds.), *A Moral Critique of Development* (London: Routledge): 253-79.

Habib, A., and R. Taylor (1999) 'Anti-Apartheid NGOs in Transition', *Voluntas* 10.1: 73-82.

Hamann, R. (2004) 'Corporate Social Responsibility, Partnerships, and Institutional Change: The Case of Mining Companies in South Africa', *Natural Resources Forum* 28: 1-13.

——, T. Agbazue, P. Kapelus and A. Hein (2005) 'Universalising Corporate Social Responsibility? South African Challenges to the International Organisation for Standardisation's New Social Responsibility Standard', *Business and Society Review* 110.1: 53-69.

Mauss, M. (1967) *The Gift* (London: Cohen and West Ltd [1925]).

Mosse, D. (2003) 'Good Policy is Unimplementable? Reflections on the Ethnography of Aid Policy and Practice', *EIDOS Workshop*, SOAS, London, 26–28 September 2003.

Quarles van Ufford, P. (2003) '"The Disjuncture of Things": Some Remarks about a New Agenda for Studying Development', *EIDOS Workshop*, SOAS, London, 26–28 September 2003.

——, A.K. Giri and D. Mosse (2003) 'Interventions in Development: Towards a New Moral Understanding of our Experiences and an Agenda for the Future', in P. Quarles van Ufford and A.K. Giri (eds.), *A Moral Critique of Development* (London: Routledge): 3-41.

Sillitoe, P., and R.A. Wilson (2003) 'Playing on the Pacific Ring of Fire: Negotiation and Knowledge in Mining in Papua New Guinea', in J. Pottier, A. Bicker and P. Sillitoe (eds.), *Negotiating Local Knowledge* (London: Pluto Press): 241-73.

Stirrat, R.L., and H. Henkel (1997) 'The Development Gift: The Problem of Reciprocity in the NGO World', *Annals of the American Academy of Political and Social Science* 554: 66-80.

Zapiro (2002) 'A Gift from the Corporate World!', in J. Shapiro (ed.), *Zapiro Bushwhacked* (Cape Town: Double Storey Books in association with Zaprock Productions): 147.

16

The digital divide and CSR in Africa

THE NEED FOR CORPORATE LAW REFORM

Judy N. Muthuri

International Centre for Corporate Social Responsibility, UK

Kiarie Mwaura

Queen's University Belfast, UK

Academics, practitioners and development partners are increasingly discussing the role of information and communication technologies (ICT) in fostering development. Indeed, as a strategy for helping developing countries to meet the Millennium Development Goals (MDGs), resources have been put aside to promote ICT. In 2002 the CEO Charter for Digital Development committed its signatories to give 20% of their annual corporate philanthropy budget to ICT projects in developing countries (United Nations 2002). In March 2005, the United Nations after years of deliberations launched a 'Digital Solidarity Fund' to finance projects that address 'the uneven distribution and use' of ICT and are aimed at enabling excluded people and countries to enter the new era of the information society (*Economist* 2005a).

In Africa, there has been an increase in partnerships between governments, the private sector and civil society aimed at enhancing the access to information and technological know-how among the poor.[1] This has been as a result of the implementation of the New Economic Partnership for Africa's Development (NEPAD), a policy framework

1 NEPAD has established an ICT Task Team, e-Africa Commission, which is responsible for developing ICT strategies, policies and projects: www.eafricacommission.org.

for African renewal which African leaders initiated in October 2001 as a means of eradicating poverty. NEPAD underscores the role of public- and private-sector partnerships as catalysts for development in Africa.

This chapter argues that, although the initiatives geared towards bridging the digital divide in Africa are laudable, corporations can play a pivotal role in helping to bridge this gap by undertaking CSR initiatives. However, this can be facilitated only by reforming corporate laws to enable companies to pursue CSR beyond their economic and legal responsibilities. This contention is elaborated more in the following section of this chapter where we locate the digital divide discourse within the CSR paradigm. In the next section, we argue that corporate laws in most Commonwealth African countries inhibit the role of corporations in bridging the digital divide. The complex, uncertain and uncodified regulatory frameworks make it difficult for company directors to understand what is expected of them with regard to pursuing social responsibilities that are not based purely on economic rationality. In the final section, we affirm that the African governments can enhance the process of bridging the digital gap by enhancing connectivity, ending any prohibitions on the use of satellite technology for social development (Panos 2005) and providing a conducive legal environment for corporations to play a more active role in social responsibility.

ICT and sustainable development

The extent to which the application of ICT furthers social goals and economic growth is largely unknown (Gilhooly 2005). We contribute to the debate around the advocacy of ICT in the developing world by relating the digital divide discourse to the sustainable development agenda for Africa. Our contention is that the digital divide is not the root problem but a symptom of deeper, more significant inequities in income, development, literacy and democracy (Norris 2001; SID 2004), which ICT can help to address.

It is notable that the digital divide is increased by inadequate telecommunications infrastructure in Africa where, for instance, many countries have only dial-up phone systems (Panos 2005). The cost of buying ICT devices and using the internet is also prohibitive given that many regions in Africa are yet to benefit from the coastal fibre optics, digital subscriber lines (DSL) internet, and very small aperture terminal satellites (VSAT). The combination of prohibitive costs and lack of basic infrastructure, such as electricity, renders ICT 'a dream' to many African people in a continent where 40% of urban households live in absolute poverty and 315 million people survive on less than one dollar a day (WSSD 2002).

Low levels of ICT penetration and integration limit economic growth and the efficient delivery of public services by the government. For example, research exploring the nature of export marketing on the internet in the Kenyan floriculture industry revealed that, despite the awareness of the benefits of e-commerce, firms are yet to fully exploit the internet as a business tool. High installation and maintenance costs of the internet, inadequate capacity and knowledge of internet use, and negative attitudes such as the perceived complexity of new technology were some of the factors thought to be inhibiting exploitation of e-commerce by the flower firms (Muthuri 2001). A study of the tour operators in Kenya also revealed that the slow pace of internet adoption was hindering full exploitation of e-commerce in the industry (Mbuvi 2000).

Whereas the use of computers and the internet appears to pose a lot of challenges to most businesses, there has been rapid penetration of mobile-phone technology in Africa. Research shows that the growth rate of mobile communication in low-income countries is twice as fast as that in high-income countries (Vodafone 2005). As a result of the rapid growth rate, mobile-phone technology is stated to have great impacts on development because the technology has been able to reduce transaction costs, broaden trade networks and serve as a substitute for costly physical transport. In fact, the use of mobile phones has enabled Coca-Cola distributors in Zambia to make payments for their deliveries by sending text messages, a process that takes 30 seconds (*Economist* 2005b). Given that ICT enables people to enhance their trade relations, embracing ICT in full could trigger economic growth in Africa as it has done in countries such as Hong Kong, Singapore and Korea, whose developing economies realised immense growth through the utilisation of telecommunications as part of their economic growth and development strategies (Saunders *et al.* 1994).

Recent research commissioned by Vodafone Plc has also shown that mobile phone technologies strengthen community ties, build social and political networks, and develop economic opportunities for the 'information-poor' (Vodafone 2005). Unfortunately, economic and social impacts of technology tend to favour people with high ICT usage and those who have both access and the capability to utilise ICT, leaving out the majority who are in poverty and lack basic skills.

The call to promote and encourage ICT in Africa needs combined efforts by the private, public and non-profit sectors. Corporations are collaborating with the government and the non-profit sectors in support of some ICT projects along thematic issues such as education[2] using the rationale of 'enlightened self-interest'. However, under the existing corporate laws, the extent to which companies can be involved in ICT as a part of their social responsibility is limited. It is the CSR discourse we now turn to.

Social responsibility of corporations in the digital divide

Corporate social responsibility refers to the role that businesses play as citizens in society. CSR is seen as having an **economic face**—going beyond the bottom line; a **legal face**—conforming to the basic rules of society including those embodied in law and ethical customs; an **ethical face**—striving to operate in an ethical way; and a **philanthropic face**—enhancing the quality of life by giving back to communities (Carroll 1998). Drawing from the long-standing debates on the social responsibility of corporations (Walters 1977; Henderson 2001), the involvement of businesses in bridging the digital divide can be a contentious issue depending on different schools of thought. Whereas business involvement in reducing the digital divide as a social initiative can be applauded from communitarian (Logsdon and Wood 2002), citizenship (Moon *et al.*

2 In 2004, the Information and Communication Technology (ICT) Trust Fund was set up. This is a collaborative initiative by companies in the private and public sector targeting ICT education and training in public secondary schools in Kenya. The Fund's aim is to provide computer technology and training in ICT to at least 80% of public secondary schools in the next five years.

2005) and stakeholder (Freeman 1984) perspectives, some economic theorists (Friedman 1970) hold that society determines and meets its needs and wants through the market. Hence, the pursuit of self-interest by business results in society's best interests being served (Friedman 1970).

These economic theorists contend that the free-market forces ensure that maximum social benefits are achieved at minimum social costs if each company tries to maximise profits. Thus corporations should engage in promoting ICT as a strategy for bridging the digital divide only if that maximises the profits of shareholders. They argue that the government, rather than business, ought to be concerned with solving social problems and providing social services, given that businesses are set up as economic associations and not as welfare agencies. They maintain that, if corporations pay their taxes, the government is able to provide social services using their capabilities and competences. Businesses, on the other hand, lack the accountability required to handle social issues, given that they are not subject to the electorate's scrutiny.

This view is consistent with an agency perspective of the corporation, which regards the main players as shareholders (who invest primarily to increase their wealth) and managers (agents), who must act in the shareholders' interests. Wealth maximisation is justified on the basis that the firm is a unit for all bargaining arrangements, which the participants in a company seek to use in order to maximise wealth through beneficial bargains. The firm is considered incapable of having other objectives, such as social responsibility, because it is a nexus of contracts, and not an individual with motivations and intentions. Therefore directors of a company have a duty to maximise the profits of a company and failure to do so may lead to their dismissal.

Although stakeholders may suffer when the sole objective of directors is to maximise the wealth of shareholders, agency economic theorists do not regard that as a sufficient basis for affording legal protection because corporate stakeholders, such as creditors and employees, are considered capable of protecting themselves through contracts (Millon 1995). This view does not recognise the inequality of bargaining power between rational economic actors within a company and society in general.

It is for this reason that communitarian theorists regard the company as an entity having both public and private roles (Stokes 1986). Communitarians recognise the need to protect non-shareholders on the basis that disparities in bargaining power and lack of information make it impossible for some non-shareholders to protect themselves through contracts. The company cannot be regarded as just the association of shareholders because it also encompasses others who affect its operations and who make commitments to it, as stipulated in stakeholder theory. Corporations become entities through which a variety of participants, who may be interdependently related, accomplish multiple and at times divergent goals (Freeman 1984). Given that stakeholders can determine the future direction of a firm, businesses have to reorient their systems and processes in order to be responsive to the needs of stakeholders. Companies can, therefore, reap long-term benefits by committing themselves to ICT projects in the community.

However, as will be seen in the following section, the social responsibility of corporations to its stakeholders is limited to some extent by the corporate laws within which corporations operate. Although this discussion applies to CSR in general, rather than to ICT specifically, it illustrates through a variety of court cases the extent to which company law is biased towards profit maximisation and how onerous it is for any corporate board, including those that pursue ICT social responsibilities, to justify socially responsible initiatives that are normative and beyond the economic objectives of the firm.

Regulatory frameworks

Most Commonwealth African countries still retain corporate laws that were inherited from the UK five decades ago. For instance, Kenya's Companies Act (the 'Act'), the basic statute governing corporate operations in Kenya, is based almost entirely on the 1948 UK Companies Act. The UK Act was introduced in Kenya in 1959 and adopted in 1962 virtually verbatim. Despite substantial economic development in Kenya since 1962, the current regulatory framework on corporate operations remains as it was in 1962.

This is not unique to Kenya, as most other Commonwealth African states have not codified the duties of directors in their company laws. Directors are governed by principles found in English common law and the common law of individual countries. For instance, Kenya's Judicature Act (section 3) permits the application of the common law and doctrines of equity in force in England as at 12 August 1897. As such, the Kenyan courts apply English common law principles and have hardly adopted a Kenyan approach to the interpretation of the 'Act'.[3] While decisions of English courts given after the reception date are not of binding authority in the courts of the territory, they are treated with the highest respect if the English law has not been subsequently modified (Amollo 1999). Due to lack of codification, the common law principles applicable to Kenya are largely inaccessible and, as such, directors and practitioners have to search through a maze of case law to understand their responsibilities.

The Act is silent on the legal obligations that directors have and, as a result of this, the common law determines whether company directors have obligations to take into account stakeholder interests. The common law requires directors to act bona fide in the best interests of the company and not for any collateral purpose.[4] As such, the directors must keep within the proper limits and avoid using powers given to them for one purpose for totally different purposes. Any exercise of the powers of directors for an improper purpose can be set aside, even though the directors may honestly have believed that they were acting in the interests of the company.[5] A shareholder, for instance, may challenge in court a company's resolution allowing directors to pursue activities that are not 'reasonably incidental' to the carrying-on of the company's business. For an act to be reasonably incidental to the business of the company, the benefit to the company must be direct and not 'too speculative or too remote'.[6] In addition, a matter can be challenged for not being expressly or impliedly authorised by a company's objects clause as contained in its constitution on the basis that it goes beyond the capacity of the company (*ultra vires*).

Since the duty to act in the best interests of the company requires directors to use powers conferred on them by the articles of association, construction of the articles

3 *Flagship Carriers Ltd* v. *Imperial Bank Ltd*, High Court Civil Case No. 1643 of 1999 (unreported).

4 *Re Smith* v. *Fawcett Ltd* [1942] Ch. 304.

5 *Australian Growth Resources Corp Pty Ltd* v. *Van Reesema* (1988) 6 ACLC 529.

6 *Evans* v. *Brunner Mond & Co* [1921] 1 Ch. 359.

determines the criteria used by the courts to determine whether a particular purpose is proper.[7] In the event that the articles are not explicit, proper purpose may be implied from the 'general obligations and duties which directors incur by the very nature of their appointment'.[8] The proper-purpose test fosters the accountability of directors by allowing courts to monitor the directors' decision-making more closely. The Act does not specify whether the duty to act bona fide in the interests of the whole company requires directors to consider the interests of the corporate entity with present members or the company as a whole, including employees, communities and other stakeholders.

According to English common law, any act considered to be bona fide by the director must be geared towards promoting the business. Gratuitous payments or gifts out of the assets of the company[9] and provision of a pension to a widow of a former employee[10] have been rendered not to be in the best interests of the company. Similarly, crediting sums to directors as a 'bonus' at a time when there were no profits available for such purposes was held in *Re The Highlands Commercial Union Limited*[11] to amount to breach of trust or duty because it was not in the best interests of the company. However, gratuitous gifts out of a company's assets for the purposes of education and charity were allowed in *Evans* v. *Brunner Mond & Co.*[12] because they were directly beneficial to the company. The passing of a resolution to give grants to scientific institutions was held to be *intra vires* the objects of the company because the company intended to make use of the reservoir of experts trained from those grants and therefore the expenditure was necessary for the continued progress of the chemical manufacturing business of the company.

Although directors who assume some ICT social responsibilities might be considered to be acting within their powers when they undertake activities that are reasonably incidental to the business of the company, lack of codification of the common law rules regulating the responsibilities of directors makes it cumbersome for directors to ascertain their actual role in social responsibility. For instance, it is unclear whether a director who sacrifices the profits of a company in the short term by assuming some ICT social responsibilities would be liable for the breach of his duties if his objectives were to enhance the profits of the company in the long term. According to *Evans* v. *Brunner Mond & Co.*, such a director would be liable for breach of his duties if he undertakes activities whose intended benefits to the company are too speculative or too remote.

As such, there is a need for the Act to specify expressly in whose interests directors are supposed to act and to whom they owe their duties in order to enable directors to ascertain their obligations easily. The drafting may follow developments in the USA where directors are required to promote the success of the company for the benefit of its members as a whole.[13] By defining expressly the term 'company as a whole' to mean the interests of all shareholders or other requisite interest groups, such as employees,

7 *Re Smith* v. *Fawcett Ltd* [1942] Ch. 304.

8 *Re The Highlands Commercial Union Limited* [1957] EA 851.

9 *Re Smith* v. *Fawcett Ltd* [1942] Ch. 304.

10 *Parke* v. *Daily News Ltd* [1962] Ch. 927.

11 [1957] EA 851.

12 [1921] 1 Ch. 359.

13 *Credit Lyonnais Bank Nederlander NV* v. *Pathe Communications Corporations* (1991) Delaware Court of Chancery LEXIS 215.

and the society within which the company operates, the Act would effectively deal with the problem associated with the interpretation of the said term.

Business involvement in ICT

Studies have shown that CSR potentially creates a win–win situation and has both tangible and intangible benefits and builds valuable assets which further business comparative and competitive advantages (Hillman and Keim 2001; Porter and Kramer 2002), including building business image and reputation, attracting a better workforce, the 'licence to operate' and a long-term improved stable context in which to do business. Companies that pursue CSR aimed at narrowing the digital divide stand to benefit immensely because they are in a position to reach more consumers. For instance, companies that will utilise the new Microsoft software tool, which will enable computer users in East Africa to use Microsoft Office programs in Swahili,[14] will be able to reach consumers that are not able to write and read in English.

Companies that embrace ICT are likely to set standards for other companies, especially if they prosper as a result of their transparency and social responsibility and the connectivity of the public. More access to ICT would also enhance communication between the company and employees, customers, suppliers and other stakeholders. Shareholders' meetings, for instance, could take place on the internet and electronic notice boards could be utilised to communicate important information (Burns 2001). Although companies may not be willing to disclose some information owing to fear of competition, adverse publicity or unwanted regulation, they are likely to seize the opportunity to deal with certain concerns by distributing additional information which may not be in the public domain.

Moreover, enhanced access to ICT in Africa would enhance public disclosure of company information. Presently, companies are required to disclose certain information, such as their constitutions, annual returns, particulars of the directors and copies of special and ordinary resolutions, all of which must be filed with the registrar of companies. However, the delay involved in obtaining such information from company registries and the cost of sending this information to shareholders is enormous.[15] Given that more access to ICT would enable stakeholders to demand and access more information than is currently available at the companies' registries, the disclosure of more information would promote corporate social responsibility (Burns 2001), regulation of companies and good corporate governance, as it would enable shareholders to scrutinise the conduct of directors more closely and enforce the liability of directors more effectively (Mwaura 2002). In summary, it would encourage the development of open and accountable societies.

14 See H-Net Network on Swahili Language and Culture www.h-net.org/~swahili, accessed 30 September 2005.

15 Company searches sometimes take a minimum of three weeks to finalise because of the lack of modern technology.

The case for enhancing e-government

Public–private-sector ICT interventions in promoting sustainable development demand that the government plays dual roles as an enabler of ICT adoption by other societal institutions through establishing conducive regulatory frameworks, and as an institutional actor in adopting ICTs through public-sector reforms. Governments stand to benefit from widened ICT access that could spin off more collaborative initiatives with corporations, and for this reason they ought to expedite the process of establishing regulatory frameworks that would enable businesses to adopt more ICT social responsibilities.

Widened ICT access would enable governments to improve the quality and cost-effectiveness of the provision of public services and to promote citizens' participation in public affairs, thus reducing the democratic divide. For instance, online discussions and civic education programmes can be used to promote e-democracy that enables citizens to have more participation in the governance of their affairs (Morison 2004). Proper use of e-government could result in more efficient services (Basu 2004), resulting in decreased costs and reduced corruption, which is often fuelled by government bureaucracy. The reduction of bureaucracy, which is also a disincentive to investors, goes a long way towards improving public-sector performance.

To widen access to ICT, a majority of African governments now have ICT task forces, which seek to co-ordinate and popularise ICT initiatives.[16] The governments are also entering into partnerships with international organisations, such as UNDP (United Nations Development Programme) and the UN, to develop online services to address problems of accessing information on development issues.[17] Many African governments are making progress in modernising their governments by putting their services online in a bid to enhance the interaction between citizens and the government. For example, the Kenyan government recently established a directorate of e-government to advise the government on ICT matters and it has also started introducing other electronic systems to increase efficiency in the payment of utility bills, registration of companies, land, deaths and national identity cards. This will not only streamline the provision of public services, but also discourage corruption, which has thrived on dysfunctional record-keeping systems.

However, in order to increase the connectivity rate and promote e-commerce and e-government in Africa, governments need to create an environment that will enable the private sector to play a more active role in bridging the digital divide. There is also a need to address broader social, economic, cultural and political issues that affect connectivity because the failure to do so could actually widen the digital divide (Pare 2004). For e-government to be effective, there is a need to train civil servants to enhance their ICT literacy and have up-to-date technology, as outdated systems are still in use in government offices.[18] The government also needs to: liberalise the communications sectors; extend communication and IT infrastructure; remove stringent regula-

16 For Tanzania, see www.moct.go.tz/ict, accessed 2 October 2005.

17 Tanzania Online is an example of such an initiative; see www.tzonline.org, accessed 3 October 2005.

18 Apart from having outdated computers, the ratio of computers in government offices is one computer for every 60 officers (see Gakunu 2004).

tions, trade barriers and inhibiting customs procedures that impede access to and penetration of ICT; and, lastly, encourage tri-sector partnership which involves entering into partnerships with government departments, schools, libraries and community centres in order to help and create more access for the citizens.

Conclusion

The benefits of embracing ICT by both the government and companies include a reduction in transaction costs, access to new markets and improved governance and efficiency (Pare 2004). Better access to ICT would enable corporations to get efficient services from the government and reach more consumers. The easier access to governmental and corporate information and the widened participation of citizens in public and corporate affairs would also enhance the accountability of both governments and corporations. This plays an important role in strengthening democracy and governance of both institutions.

Besides their direct involvement in enhancing connectivity, governments can enhance the process of bridging the digital gap by providing an enabling environment for the exploitation of ICT and creating a conducive legal environment that would provide incentives for corporations to play a more active role in social responsibility. Common law rules that enable directors to assume social responsibilities need to be codified, as they remain largely inaccessible, making it difficult for directors to understand their social responsibilities. Their scope also needs to be widened in order to allow directors to assume social activities that might not be of immediate benefit to their companies.

These recommendations would not only benefit companies in the long run but also go a long way towards helping governments to bridge the digital divide and enhance e-government. However, in the absence of clear regulatory frameworks that encourage companies to be involved in CSR, business executives ought to pursue ICT initiatives that create business value and can be linked to the companies' sustainability objectives.

References

Amollo, O. (1999) 'Reviewing 100 years of Common Law in Kenya', *The Advocate*, January 1999: 16-17.
Basu, S. (2004) 'E-Government and Developing Countries: An Overview', *International Review of Law Computers and Technology* 18: 109-31.
Burns, T. (2001) 'Implications of Information Technology on Corporate Governance', *International Journal of Law and IT* 9: 21-38.
Carroll, A.B. (1998) 'The Four Faces of Corporate Citizenship', *Business and Society Review* 100.1: 1-7.
Economist (2005a) 'The Real Digital Divide', *The Economist*, 12 March 2005.
—— (2005b) 'Calling across the Divide', *The Economist*, 13 March 2005.
Freeman, E. (1984) *Strategic Management: A Stakeholder Approach* (Boston, MA: Pitman).
Friedman, M. (1970) 'The Social Responsibility of Business is to Increase its Profits', *New York Times Magazine*, 13 September 1970.

Gakunu, G. (2004) 'e-Government Strategy for Kenya', www.apc.org/apps/img_upload/6972616672696361646f63756d656e74/egov_Presentation_for_ICT_Convention.ppt, accessed 3 October 2005.

Gilhooly, D. (2005) 'Creating an Enabling Environment: Toward the Millennium Development Goals', Proceedings of the Berlin Global Forum of the United Nations Task Force, 2005; available at www.unicttaskforce.org/perl/documents.pl?id=1489, accessed 1 October 2005.

Henderson, D. (2001) 'The Case against Corporate Social Responsibility', *Policy* 17.2: 28-32.

Hillman, A.J., and G.D. Keim (2001) 'Shareholder Value, Stakeholder Management and Social Issues: What's the Bottom Line?', *Strategic Management Journal* 22: 125-39.

Logsdon, J.M., and D.J. Wood (2002) 'Business Citizenship: From Domestic to Global Level of Analysis', *Business Ethics Quarterly* 12.2: 155-87.

Mbuvi, M.M. (2000) *The Potential Adoption of E-commerce by Tour Operators: A Case of the Kenya Association for Tour Operators (KATO) Members* (MBA dissertation, University of Nairobi).

Millon, D. (1995) 'Communitarianism in Corporate Law: Foundations and Law Reform Strategies', in L. Mitchell (ed.), *Progressive Corporate Law* (Boulder, CO: Westview Press): 1-34.

Moon, J., A. Crane and D. Matten (2005) 'Can Corporations be Citizens? Corporate Citizenship as a Metaphor for Business Participation in Society', *Business Ethics Quarterly* 15.3: 427-51.

Morison, J. (2004) 'E-Democracy: On-line Civic Space and the Renewal of Democracy?', *Canadian Journal of Law and Jurisprudence* 17: 129-41.

Muthuri, J.N. (2001) *Export Marketing in the Internet: The Case of the Horticulture Industry in Kenya* (MBA dissertation, University of Nairobi).

Mwaura, K. (2002) 'Regulation of Directors in Kenya: An Empirical Study', *International Company and Commercial Law Review* 13: 465-79.

Norris, P. (2001) *Digital Divide: Civic Engagement, Information Poverty, and the Internet Worldwide* (Cambridge, UK: Cambridge University Press).

Panos (2005) 'Why Calls in Africa Cost More: The Need for VSATs' (PANOS Media Toolkit on ICTs, No. 2; available at www.panos.org.uk/files/wsistoolkit2.pdf, accessed 2 October 2005).

Pare, D. (2004) 'The Digital Divide: Why the "The" is Misleading', in M. Klang and A. Murray, *Human Rights in the Digital Age* (London: Glasshouse Press): 85-97.

Porter, M.E., and M.R. Kramer (2002) 'The Competitive Advantage of Corporate Philanthropy', *Harvard Business Review* 20.12: 56-68.

Saunders, R., J. Warford and B. Wellenius (1994) *Telecommunications and Economic Development* (Baltimore, MA: John Hopkins University Press, 2nd edn).

SID (Society for International Development) (2004) *Pulling Apart: Facts and Figures on Inequality in Kenya* (Nairobi: Society for International Development).

Stokes, M. (1986) 'Company Law and Legal Theory', in W. Twinning (ed.), *Legal Theory and Common Law* (Oxford, UK: Oxford University Press): 155-83.

United Nations (2002) 'CEOs pledge no less than 20 per cent of philanthropic budgets to ICT for development', United Nations Press Release of 17 July 2002; www.un.org/News/Press/docs/2002/ga10029.doc.htm, accessed 1 October 2005.

Vodafone (2005) 'Africa: The Impact of Mobile Phones: Moving the Debate Forward', *The Vodafone Policy Paper*, Series 2.

Walters, K.D. (1977) 'Corporate Social Responsibility and Political Ideology', *California Management Review* 19.3: 40-51.

WSSD (World Summit on Sustainable Development) (2002) 'Facts about Africa', Johannesburg, South Africa, 26 August–4 September 2002; www.un.org/jsummit/html/media_info/press_kit/fact11_africa.pdf, accessed 25 September 2005.

Part VI
Supply chain and SMEs

17

Up-lifting power

CREATING SUSTAINABLE CONSUMER-DRIVEN SUPPLY CHAINS THROUGH INNOVATIVE PARTNERSHIPS IN GHANA

Suzanne 't Hooft*

Former Ahold Trainee

At the World Economic Forum in Davos some years ago the Secretary-General of the United Nations, Kofi Annan, spoke to the leaders of multinational corporations and in his speech he addressed their responsibility to the world and in particular to Africa. At this meeting the former CEO of Royal Ahold, Cees van der Hoeven, was present. Ahold is one of the largest retailers worldwide and as one of the biggest food providers in the world, the former CEO recognised the potential and the responsibility of the company to try to make a difference in Africa.

Ahold started a project with just this general idea to contribute 'something' to poverty alleviation in Africa. The corporate social responsibility department became responsible for the project and ideas began to run as widely as providing funding to hospitals or other institutions, but never with an intention to start commercial operations in Africa. During consultations with various development agencies and after a fact-finding mission, it became clear that, for Ahold to make a difference, the company should bring something to the table that would make a long-lasting impact based on its own experience. Initially Ahold did not have any intention to buy African produce, but wanted to act as a knowledge and expertise provider. Expert missions with buyers from various Ahold operating companies revealed that it was very difficult to have an impact and build commitment with the target groups without the physical flow of products

* With the co-operation of Maresa Oosterman, Netherlands Ministry of Foreign Affairs.

going to Europe. Also, Ahold would then be able to concentrate on what the company is best at: buying and selling produce and giving valuable advice on marketing and logistics.

The fact is that Africa plays a very minor role in the world's economy and little African produce can be found on our supermarket shelves. Nevertheless, opportunities were soon found given that agriculture plays an important role on this continent and it is much closer to Europe than Latin America or Asia (which can allow for much cheaper transport by sea). This opportunity formed the backbone for the creation of consumer-driven supply chains from Africa, which turned out to be successful both in experience and in actual product offerings.

In order to create these consumer-driven supply chains Ahold sought partners from different backgrounds and in various parts of the supply chain. This resulted in a multitude of parties involved in the project such as governments, non-governmental organisations (NGOs), educational institutions, trade associations and other private companies. Through the involvement of these different partners, co-operation became rather complex. Many obstacles needed to be overcome and the experiences obtained through successes and failures along the way are a part of this study.

The model

Core competences, efficiency and synergy effects are all important elements in today's business society. Setting clear targets and focusing on what each person and each organisation does best results in greater efficiencies. These principles formed the basis of the partnerships that were sought in this project. It seems logical to focus on things you're good at, but it is important to stress the relevance of this principle. When linking corporate social responsibility values into a company's everyday practices it is important that they are linked to the organisations' core competences. Keijzers *et al.* (2002: 15) provide a definition of corporate social responsibility in which this relation becomes apparent: 'CSR is the strategic process in which a business integrates the ecological and social aspects of its activities in its day-to-day management.'

For this project's success it was very important to link the efforts of Ahold to its core competences. It brought a sense of ownership for Ahold and showed commitment to producers in Africa so that even when Ahold was to leave Africa the linkages made through the exchange of goods were there to last. This means that if companies are serious about these types of projects they should create opportunities through commercial activities instead of mere philanthropic giving.

Ghana and the project start-up

Soon after the decision was made to start a project in Africa, Ghana was chosen to start the pilot project. This country was chosen for its political and economical stability. In this country conversations were started with various NGOs and governmental institutions in order to seek opportunities for development. The technicalities of development aid were in a different league from what was known to the Ahold managers. It soon became clear that, if a development focus was to become a part of the project, organisations from this field of business were necessary to assist and play an active role.

Several organisations were found in Ghana that are active in giving management and technical advice to farmers in order to assist with their production. However, a large gap was found between the African produce and what was required by Western retailers. In general, the technical assistance provided by development agencies focused on improving existing practices. This means being production-driven instead of consumer-driven. Also, creating market access in Western markets is not a part of these development agencies' work and the products that are produced through hard work might not even find a market.

Project starting-points

Through consultations with these organisations Ahold managers saw an opportunity to lift Ghanaian suppliers to Western market standards by linking development assistance to suppliers in areas where these companies needed help. Once the supplier could comply with Ahold standards (and in this respect to most other Western markets), the supplier would be rewarded with market access and concrete results. This market-based instead of ideologically steered construction was not always easy to explain to NGOs.

Another important foundation of this project is the consumer orientation of Ahold's Africa Sustainable Assistance Project (ASAP). The route taken by this project starts with the consumer and creates concepts based on the consumer *and* the available ingredients in Ghana. Normally, product development in these markets would be steered by production-driven development, meaning creating value through additional processing of existing products (for instance, by making pineapple juice from pineapples). Although this process creates added value it is not necessarily driven by consumer needs.

In summary, key elements within the model are the market-driven approach, consumer needs and partnerships with the public sector. Figure 17.1 shows a visual representation of this model.

The goals

With the foundations of the model in place for the Africa Sustainable Assistance Project, the multinational was able to show how it was going to reach its main objective: 'To utilise the know-how and expertise of Ahold's people around the world to make a positive impact in Ghana by creating sustainable business relationships with suppliers.' On the basis of consultation in Ghana, ASAP had three initial targets:

1. Develop the viability of Ghanaian growers to export tropical fruits and vegetables (through buying Ghanaian products based on European standards):
   - Utilise Ahold purchasing expertise to upgrade competitiveness
   - Utilise Ahold buying as a beachhead towards buying by other retailers

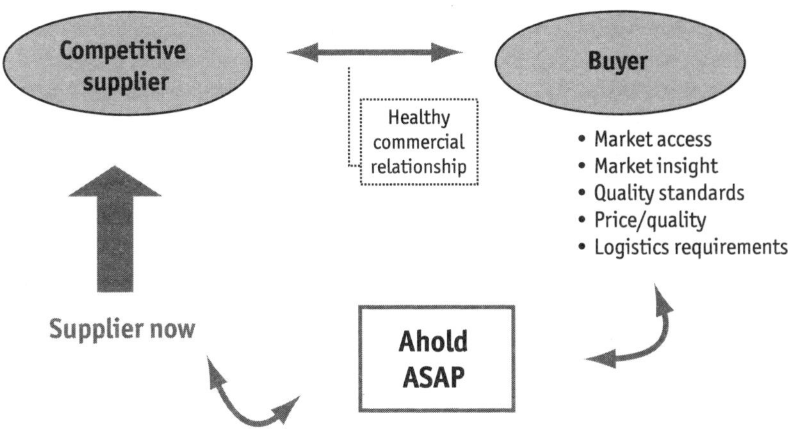

FIGURE 17.1 The ASAP model

2. Develop value-added shelf-stable product(s) for local and/or export markets to be manufactured by local entrepreneurs. Use Ghanaian and Ahold's product development resources to develop value-added product(s), made in Ghana from Ghanaian ingredients, to be marketed in Ahold's stores (and potentially other retailers) under corporate brands and/or in the Ghanaian and/or regional markets
3. Consult on demand of governments, NGOs and trade associations: Provide Ahold manpower and knowledge as needed on a consulting basis to local trade organisations and NGOs in support of the other ASAP targets

Ahold committed itself to three years for the pilot project by sending a senior manager, Roland Waardenburg, to Ghana. He moved to Ghana to shape the project and started making progress along the lines of the proposed targets. The programme director was new in the field of development assistance and started out by talking to a lot of different parties. This resulted first in enough exposure of the fact that Ahold had arrived on the continent: not unimportant to the initial phase of the project. However, along the way it also became difficult to choose which parties would be most valuable for a constructive outcome of the project.

Another challenge at the beginning of the project was that the work could not be confined to Ghana. Ghana produces a limited variety of products in limited seasons, bound as it is by local constraints such as soil and climate. Therefore, to make a meaningful contribution to development and commerce, the scope was widened to the rest of Africa and even other parts of the world.

The results

When looking at opportunities to source products from Ghana and to create new product development opportunities, the retailer explained that it would need to find products that are attractive for consumers. A product survives on the supermarket shelves only if it is either: Attractive and new, or Better quality, and/or is a Cheaper offering (ABC). Explaining these ABCs did not cause much trouble, but it was getting the right products under these headings that brought the most challenges.

Target one: sourcing products

In the first target area, 'develop the viability of growers to export tropical fruits and vegetables', the most results were achieved. One of the greatest successes was the introduction of certified fair trade (Max Havelaar) and organic fresh-cut pineapple in the Dutch supermarket Albert Heijn. This product is attractive and better, because it does not drip and tastes sweet. Also the product is processed locally which allows for more value adding locally. Furthermore the fair trade[1] and organic[2] certification made the product even more attractive, because this is currently a growing consumer market.

Ahold worked together with a USAID[3]-financed consortium called Trade and Investment Programme for Competitive Export Economy (TIPCEE). In this consortium various development organisations work together for the improvement of Ghanaian producers. Linkages had already been made with a company called Blue Skies that works with farmers and sells fresh tropical fruit products to leading retailers in the UK. Soon after the project was started in Ghana, the link between Blue Skies and the Dutch supermarket was made and fresh-cut fruit salads were sold in Dutch stores. In order to create a fair trade and organic product and to obtain certification for the farmers that supplied Blue Skies, a project was started with TIPCEE. This meant the certification and development of over 70 farmers for their pineapple production. Now these farmers receive a guaranteed price for their produce and have been able to raise their standards and find access to a new export market.

Pineapple is one of the largest Ghanaian agricultural products and is available year-round. However, when trying to sell this product to Ahold operating companies it became apparent that the variety that was produced in Ghana was different from the one that Western consumers are used to. Ghana mostly produces the Smooth Cayenne variety whereas in Latin American countries the MD2 variety is produced. In a large-scale market research organised by the Michigan State University in co-operation with USAID, consumer preferences were researched in eight different countries. This resulted in a changeover of producers to the MD2 variety as consumers clearly indicated their preference for this variety.

1 'Fair Trade is an alternative approach to conventional international trade. It is a trading partnership which aims at sustainable development for excluded and disadvantaged producers. It seeks to do this by providing better trading conditions, by awareness raising and by campaigning' (www.fairtrade.org.uk). Further information can be found on www.fairtrade.net.

2 'Organic food is produced using methods that avoid the use of man-made fertilisers, pesticides, growth regulators and livestock feed additives' (www.food.gov.uk).

3 United States Agency for International Development: www.usaid.gov.

Another product that was sold (in season) in Dutch supermarket stores was mangoes from Burkina Faso. This product was attractive because Burkina Faso provided the product in a 'new' season, when the rest of the world had no mangoes to offer. ICCO, a Dutch NGO, is a partner in the ASAP project and was able to assist the company Agrofair to get the mangoes to the Dutch supermarket shelves. The farmers in Burkina Faso needed EurepGAP certification[4] in order to comply with Western retailer quality standards. Partly through this Ahold requirement the certification was organised and can now also be used when dealing with other retailers.

Various other African products have been able to find their way to Dutch or Swedish consumers in the Albert Heijn and ICA supermarkets. Particularly in the fair trade and organic fruit calendar there were gaps which could be filled in by this project. Through the invested time and effort of many parties new African producers were linked, certified and offered market access to Western supermarkets.

Target two: developing shelf-stable products

In the second target area, 'develop value added shelf-stable products', the challenges were even greater and this resulted in many initiatives but very few tangible results. At present Ghana produces only a limited number of shelf-stable products. All of these products can easily fit on only a few supermarket shelves. Opportunities, however, are abundant through the availability of various raw materials such as cocoa, coffee, shea nuts and fruits. These products can be further processed to create value-adding activities locally.

A product development process is already difficult as many ideas are exchanged between the retailer and the producer. Since Ahold did not know with whom to start these processes it became even more challenging. To overcome these challenges at first an exploration of the local market opportunities was made through a feasibility study which was financed by the local branch of the International Finance Corporation, APDF. This resulted in valuable information on products available in Ghana and the state of the companies active in further processing.

Not surprisingly, the general state of the Ghanaian further processing industry was found to be very poor. Basic requirements on packaging, marketing of products and quality could not easily be met. This meant a very great challenge in working with local producers because of a lack of knowledge and financial means. Also, Ahold itself is not a producer of goods; it merely sells products and its expertise lies in logistics and marketing products to consumers.

In co-operation with experts from the local university through a sponsored activity by USAID, Ahold worked to start developing products for the local market. Michigan State University has a Partnership for Food Industry Development, Fruits and Vegetables (PFID-F&V) that was also linked with this project. The products that were identified seemed promising but local producers did not pick it up.

4 EurepGAP is an initiative of retailers belonging to the Euro-Retailer Produce Working Group (Eurep) and stipulates standards and procedures for the global certification of Good Agricultural Practices (GAP), www.eurep.org.

All in all, the activities under target one were more easily established and have generated valuable output. The second target was a bridge too far for the ASAP scope caused by a limited budget and time span.

Target three: consultation

With regard to the last target, 'to consult on demand of governments, NGOs and trade associations', the project was valuable as well. One of the concrete examples is the co-operation with ICCO on the commercial expansion of a women-driven art village, Sirigu, in the north of Ghana. By working together in these public–private partnerships each partner has learned from the other and created insights into each other's way of working.

The challenges

In relation to the largest challenges that needed to be overcome, a division is made between the African context and the partnership context. The first brings forward challenges related to African culture, governance and economic impediments. The second brings forward challenges related to cultural backgrounds, trust and working processes.

The African context

The African business environment was a completely different surrounding for the multinational retailer, first of all because of the structural problems within the supply chains in which the standards of production were found to be quite low. Often the variety of produce was not right, the quality was nowhere near right, the quantity was not enough, the continuity and timely delivery was a huge problem (not only because of the farmers but also others in the chain, involved, for instance, in packaging, cooling or customs) and certification was a long way off. To add more complexity to these problems, the inexperience of Ghanaians and their way of looking at life made it quite difficult to get the business off the ground. Furthermore, existing trade restrictions on African produce hampered the possibilities for export of certain goods.

All in all, one of the most frustrating aspects of doing business in Ghana was the fact that Ghanaians do not seem to want to work together. Especially in this type of project where it was necessary to build scale through the co-operation of various producers, it became a difficult process. It seems as though co-operation in Ghana is limited to the extended family circle. In business, partnerships are hardly found and competition is more important due to a general lack of business opportunities. Under-selling and aggressive competition are thus more likely to play a role.

Understanding these cultural differences is a first step in being able to work together and to start reconciling these differences. Hofstede (1994) provides an overview of dimensions that are aspects of cultures that can be measured relative to other cultures. One of these dimensions is 'collectivism versus individualism'. Ghana is presumably a more collectivist society meaning that personal relationships are very important but chosen based only on a moral or family attribute. Forming groups based on business transactions only probably does not create enough common ground to establish co-operation.

Another cultural aspect that differs greatly from the Western perspective is the way in which Ghanaians perceive time. Trompenaars and Hampden-Turner's (1997) work on intercultural relationships describes a dimension that relates to time perception. Ghanaians very much live in the present with an extremely short time-span. In our business society most planning and organisation focuses on the future; strategies, goals and objectives are all future oriented. Planning therefore to us relates to aspects that are to be achieved in the near future (e.g. days, months). Ghanaians were found to plan as they move along and very much deal with the present state of affairs.

By working closely together these cultural differences became apparent. In seeing these differences, understanding them and yet striving to remain ourselves, it is possible to create common ground and see how others' perspectives can help our own.

The partnership context

Many parties were contacted right at the beginning of the project in The Netherlands and Ghana in order to establish partnerships. Development agencies and governmental institutions were targeted to bring forward experience of development aid and to channel existing programmes into the project.

At the outset there were some issues relating to the newness of the project and the lack of trust in a multinational corporation. It did not really become clear to some development agencies what Ahold wanted to do for Africa. The general outlines of the project could not, for instance, stipulate which African produce would be bought and how this process would work exactly; being a pilot programme, it was not altogether too clear for the Ahold managers as well. When starting an adventure in which the outcome may not be too clear, only trust can bridge the gap between partners. A development agency is more likely to expect a corporation to abuse public funding than to be genuinely concerned about the state of development of Africa. Also, the idea that through co-operation the carefully built image of an NGO could be easily damaged is a key element because reputation is important for safeguarding an NGO's future funding. Also, these organisations were afraid that the company would pull out of the project unexpectedly if its business focus shifted.

NGOs were also hesitant to support a large multinational with enough financial means. Ahold's largest investments were made in terms of manpower and the creation of supermarket shelf space and giving opportunities to products that would otherwise not have been considered. The fundamentals of the partnership were that all partners could contribute their own share and in doing so focus on their competences. This meant that each partner financed the means necessary to do its own work.

Sometimes no co-operation could be initiated because the project did not fit into any existing programmes and if project proposals do not fall under specific policy measures applications seemed futile. No common ground for instance could be found with the Dutch government at first owing to the cultural differences between the two parties. The very fact that the Dutch government focuses on co-operation with governments on entire sectors (e.g. health or education) or even on the whole budget (with the Ministry of Finance) to reach long-term goals, did not make it easy to establish common ground. It contradicts the targeted project of Ahold in many ways. Also, the dynamics of government, in which individuals cannot be made accountable for policy, take a rather long-winded approach to constructing policy, have to involve many players (other governments and ministries, NGOs and the private sector) and with its bureaucratic decision-making processes, are very different from the dynamics of the private sector. Large corporations can show many of the same characteristics, but a targeted programme such as ASAP did not—a world of difference. However, interest in the project was captured and ways were sought to start collaborating.

To begin with, ASAP was put in touch with relevant existing facilities and organisations, such as PSOM (subsidies for private pilot projects) and ICCO (a co-funding NGO). All in all, opportunities to use experience from working with the private sector and to offer experience from working in development co-operation were considered too valuable to miss. These experiences could be put to use to a wider public if the government could start disseminating best-practice experiences with private-sector parties. Maresa Oosterman, working for the Dutch Ministry of Development Co-operation (DGIS) was sent to Ghana on a pilot secondment to exchange experiences with the project by working actively with the Ahold programme director. As a result, ideas have been put forward by both the private and the public sector to create more common ground and to co-operate more closely in order to reach the common goal of sustainable economic development in Africa more efficiently and effectively. These ideas include an expansion of ASAP, co-operation with universities to explore the potential of horticulture in Africa, the necessity of a chain manager to link up development and private organisations in certain product chains, co-operation with third parties such as fair trade organisations, and finally a focus on Africa (in shops, in programmes, in personnel exchange).

In most cases, throughout the partnership process, co-operation with development agencies (NGOs, banks, donors) progressed slowly. Differing time-frames, cultures and working levels caused delays and frustrations that could not easily be overcome. Development organisations wanted structural improvements (in terms of better-trained farmers, better business environment, etc.) in, say, 3–10 years, whereas Ahold's ASAP initiative could also be referred to as: As Soon As Possible. To achieve its own goals within its own time-frame, ASAP made the rational choice of focusing on getting products into the shops fast, by itself if no help was readily available. The scope of these development organisations was often too broad to fit with the specific needs that ASAP identified for each farmer. This targeted approach led to the fact that Ahold now needed to focus on areas in which it did not have any expertise: the support of farmers. However, this do-it-yourself approach did give concrete results.

There were also cases in which it did not turn out to be necessary to bring development agencies into the project. Ahold could work together with nucleus farms or factories that supported the farmers working with them and delivering to them. These nucleus farms support the independent farmers in various ways: for example, schooling, lending machinery, providing seeds, setting up saving schemes and, most importantly, giving a buy-back guarantee. This worked for all parties involved: the farmers could increase their sales, improve standards and expand the number of farmers involved as a result of the deal with Ahold. And, finally, there were cases in which ASAP identified producers that were ready for export but could not get access to international markets. In those cases, ASAP made the link with buyers at the operational companies of Ahold and gained the buyers' interest and trust. In these cases it was essential that an Ahold manager was active in Africa because he understood the local situation and could gain the trust of colleagues abroad.

Why couldn't ASAP negotiate successfully with more development agencies to gain support at the beginning of the chain? The parties were quite interested at the start and needed to operate in a no man's land where existing boundaries and work procedures no longer sufficed. However, some development agencies were more reluctant to set their origins aside and work with new procedures. The short-term goals of ASAP did not coincide with the more long-term perspectives of these agencies. The fact that organisations did not want to lose touch with their dedication to structural improvements in the agricultural sector is understandable. But the opportunities that were explored at first to link up with direct access to a market, making their efforts economically sustainable were lost through conflicting time-frames.

The practical mind-set of the private sector versus the more policy-oriented vision of the public sector also caused differences in views. Furthermore, the background of the private-sector manager who is judged on his or her ability to take risks and explore opportunities is quite different from that of the person who is judged on avoiding risks and his or her ability to design processes towards complicated goals by carefully co-ordinating activities with different parties. These cultural differences caused gaps that were sometimes too wide to be bridged.

Something can also be said about the right choice for partnering in some cases: as a pilot programme it was difficult to establish which groups to work with. The NGOs and Ahold provide development and knowledge facilities, but working capital and, for instance, equipment finance are not a part of these investments. Ultimately, and especially in the case of companies in further processing, these investments are necessary to uplift the state of the production capacity. In this respect it might well have been more convenient for Ahold (and for the selected Ghanaian producers) to work more closely with financial institutions from the outset.

Short-term versus long-term visions, opportunity seeking versus risk avoiding, result orientation versus process orientation are the different ends of the spectrum on which the private and the public sector find themselves. Sometimes these partners could find and meet each other somewhere in the middle. Ultimately, the successes brought forward in this case are the result of the dedication of people from these two 'worlds' to make a difference and their ability to set aside their cultural differences and differing work procedures in order to work together.

The lessons learned

Some of the most important factors that were critical for the success of ASAP are listed here. By outlining these valuable lessons some form of guideline is created for future public–private partnerships that aim to target a specific area of sustainable business development. Matthijsens *et al.* (1998) describe critical success factors as those characteristics, conditions or variables that, if managed appropriately, can determine the success of the organisation. The critical success factors listed here focus mainly on the establishment of a partnership between a company and a public entity. Furthermore the role of the project manager is very important in the success of the project.

Nelson and Zadek (2000) recognise several elements that contribute to the success of a partnership. 'It is the quality of the dynamic relationship between a partnership's context, purpose, participants, organisation and outcomes that makes the difference between success or failure.' So there are many more lessons that could be learned from ASAP, but Box 17.1 is restricted to the partnering process. These critical success factors are based on experiences distilled from the ASAP project.

- Mutual formulation of the project's mission statement
- Understand each other's background and working methods
- Partners need to be aware of their own and their partner's core competences
- An exploration of each other's field of action is planned before starting to work together
- Business motives to participate involve both business and social benefits to promote long-lasting win–win situations
- Focus on project outputs during partnership exploration and implementation
- Project outputs need to be specified in terms of tangible business results and intangible knowledge creation areas
- Tangible business results are measurable and feasible
- Areas of responsibility need to be indicated for each partner. These areas need to be linked to specific targets to measure the results.
- Regular consultation speeds up the partnering process. All partners should be active locally.
- Openness, curiosity, values, integrity, vision, leadership, commitment and risk taking characterise all partners
- Methodologies need to be constructed for the evaluation of the partnership processes and outcomes against common and individual agendas
- The project manager needs to have enough authority in the organisation to embed the programme internally
- The project manager uses innovative working methods and thinking patterns to target problems

Box 17.1 Critical success factors

The future

The ASAP pilot programme has come to an end in its current form. The company has chosen to prolong the programme by starting a new programme from September 2005 called Ahold Sustainable Trade Development (ASTD). This programme will focus on 11 countries in Southern and West Africa and is based on the evaluation of the ASAP programme. Many promising opportunities have arisen from ASAP which can now be coordinated through the ASTD initiative. The experiences that have come from ASAP can be put to use and the contacts with producers and development agencies in Africa will hopefully materialise.

It may be on a small scale, but for some producers in Africa this initiative has already been successful. By providing enough flexibility and adopting a more feet-on-the-ground approach these types of arrangement between the private and the public sector can make a meaningful difference to those in Africa who do not have the same opportunities as we have in Europe.

References

Hofstede, G. (1994) *Cultures and Organisations: Software of the Mind. Intercultural Cooperation and its Importance for Survival* (London: HarperCollins Business).

Keijzers, G., F. Boons and R. Van Daal (2002) *Duurzaam ondernemen: Strategie van bedrijven* (Dordrecht, Netherlands: Kluwer).

Matthijssens, P., R. Martens and K. Vandenbempt (1998) *Concurrentiestrategie en marktdynamiek: Op weg naar concurrentievoordeel in industriele markten* (Deventer, Netherlands: Kluwer BedrijfsInformatie).

Nelson, J., and S. Zadek (2000) *Partnership Alchemy: New Social Partnerships in Europe* (Copenhagen: The Copenhagen Centre).

Trompenaars, F., and C. Hampden-Turner (1997) *Riding the Waves of Culture: Understanding Cultural Diversity in Business* (London: Nicholas Brealey Publishing).

18

Women's Gold

FINDING A MARKET FOR DAGARA SHEA BUTTER

Corina Beczner, Bob Gower and Palma Vizzoni

Presidio School of Management, USA

Emerging development models

Business is now being seen as a key partner and solutions provider in the move towards sustainable development in emerging markets. Emerging from the traditional trade-aid programmes established by the WTO (World Trade Organisation) and institutions such as the International Monetary Fund (IMF) and the World Bank Development Fund are hybrid models that bring together the social intentions of non-profit development projects with the scalability of a business. Business itself is also seeing the opportunity presented by the world's poor. Success in these emerging markets can happen only by thinking beyond conventional wisdom, and a new trend supports new business prospects and demonstrates how to 'do well by doing good'. This blended value approach is known as corporate social responsibility, translated as doing business within the norms, laws and expectations of society. Business cannot succeed in a society that fails. Therefore business has much to gain by creating social change and bringing much-needed solutions to the emerging markets of the developing world.

The World Business Council for Sustainable Development (WBCSD) Sustainable Livelihoods programme is working to create the conditions for 'pro-poor' business models to emerge in developing countries (WBCSD 2004). It has positioned itself as a broker by encouraging novel partnerships between investors, donors and companies. But mainly it is offering mainstream businesses a 'safe' place to 'learn by doing', and providing them with the tools they need to constructively work with other development actors, such as NGOs (non-governmental organisations) and governments, to successfully create business opportunities that provide value for both the company and the people. Although not a WBCSD project, the Women's Gold initiative reported on in this chapter is an example of the partnership approach advocated in their Sustainable Livelihoods programme.

Shea butter

In the semi-arid Sahel region of West Africa there is a substance known as 'women's gold' that comes from the seed of a wildcrafted fruit tree called *shea* (also known as *karite*). Shea butter has extraordinary traditional medicinal and nutritional uses and is extracted from the seed kernel of the shea fruit. It is a common local ingredient in food, soaps and medicines, but also has qualities that make it a valuable export that is used frequently in chocolate and cosmetics. Although the tree grows throughout the Sahel, its largest concentration occurs in Burkina Faso (Harsch 2001). Shea is an abundant and important resource and is considered sacred among many cultures in the region.

The tree is not cultivated but grows wild, begins to bear fruit after about 20 years, reaches maturity at 45 years and may produce fruit for up to 200 years after that (McLymont 2005). The area of the world where the shea tree grows is intensely sunny. Coincidentally, according to first-hand conversations with small-scale shea butter manufacturers in West Africa, it is likely that shea butter has the capacity to penetrate the epidermal layer and repair human skin cells damaged by the sun. Traditionally, shea has been used to treat a wide variety of skin conditions including cuts, grazes, burns, stretch marks, blemishes, eczema, psoriasis and more (Durand 2004). 'Natural, environmentally friendly and traditional beauty products are more and more in demand,' according to a skincare adviser at a Sephora beauty store in Paris. 'Shea butter is popular because it has so many different qualities and uses' (Durand 2004). Such properties have fomented an increased international awareness of, and demand for, this commodity by the beauty, health and skincare markets.

Traditional shea butter is produced in a cultural community system with specific characteristics. Shea butter is hand-extracted exclusively by women through a labour-intensive process that allows them to harvest and utilise only about 50% of kernels in a given season. Shea production is confined to the dry, agricultural off-season when there is low demand for labour in the fields. The seasonal nature of production is a potentially limiting factor in an international commodity market concerned with consistent supply. According to direct conversations with small NGOs working with shea production in West Africa, the availability of clean, potable water in the region can limit the quality of the finished product.

These concerns aside, what sets shea butter apart as a commodity is that it has the potential to support the most marginalised of the marginalised: rural women. The production, sale and use of this product benefits not only these women, but also their children and families, and gives them status in their communities that they might not otherwise have; they become businesswomen.

The Dagara

The following summary of Dagara farming and cultural conditions is based on experiential study and travel to Burkina Faso with Dr Malidoma Patrice Somé, a scholar, initiated elder and shaman of the Dagara tribe.

The Dagara people, an indigenous tribe native to West Africa, live in an area that crosses the borders of Burkina Faso, Ghana and the Ivory Coast. Historically, the Dagara have practised rain-fed, subsistence agriculture and animal husbandry. But three decades of drought conditions, combined with the cumulative effects of deforestation and the diversion of traditional waterways, have created serious challenges to the ability of the Dagara to continue to survive as subsistence farmers.

Among the many unfortunate legacies of colonisation is the degradation of the soil. Persuaded to participate in the market economy of Europe, the Dagara people in Burkina Faso turned over a significant portion of their croplands to the cultivation of cotton. This experiment has had disastrous consequences. A people historically capable of supporting themselves on their own land are now threatened partially due to damage of the fragile sub-Saharan soils as a consequence of the industrial agricultural methods used in cotton production.

Currently, the Dagara, like many people living in marginalised nations, suffer from malnutrition and illnesses from mostly water-borne diseases. They also endure the societal breakdown caused by the exodus of family members who, in search of paid work and city lifestyles, abandon villages for urban centres.

While the contemporary existence of the Dagara is difficult, their incredible strength must also be acknowledged. Like many African peoples, they have survived a harsh history of slavery and oppression with much of their ancestral, cultural and spiritual traditions intact. However, the lingering legacy of colonialism and the current pressures of globalisation continually threaten the survival of a society that holds spiritual and social technologies that can serve the equally threatened Western world. The needs of both communities are different but significant and mutually interdependent.

Echoes of the Ancestors

Echoes of the Ancestors is an NGO providing human capital to leverage support for the Dagara, in an effort to foster social equity and sustainable livelihoods. Its special relationship with this indigenous tribe was fostered through Malidoma Somé, a traditional Dagara Shaman and initiated elder who holds three masters' degrees and two doctorates from The Sorbonne and Brandeis University and is working to bridge the modern and indigenous worlds. Currently, Echoes of the Ancestors provides a vehicle for the unfolding of this relationship between Dagara people and Westerners through its two main projects, Women's Gold, focusing on shea butter production, and SpiritWater, focusing on the drilling of wells for drinking water.

The story

Unlike typical aid or development projects, Echoes of the Ancestors initiatives originated from the building of relationships—the merging of two cultures considered by most to be worlds apart. In 2001 a number of American women travelled to Dano, a small, rural village in Burkina Faso, at the invitation of Malidoma Somé. In Dano the women of the village approached the visitors declaring their need for clean water, medicine for their children and a way to educate themselves. The visiting women saw this request as an opportunity to respond with gratitude to a people who had offered them profound healing, welcoming them into their homes and sharing some of their most intimate and precious cultural and spiritual practices. Together, the women have explored ways in which the Dagara women might achieve their goals using existing resources and their many skills. Out of this meeting, Women's Gold was born.

We are MBA students researching the opportunities for sustainable new business pilot projects for the Dagara people through Echoes of the Ancestors. 'Sustainable' in this case refers to businesses that are financially sound, culturally appropriate and environmentally sensitive. Our intention here is to utilise our knowledge and skills to make recommendations so that Women's Gold can grow into a prosperous business and create sustainable livelihoods for this extraordinary indigenous culture.

Throughout our research and inquiry we have noted that the truly sustainable approach is one arrived at by the stakeholders themselves. As outside observers, we can serve this project by helping to define the issues to be addressed and providing information, contacts and insights. It is not our intention (or within our abilities) to provide a solution, only to offer our work and collaborate with the stakeholders as they arrive at their own solutions.

The market conditions

The global context

Burkina Faso is considered to be one of the poorest countries in the world, ranking in third-to-last place on the Human Development Index. Disease and hunger are a part of everyday life for many of its 11 million inhabitants. There are numerous aid projects operating in Burkina Faso designed to alleviate human suffering and hopefully pull people out of poverty. There is also a new paradigm emerging that does not focus on one nation *gifting* to another but recognises that truly effective solutions are ones in which each player receives value. Sometimes referred to as synergy or synergistic, this paradigm was clearly articulated by President Joaquim Chissano of Mozambique: 'In Africa, we believe in the principle of reciprocity, we will do something for you today, and you will do something for us tomorrow. But this raises the question, "what do the poor have to give to the rich?" ' (Gerzon forthcoming).

What indeed? One of the things that has attracted our team to working with Echoes of the Ancestors is that the organisation is operated by those who already feel they have received something from the Dagara people and are intent on cultivating an ethic of reciprocity, equality and dignity in their atypical 'aid' projects. Another aspect of this reciprocal arrangement is that Echoes of the Ancestors seeks not only to provide services but also to empower the Dagara to provide for themselves. Echoes of the Ancestors does not suggest projects but arrives at them collaboratively with the Dagara, allowing the recipients of the 'aid' to define what form it will take.

Commodities crisis

Many of the marginalised countries in the world, often referred to as the 'less-developed countries' (LDCs), rely on the export of specialised commodities to support their national economies. There is a crisis in world trade. As globalisation gains momentum, the majority of poor countries have not only missed out on its benefits, but have also become even more marginalised and impoverished. While the rich grow richer, six of the ten poorest countries in the world are now less prosperous than they were 20 years ago (Muriu 2003). This situation can be partially explained by the reliance on exports of commodities such as coffee, cotton and cocoa. Prices of these monoculture commodities have plummeted in the last decade (Muriu 2003).

Also, it cannot be ignored that the world trade system is subject to rules that clearly favour the wealthy. The WTO makes most of the rules that determine how countries trade with each other. WTO talks have been stalled since the ministerial summit in Cancún in September 2004. Some blame this stalemate on the refusal of rich-country governments to deliver on trade reforms they had promised (Barry 2004).

There are many issues that need to be addressed to even broach the subject of fairness in trade and income stability for the world's poor. The World Bank estimates that 1.1 billion people live on less than US$1 a day, which it defines as extreme poverty, meaning that such people lack the resources necessary for survival (Sachs 2005). World trade has the potential to be a source of balancing these inhumane gaps, and there are some very clear areas in which to begin such work. With regard to the commodities crisis, the continuing iniquity of rich-country agricultural subsidies and export dumping that undermines farming deserves urgent attention. Agricultural dumping onto the world market can only be effectively eliminated by major reform of the subsidy practices of rich countries. In reality, subsidies should genuinely pursue domestic goals of greater social equity and rural development rather than defend agribusiness exports and profits.

Burkina Faso has a population of 11 million, 2 million of whom depend directly on cotton farming. About another 5 million people depend on cotton indirectly. Cotton is the leading cash crop and accounts for about 60% of exports. In Burkina Faso, it is known as 'white gold'.

In Burkina Faso alone, harvesting and processing shea is done by between 300,000 and 400,000 rural women (Harsch 2001). Earnings from the butter of shea nuts directly benefit the poor of Burkina Faso. This sets shea aside from other commodities such as coffee, cotton, cocoa and copper because its sale boosts the livelihoods of rural women and their families. Exports of shea butter and unprocessed shea kernels brought in CFA5 billion (*cifa* is the currency of Burkina Faso; 5 billion CFA equates to US$7 million) in 2000, making it Burkina Faso's third most important export, after cotton and livestock (Harsch 2001).

The world price for shea nuts plummeted in 1986–87 and the quality of Burkina's output declined as well, bringing a reduction in its share of the world market. By 1990, Burkina was exporting only 22,000 tons, just a fraction of the shea nuts grown each year. In April 2003, the state company that markets cotton for Burkina Faso reported that the country would receive less for its cotton because the US and the European Union were pumping heavy subsidies into the agricultural market, causing a sharp fall in prices on the international market (Muriu 2003). American farmers receive more in subsidies each year than the entire GDP (gross domestic product) of Burkina Faso.

The solution the Burkinabe government proposed was that its farmers should produce more cotton to make up the shortfall. This, however, assumed that there was unutilised capacity. One of Burkina Faso's cotton farmers, Drissa Ouattara, was reported as saying about commodity dumping by wealthy nations:

> Their policy prevents us from keeping the little we get after working so hard, in such difficult conditions. The irony . . . is that it is these same people who advise our governments to elaborate poverty reduction programs, elaborate plans to reduce poverty while at the same time they take measures to make us poorer (Muriu 2003).

While shea butter shows more promise than other commodities for having a positive impact on the lives of some of the world's poorest people, particularly women and children, it is evident that the shea market must be consciously structured to promote this service.

Creating a market

Supply chain

The ideal supply chain is a non-zero-sum-game system with each player adding value to the chain but not *extracting* value at the expense of another player. The goal is to create a business that generates its own operating budget—not an aid project dependent on a constant influx of dollars or charity labour. There are potentially several players in the shea supply chain and all must receive benefit commensurate with their effort. It is the producers in the developing world who are frequently short-changed in commodities markets, but creating a system that benefits them in the long term means making sure all players are adequately compensated.

The term *supply chain* refers to the steps that transform raw shea nuts into products consumed by end-users. We can also call this the *value chain* because we are concerned with the value all players in the chain add to the finished product and also the value each receives. Value added can come in the form of information, additional processing or specific skills such as marketing or import/export law.

The primary value received is financial for all but the end-user, whose benefit is increased health and well-being. However, there are also other forms of value exchanged. The opportunity to give back to people from whom spiritual knowledge has already been received is a primary motivation for all of the current players in the US. And the reciprocal relationship itself can add value by creating satisfying relationships across cultural lines. This secondary added value is connected to the supply chain itself, not to the money or goods that change hands, and is passed on to the end-user in the form of information about the Dagara and the sense of fulfilment that many feel when they help others.

As the specific players in the supply chain are determined, it will be important to assess and negotiate what kind (and quantity) of value each needs to receive in order to create the most sustainable arrangement. For all, except those with an independent income, long-term involvement will probably not come without a certain amount of financial compensation. Likewise, steady customers will develop only if they find the products useful. Therefore, when creating trading relationships the focus should first be on these tangible benefits. However, the nature of the product and business also seem to dictate that those interested only in money are likely to be a drain on the system.

The current market

Country	Estimated total potential production	Estimated actual collection	Estimated consumption	Total exports	Export as shea kernels	Export as shea butter
Benin	80,000	50,000	14,900	35,100	35,000	100
Burkina Faso	150,000	75,000	35,000	40,000	37,000	3,000
Côte d'Ivoire	150,000	40,000	15,000	25,000	15,000	10,000
Ghana	200,000	130,000	70,000	60,000	45,000	15,000
Mali	250,000	150,000	97,000	53,000	50,000	3,000
Nigeria	250,000	100,000	80,000	20,000	20,000	0
Togo	50,000	40,000	10,000	30,000	15,000	15,000

TABLE 18.1 Shea kernel production and utilisation in metric tons per annum

Source: West Africa Trade Hub

Currently, it is estimated (these are rough estimates by a trade association in the region) that as much as 80% of the shea exported from West Africa is in the form of raw kernels that are processed into shea butter in large plants, primarily in Europe. It is also estimated that nearly 50% of the *potential* shea harvest is not collected (see Table 18.1). This means it is possible for the women of Burkina Faso to reap greater economic benefits by adding value via refining before export, and by increasing the amount of shea harvested. By creating a viable market for this hand-processed (sometimes called unrefined) shea butter, we expect producers to harvest more.

There are, of course, limits to the shea harvest, and long-term planning scenarios should look forward to a time when peak production has been reached. That time is far off and is not likely to affect current actions. However, a vision for a developed market, ecological conservation plan and a culturally appropriate financial arrangement for primarily women-operated businesses would be a helpful guide in the ongoing planning process. Of particular concern is the protection of the trees. Currently, government has very little influence in the region, so increasing the political stability of the country is of importance. However, there is also no known incentive for people to cut down the trees, so the situation is stable for the foreseeable future. That said, little is known about the seasonal cycle of the shea tree, and further study is needed to determine sustainable harvest levels.

Traditional gender roles in the Dagara community are another matter, and need to be carefully considered. Though the project was founded by women, they may not be able to retain control of it. Therefore business skills will need to be transferred to the women so that they can both retain control of the business and participate fully in its growth.

Perhaps the main factor in creating a sustainable shea business for the women of Burkina Faso is the price at which they sell the product. Currently, large exporters pay around US$0.75 per kg (2.2 lbs) for unrefined shea butter. A single kilogram represents about 20–30 hours of labour. For the producer, these prices translate as receiving less than US$1 for a week's labour, which is far from a living wage. According to individuals working in the industry, shea sells for at least US$3 per kg in the US, with high-quality shea from a verifiable source fetching as much as US$10–15. Getting as much as possible of this value to the producers is the key to creating a sustainable business.

The players

Currently, the shea butter produced by the Dagara women is not ready for the retail market, and setting up a direct-to-market sales system is not feasible. Therefore, there needs to be at least one other entity between the producers in Africa and the consumers in the US or EU to provide packaging and consumer marketing. It is also possible that wholesalers and export/import firms could be involved between producer and packager/marketer, and packager/marketer and consumer.

There are several possible scenarios linking Dagara shea to a market in the industrialised world each with its own strengths and weaknesses. Choosing the right one will require conversation among the stakeholders and consultation with legal professionals. Here our purpose is to outline a few distinct possible structures pointing out the pros and cons we see in each. We suggest the primary criterion used in choosing a course of action be sustainability, including financial viability and cultural and environmental appropriateness.

All but one of the scenarios below focus on situations of the industrialised world. In each case it is assumed that the Dagara are able to export the shea directly, or that some entity in the US will import it directly. However, as with all commodity trading, there is likely to be a significant amount of arcane knowledge necessary to navigate import/export restrictions. For this reason all the scenarios below will possibly require an arrangement with a company or individual with this specialised knowledge.

Scenario 1: the long and winding road

Perhaps the easiest choice would be to sell the shea butter in Africa to an exporter or to a consolidator who then sells to the exporter. This is the easiest path, yet it produces an unsustainable financial flow for the Dagara women owing to the low price paid by these exporters and consolidators and the value they *extract* from the process. True, they add value in the form of export knowledge and skills, yet it seems they are in a position to arbitrage out more value than they add.

Scenario 2: Women's Gold™

In this scenario a for-profit entity is created in the US and/or EU that develops a consumer brand centred on Dagara shea. This brand is able to leverage the story of the Dagara women as a marketing tool as well as control the quality from tree to market. The transfer of value in the form of quality product and cultural information is maximised in this model. However, so is the expense and risk. Creating consumer brands is not easy and many fail. There are also a few legal hurdles to overcome in this scenario, as the relationship between for-profit and non-profit entities is tightly controlled in the US. When developing this model, retaining legal counsel will be essential to ensure that the tax-exempt status of Echoes of the Ancestors is not threatened.

Scenario 3: Women's Gold™—wholesale

This scenario is very similar to scenario 2 but involves the creation of a wholesale entity in the US or EU that then sells to small or medium-sized cosmetic producers on a wholesale basis. It has all the strengths of the retail model and dramatically curtails the expense and risk. However, it also, potentially, lowers the price received for the butter. In the final analysis this may not be a problem because the lost financial value may be quite small and the decreased risk and increased flexibility will more than make up for it.

Scenario 4: direct supply

In this scenario the Dagara women become a part of a large, established supply chain for either a wholesaler or a retailer such as The Body Shop, an international cosmetics company. In this case, an agent acting on behalf of the women's groups would approach a large importer who was able to purchase the entire production flow as well as handle its export. Provided that an agreeable, fair-trade price could be decided, there is little downside to this arrangement. It could have limitations regarding the transfer of information about the women, but this could be mitigated by negotiating with the buyer to provide information about the Dagara women on its website or even at point of sale. The strength of this scenario lies in the quick transfer of financial value, knowledge of quality control and international markets, and ease of set-up. The limitations are that dependence on a single customer is a potentially vulnerable position, and negotiating a good deal with the right customer may be quite difficult.

Conclusions

Businesses, it is easy to forget, are simply a means of transferring and, one hopes, increasing value for people. The business exists for the players in the supply chain and should serve their needs, not the other way around. When choosing an initial structure for this business, the primary stakeholders should seek to maximise value and minimise expense. Saying this is easy; however, doing it is more difficult.

Our recommendation would be first to create a wholesale business within the United States. This structure has the benefit of being quick to set up, and is an arrangement that will hopefully provide some initial capital to be utilised in creating a stable production facility with predictable output in terms of both quantity and quality. A direct supply relationship with a large marketer would provide additional benefit of knowledge transfer and, if an appropriate partner can be found, should be carefully considered.

In addition to developing a business, Echoes of the Ancestors can help by continuing its effort and expanding its support of the larger systems on which the society depends, particularly the basic needs of health and sanitation. Arranging a direct transfer of business knowledge to the women in the form of seminars will also be important as well as helping the women create relationships with NGOs, trade associations, other producers and industry groups, both in Africa and internationally.

There is a great opportunity presented here and one that can bear fruit quite soon. As the business grows it will be important to build in a planning process that allows the business to adapt to changing market conditions. We look forward to what we hope is a long relationship with a growing and productive business.

Bibliography

Barry, A. (2004) 'Can Trade Work for the Poor? The Challenge for UNCTAD XI', maketradefair.com, accessed 11 April 2005.

Durand, I. (2004) 'Shea Butter: Africa's Beauty Secret', iafrica.com, 10 August 2004.

Gerzon, M. (forthcoming) *Leading Beyond Borders: Thinking Globally and Acting Locally for a Just, Sustainable World*: 137.

Harsch, E. (2001) 'Making Trade Work for Poor Women', *Africa Recovery* 15.4: 6.

Lines, T., G. Fanjul, P. Fowler and C. Charveriat (2004) *The Rural Poverty Trap: Why Agricultural Trade Rules Need to Change and What UNCTAD XI Could Do About It* (Oxford, UK: Oxfam International).

McLymont, R. (2005) 'Shea Butter: What-all is the Big Deal', *The Network Journal*, March/April 2005; TNJ.com, accessed 11 April 2005.

Muriu, M. (2003) Speaking notes for WTO Panel: Road to Cancun, Oxfam International, 26 January 2003.

Peronny, H. (2000) 'Improving Shea Butter Production in Burkina Faso', *Reports Magazine*, 10 March 2000 (The International Development Research Centre).

Sachs, J. (2005) 'The End of Poverty', *Time* magazine, 14 March 2005.

WBCSD (World Business Council for Sustainable Development) (2004) *Doing Business with the Poor: A Field Guide* (Geneva: Atar Roto Presse): 48-50.

19

Elements of SMEs' policy implementation in sub-Saharan Africa

THE CASE OF BOTSWANA

Mengsteab Tesfayohannes

University of Waterloo, Canada

During the past ten years, the resurgence of development policies and strategies for sub-Saharan Africa (SSA) nations has dominated the themes of world conferences and the headlines of major media networks. SSA nations themselves and world institutions such as the United Nations and the World Bank in part, have recognised the need to reformulate and adjust the adopted development policies and strategies in a manner to alleviate poverty, generate mass employment and advance the social fabric. In fact, after considering the seriousness of the scenario, the United Nations Conference on Trade and Development (UNCTAD 2001) put out a press release, entitled 'Economic Development in Africa: Performance, Prospects and Policy Issues'. SSA nations are now attempting to critically appraise and reformulate their national economic development policies and strategies. The objective is to pull themselves out of the quagmire of poverty and backwardness and enhance growth and sustainability.

Innovation and entrepreneurship are the major deriving forces of growth and prosperity, and the core elements of national economic development policies in both developed and developing nations (Tesfayohannes 1998). To highlight their importance, the behavioural guru, Maslow (1968), said, 'The most valuable 100 people to bring into a deteriorating economy are not politicians, economists, scientists, engineers but self-motivated, talented and forceful entrepreneurs.' This indicates that SSA nations need to redirect their socioeconomic development policies and strategies towards this trend to achieve economic diversification and universal basic needs fulfilment and to minimise vulnerability in the current turbulent and uncertain global business environment. Innovation and entrepreneurship are predominantly linked with the promotion of SMEs, which are recognised as the engine of sustainable economic growth. SMEs' vitality is more prevalent in the developing economies as they constitute a significant part of national economic productivity. They are also known for creating employment for a large segment of the productive population.

SSA nations are aware of the potential contribution of SMEs (small or medium-sized enterprises) to sustainable economic development and their role as means of livelihood for millions of young and innovative Africans (Briscoe 1995). Most importantly, SMEs play a pivotal role in accelerating the evolutionary transition from agrarian to industrial society (Briscoe 1995). Although many of the SSA nations have already formulated and adopted SME promotional policies as part of their national economic development agenda, the changing world economy calls for more articulated policies to extend facilitative support through the joint collaboration of government, the private sector and other stakeholders. This is especially true for SSA nations (Visagie 1997). It is easy to formulate sound policies on paper, but policy implementation is a most challenging task. Formulating effective and savvy policy implementation strategies is instrumental for the realisation of development goals. Hence, policy-makers in each country are required to initiate and design appropriate schemes and programmes of policy implementation as the driving forces of policy implementation endeavours.

This chapter proposes schemes, action programmes and regulatory acts as elements of an SME promotional policy implementation framework. The chapter is limited in its scope. The proposed elements are hypothetical and solely for 'brainstorming' purposes. Although the proposed elements are useful for SSA countries in general, Botswana is selected for a closer look.

Botswana's developing agenda

Botswana is a small country located in southern Africa. Its socioeconomic growth has been remarkable during the past 40 years. The country is one of the few countries in the SSA to have achieved sustained socioeconomic growth and established a solid democratic governance system. Botswana was one of the 25 poorest countries in the world in 1966, but graduated to a middle-income country, with an income per head of over US$4,000 in 2004 (Botswana Statistical Report 2004). The country has already formulated a comprehensive development vision in line with the Millennium Development Goals through a self-reliant approach to development (Government of Botswana 1997, 2001a, 2001b; Ministry of Finance and Development Planning 2005).

The core development agenda of Botswana is to enhance gender equity-based economic empowerment of citizens and foster private sector-led and diversified sustainable economic development. This is evidenced by the goals of its national development macro policies (Government of Botswana 1997, 2001b). The country's goal in 2016 is to reduce the current level of poverty and backwardness by half, through fostering gender equity-based indigenous managerial and technical expertise, innovational capacity and entrepreneurial acumen (UNDP 2000). The Government of Botswana (GoB) has attempted to strengthen its institutional capacity to facilitate a conducive environment for private initiatives and innovations. Sectoral development policies and the national development plans of the country have given substantial attention to the support of SMEs as promoters of innovation, entrepreneurship and business skills (Government of Botswana 1999, 2001a). About 10% of the development budget of the country is earmarked for this purpose every year (Ministry of Finance and Development Planning 2000, 2003).

The need for SME promotional policies formulation and successful implementation

SME contribution to Botswana's economy and corporate citizenship

The pivotal role of SMEs to the building of indigenous-based and -developed national economies and advancing technological innovations has created the scenario in which SMEs collectively have a greater stake in promoting corporate citizenship in general (Liedholm and Mead 1999; IISD 2004; Taylor 2004; Luetkenhorst 2004; Coskun 2004). They are known for generating mass employment, promoting indigenous entrepreneurship and meeting broad local demands for goods and services. Due to the important contribution they make, they are recognised as the *driving forces* of economic growth and social development as pillars of corporate citizenship (Owualah 1988; De and Maria 2003; Luetkenhorst 2004). They are also instrumental in accelerating the process of transforming traditional industry into a modern industry whose supporting props or pillars are deeply rooted in the culture and ethics of the indigenous people (Owualah 1988; Trulsson 2002; Liedholm 2002; Robertson 2003; Yumkella and Jebamalai 2003). Unfortunately, this noteworthy contribution of SMEs towards promoting corporate citizenship has so far received nominal recognition by the national development policy-makers and stakeholders of private-sector development (World Economic Forum 2005).

SMEs in Botswana are not well documented. Figures are only estimates based on some previous studies and crudely aggregated official statistical data. Some previous studies expressed that their potential contribution to Botswana's economic development is enormous. As a result, the Government of Botswana has attempted to improve their current precarious position (Government of Botswana 1998; BIDPA Briefing 2000; Chandrasekar 2000; Chengeta 2003). The definition of SMEs varies from country to country, as it should reflect the existing socioeconomic objective realities and suitable parameters for promoting SMEs in each country. The defining process should consider macro- and micro-related issues such as: sociocultural tradition; the general economic standard; legal decrees and other regulations; and nationally adopted development policies and strategies (Rempel *et al.* 1994; Tesfayohannes 1998; Chandrasekar 2000). Therefore, enterprises employing fewer than 100 workers are generally defined as SMEs in Botswana (Government of Botswana 1999; BIDPA Briefing 2000). There are currently approximately 70,000 SMEs engaged in all economic activities of the country. They account for 50% of private-sector employment, which is more than 150,000 people in absolute figures, and their contribution to GDP is about 25% (Botswana Statistical Report 2004). The current contribution of SMEs to the national economic development of Botswana is low in comparison with other emerging middle-income countries in the developing world at large (BIDPA Briefing 2000; IMF 2002; United Nations 2002). This scenario has led the GoB to initiate various programmes fostering the development of SMEs in the country (BIDPA Briefings 2000).

The need to introduce a national SME policy

The GoB issued SME promotional policy to enhance the development and outreach activities of SMEs and solve their infrastructural, organisational and technical problems (Briscoe 1995; Government of Botswana 1998; BIDPA Briefings 2000). The following evidence clarifies why introducing a comprehensive national SME policy was necessary: More than 50% of annual total imports of the country for the last six years were consumer goods such as food, beverages and tobacco, textiles and footwear, wood and paper products, metals and metal products, leather products, chemical and rubber products and related others (Botswana Statistical Report 2002). The country spends a large amount of hard currency on importing goods that could have been easily produced and sold locally. For example, Botswana is known for its livestock, but almost 80% of its diary and milk products are imported from South Africa (Botswana Statistical Report 2003). On the other hand, more than 90% of the annual exports during the same period were predominantly prime products such as diamonds, copper-nickel-matte and beef (Botswana Statistical Report 2003).

Botswana's SMEs have the potential to substitute many of the currently imported consumer goods by producing them locally. This can help the country to divert its resources to finance vital development projects including empowerment of SMEs. Many firms have suffered from debilitating debt burdens and financial liquidity risks as a result of unwise resources utilisation attributed to improper planning and lack of knowledge in adaptation of appropriate technology. More than 90% of SMEs are currently affected by a lack of finance. This is one of the major hindering factors for the successful start-up and competitive sustenance of SMEs. The financing problem is aggravated by a lack of information on available sources of finance and the reluctance of financial institutions to grant loans to SMEs because of the perception of high risk of defaults (Daniels and Fisseha 1992; Briscoe 1995; Government of Botswana 1998).

Sociocultural attributes have a strong impact on the entrepreneurial development of a given environment. One can express the sociocultural attributes in terms of the following attitudes and norms: work and work ethics, self confidence, creativity, the ability to face challenges, efficiency and effectiveness in time usage, spending habits, individualism versus collectivism, knowledge-seeking mentality, risk-taking attitudes, decision-making approaches, managerial style and bureaucracy, degree of affiliation and loyalty to ethnic group, power distance, and political environment (Briscoe 1995; Government of Botswana 1998). Unfortunately, the negative impacts of sociocultural attributes have played a regressive role in the socioeconomic development process of Botswana and other SSA nations. The GoB has taken measures to dismantle the socioculturally instigated obstacles and advance human development and citizen empowerment, and the country has so far scored remarkable achievements in this respect, but more should be done.

Another sad reality is the lack of interest of young citizens in entrepreneurship and self-employment but eagerness and preference to work in the public sector. This colonially instigated collective attitude has been aggravated by the absence of a viable education system that can create a fertile ground for self-employment and entrepreneurial innovation (Government of Botswana 1998; BIDPA Briefing 2000). Many handicraft-related professions, such as blacksmithing, have been considered inferior and many people have not been enticed into them. Women entrepreneurs are still the prime victims of the prevailing sociocultural influences (Maini 2002). The general impression asserting that 'Women should stay at home taking care of their children and fulfil family responsibility' is still alive in its detrimental shape in the minds of many people particularly in the rural and semi-urban areas. In many localities, husbands are deliberately hostile to the entrepreneurial successfulness of their wives. Most of them think that they may lose their control and supremacy at home if the wife is successful economically. SMEs in Botswana are also not active in establishing viable networks and partnerships with local and foreign ventures. Many of them produce and sell their products without bothering about the impacts of current market trends and competition. Even they may not be aware of the available government assistance programmes (Chengeta 2003). This is partially due to the lack of adequate technical assistance and training service facilities in the country (Government of Botswana 1998). The dearth of appropriately qualified and experienced professionals in this area is also another cause for concern.

To improve this unfavourable situation, the GoB introduced a national SME promotional policy in 1999. The policy was comprehensive in its content and contained policy goals and provisions specifying the role of SMEs in the process of: developing an export-led national economy; encouraging the development of a competitive and sustainable SME sector in line with the fundamental dynamism of the competitive market economy; creating sustainable employment opportunities for the local populace; promoting the development of vertical integration and horizontal linkages between SMEs and primary industries in agriculture, mining and tourism; and improving efficiency in the delivery of services such as training and business promotions to SMEs (Government of Botswana 1998, 1999; Chengeta 2003). Strategic policy considerations were also issued under five major categories: institutional arrangements and regulatory environment; education, training and entrepreneurship development; access to finance; market opportunities; and technology support. The proposed elements of the policy implementation framework in the form of schemes, regulatory action and action programmes are categorised based on the above five strategic policy considerations. Some years have passed since the issuance of the SME policy. However, the government and other stakeholders have repeatedly revealed that the policy has so far largely remained on paper and failed to give the desired outcome (Duncombe 1999; Ministry of Finance and Development Planning 2002, 2003, 2004; Chengeta 2003). As reported, this happened because of the lack of proper policy implementation initiatives.

Recommended conceptual elements of an SME policy implementation framework

Complementarity of policy formulation and implementation strategies

Policy formulation and implementation processes are complementary. Effective SME policy can give a solid foundation for successful policy implementation endeavours. Consideration of the objective realities and cultural values of the local environment is vital in the policy formulation process. To emphasise this, Sunkel (1972) said a long time ago: 'A nation must use its traditions, culture, values, institutions and history to create and achieve its own process of development and national realisation.' Appropriate and locally initiated development policies can pave the avenue for designing successful policy implementation strategies. SSA nations have so far been confronted with policy implementation problems owing to the absence of co-ordinated policy implementation strategies (Wolgin 1997; Temtime *et al.* 2004; Nwankw and Richards 2004). Previous studies have acknowledged that, if a policy is not supported by details of implementation modalities and appropriate institutional arrangements, realisation of policy can be very challenging if not impossible (Lebre La Rovere 1996; Nugent and Seung 2002). Therefore, the design of articulated and logically synchronised conceptual schemes, action programmes and regulatory acts is instrumental for successful policy implementation endeavours in Botswana and other SSA nations (Temtime *et al.* 2004). The implementation process of Botswana's SME policy can then be appraised against these ideal elements for taking corrective actions.

Foundations for the elements of a policy implementation framework

For almost four decades SSA nations have been in the spotlight over how to design lasting and meaningful development policies and overhaul their economies. However, none of the grand policies and strategies came to fruition except for some strategies that were materialised temporarily but vanished like a phantom due to the lack of sound and operable economic policy which ought to have been holistic (Araia 2001). In fact, it has become more difficult for the SSA nations to achieve the desired progress by strictly adopting the conventional paradigms of development advocating pure economic growth merely from an input–output point of view. These are, in most cases, inappropriate to the realities on the ground. We have seen that the adoption of this trend has become responsible for unjustified economic and social inequalities and depressing realities of dualism in the economies of SSA nations (Todaro 2000; Jalilian *et al.* 2000; Nwankw and Richards 2004). This depressing situation has left a solid syndrome of self-confidence deficiency and a stark fact of economic life for the majority of these nations. Furthermore, the SSA nations should skilfully confront the current rapid globalisation of the techno-economic system and internationalisation of the financial markets to secure their mere survival. This formidable task demands the design of strategies that are instrumental to achieving sustainable economic development goals. Nurturing the business sector should be the prime agenda in all SSA nations. In line with this basic concept, we need to link the SME promotional policy with the macro-economic development structural map as shown in Figure 19.1.

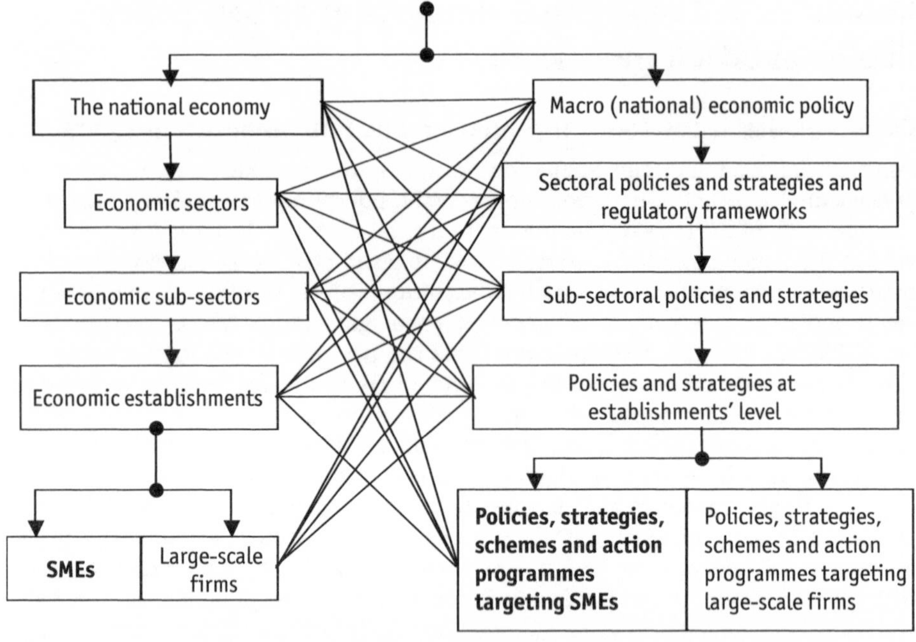

FIGURE 19.1 The dynamics of policies and strategies at different levels of economic structure and their relationships

SME promotion policy is part of the overall national economic development structure, and we should realise the establishment of forward and backward linkages with the other macro-economic and sectoral policies and strategies of the national economic structure. This linkage is important for the effectiveness of policy formulation and implementation tasks. Failing to understand this vital link does not guarantee the effective realisation of policy goals.

SME policies should be complementary to the other vital sectors of the national economic development structure (Government of Botswana 1999; Chandrasekar 2000). This means we have to ensure that the SME policy formulation process should reflect the determinants of SME development at meta, macro, meso and micro levels (see Fig. 19.2). The failure or success of SMEs in any SSA nation in general and in Botswana in particular is directly and indirectly dependent on these determinants. Therefore, SME development policies and implementation strategies should be evaluated in the light of these determinants. They are crucial for creating a conducive environment for firms to be sustained and eventually grow. Governments and all other stakeholders should make them conducive to SME development. Therefore, we need to understand how the major determinants of SME development are structured, and know the responsible executers (or performers) at all levels.

Organising SME policy goals in the form of super and base structures is recommended to facilitate effective implementation of policies and strategies. The elements of the super structure are required to regulate the economic motive forces as the prime push

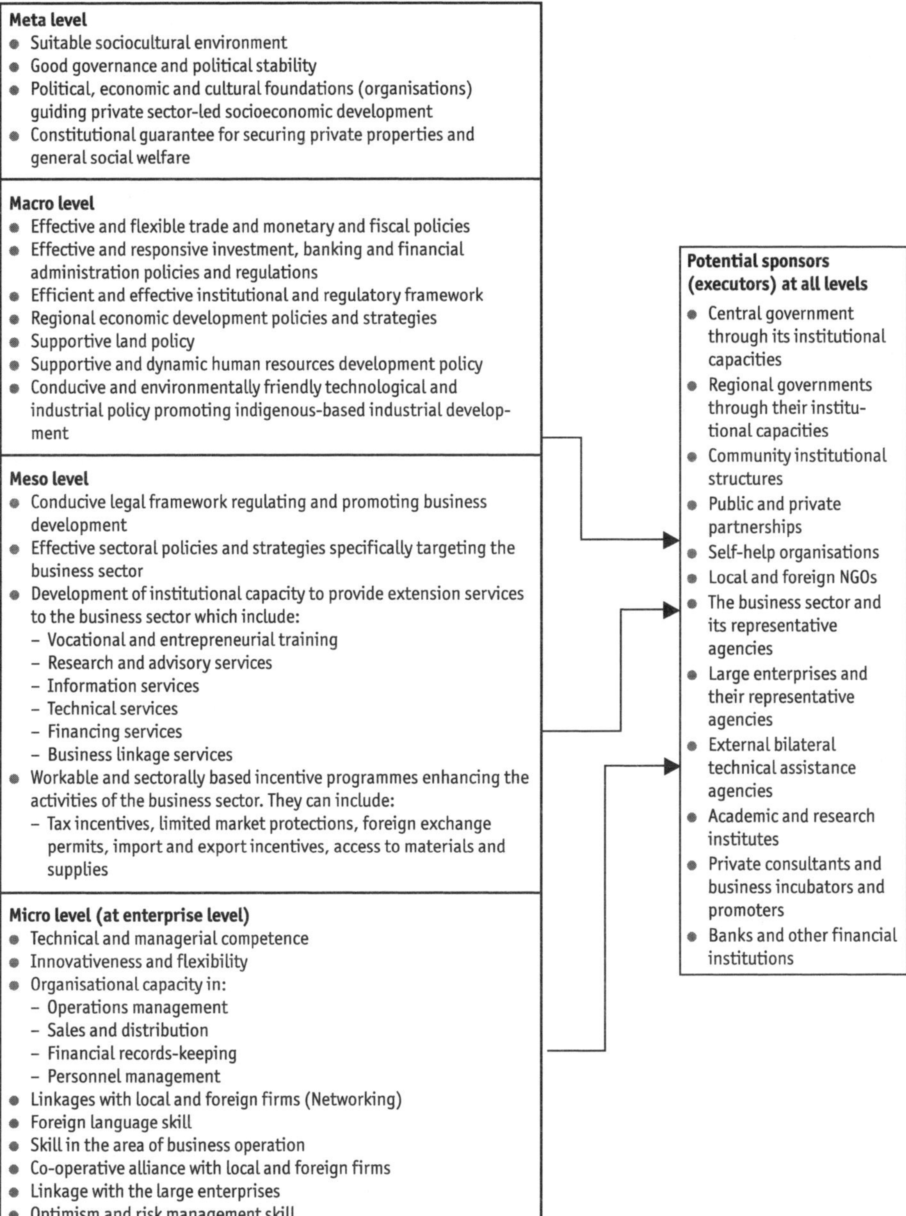

FIGURE 19.2 Determinants of SME development

factors of socioeconomic development and capacity building. The economic motive forces are elements of the base structure of the mode of socioeconomic development of a society. This categorisation is essential to synthesise and recommend appropriate implementation action programmes. As shown in Figure 19.3, the institutional capacity and regulatory framework-related policy objectives are categorised as elements of the super structure. Training and entrepreneurship development, access to finance, market opportunities and technological support are categorised as elements of base structure. This classification is a prerequisite for priority settings in the process of designing specific schemes and action programmes as the principal elements of policy implementation.

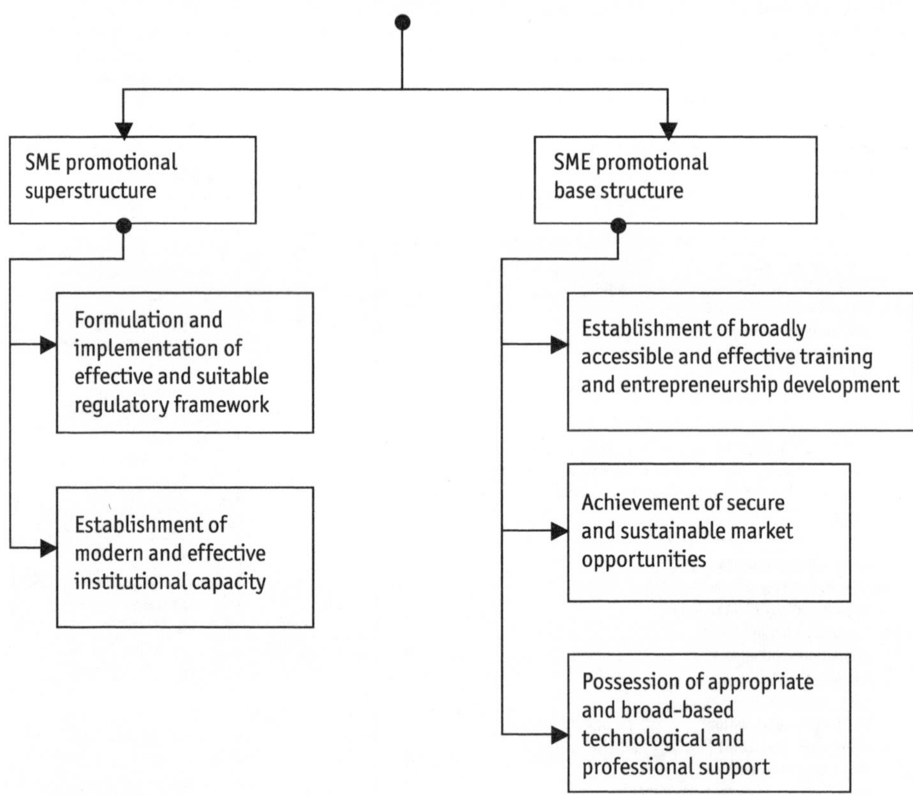

FIGURE 19.3 SME promotional super and base structures

Recommended schemes, action programmes and regulatory acts as elements of an SME policy implementation framework

In this section, numerous schemes, action programmes and regulatory acts are recommended. The author believes that these elements can serve as references for the policy implementation endeavours. Policy implementation is an important task that should be performed with care and prudence. Many of the schemes, action programmes and regulatory guidelines are self-explanatory and some others need interpretation. The purpose of this chapter is to introduce them to Botswana and SSA policy-makers. The author recognises that each proposed act and scheme should be supplemented by tech-

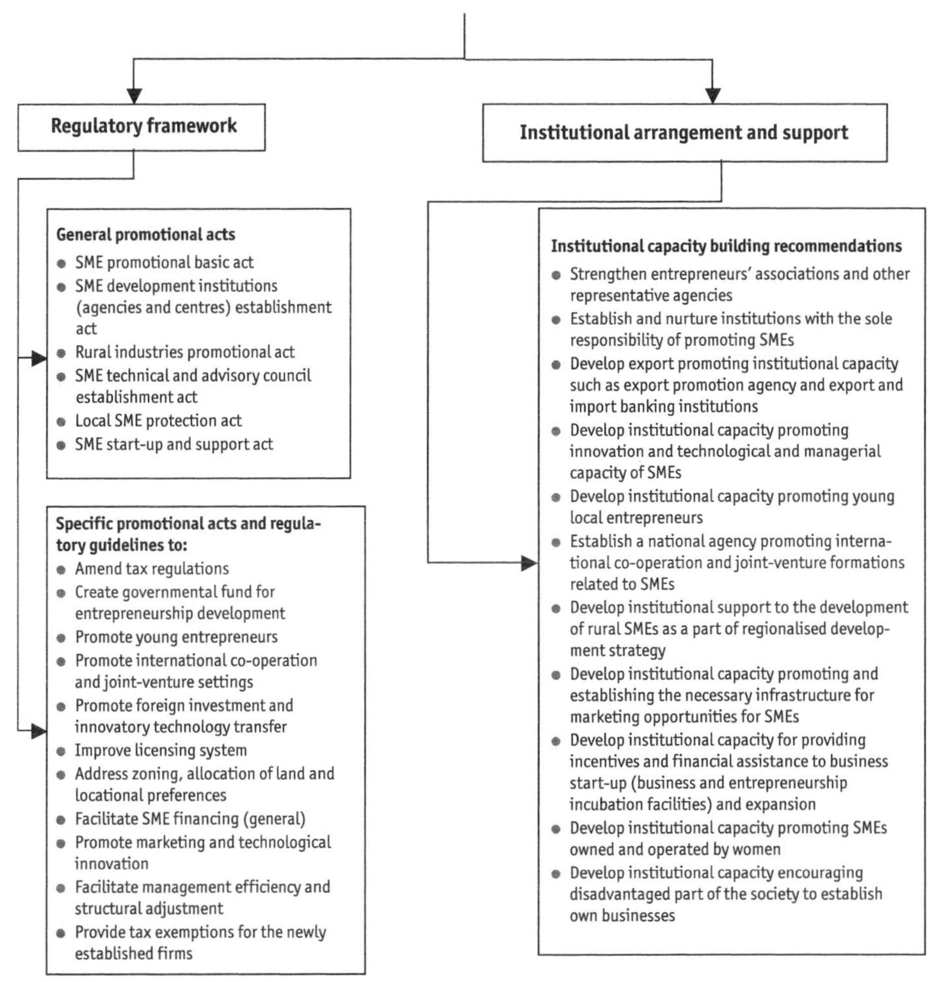

FIGURE 19.4 Action programmes targeting the promotional super structure elements

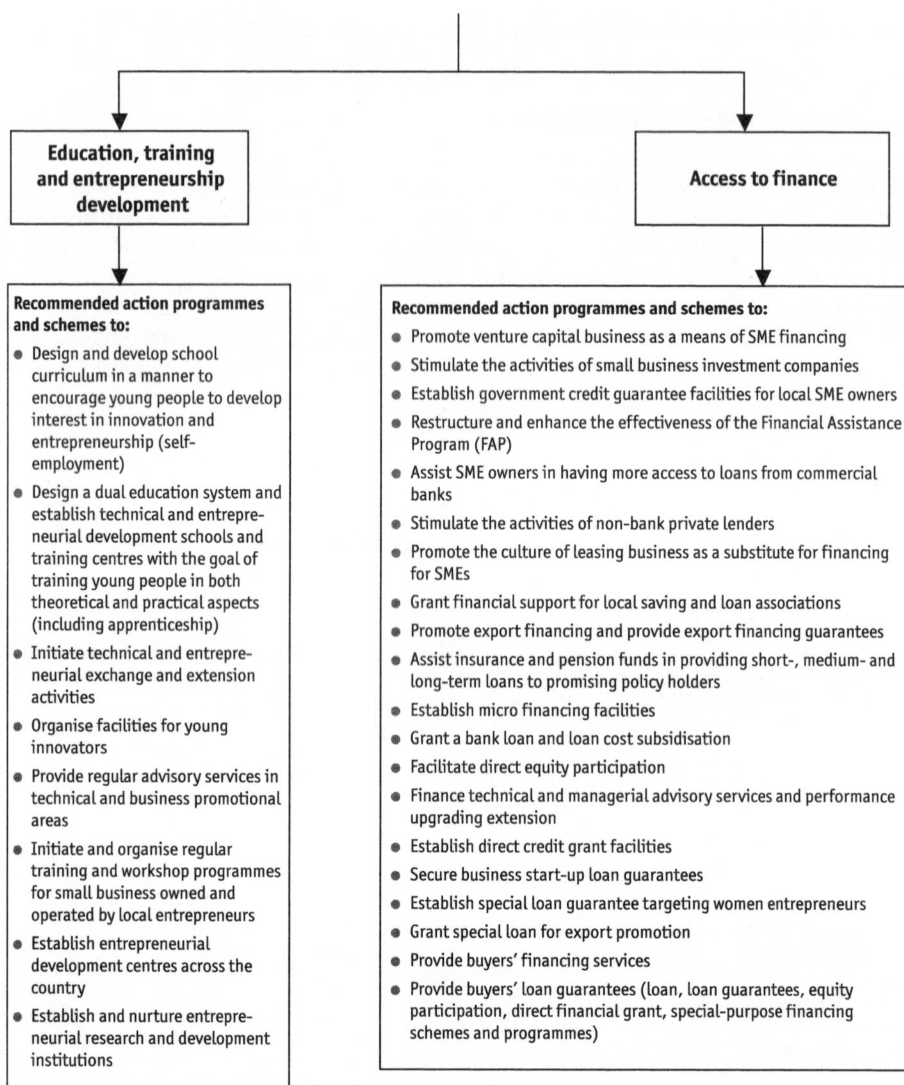

FIGURE 19.5 Proposed schemes and action programmes targeting the base structure elements (part 1)

nical details necessary for successful implementation, and those that need interpretations should be interpreted. This task is beyond the scope of this chapter. However, the author will deal with this challenge in the next phase (in another paper). The author fully realises that Botswana and other SSA nations have their own SME policy implementation initiatives. But the proposed elements of the policy implementation framework shown in Figures 19.4–19.6 can serve as a supplemental help in the process of designing effective SME policy implementation strategies reflecting the objective reali-

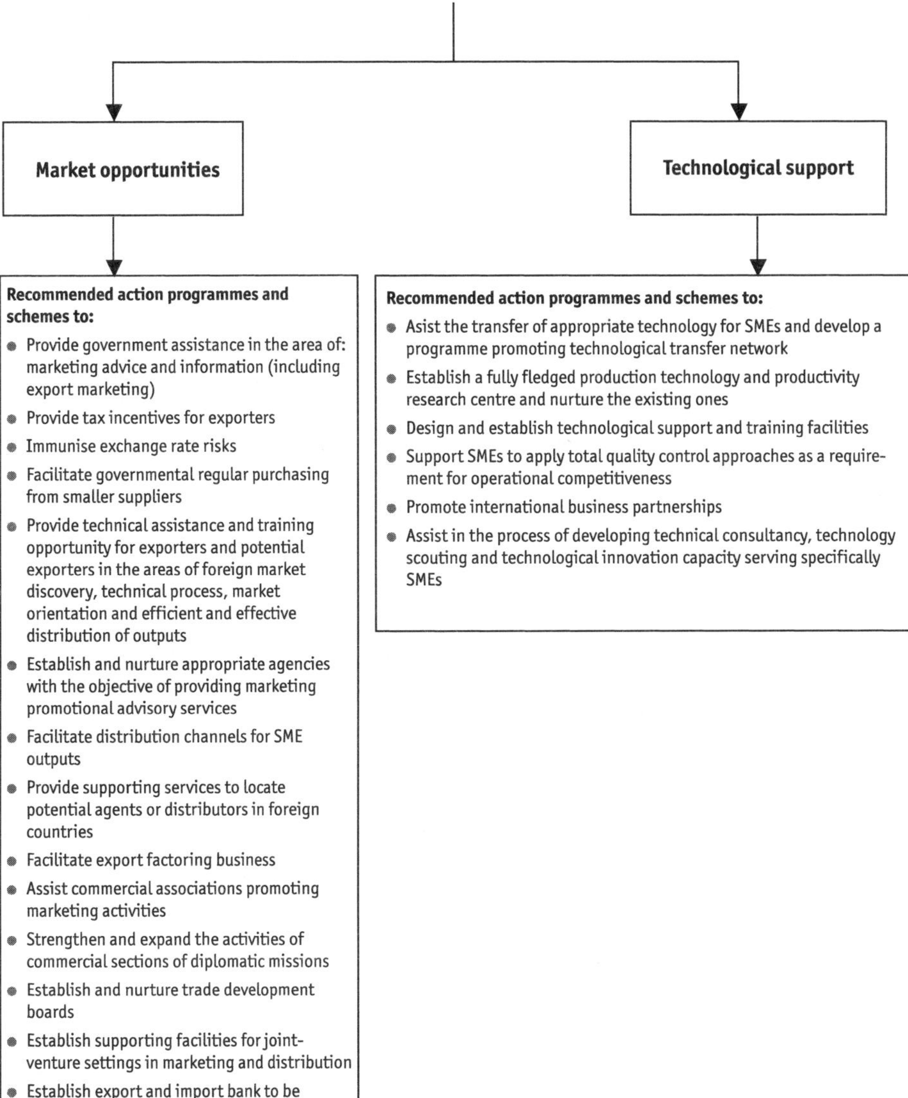

FIGURE 19.6 Proposed schemes and action programmes targeting the base structure elements (part 2)

ties and peculiarities of their environment. Botswana and other SSA nations can then adopt many of those elements shown in Figures 19.4, 19.5 and 19.6. Implementation strategies are country-specific, but well-crafted conceptual elements of the implementation framework with the necessary interpretations and technical modalities and details can help to foster innovation and trigger initiative in the process of SME policy implementation.

Conclusion

The issue of SME development has continued to occupy centre stage in the core development agendas of SSA nations. This shows that SMEs are regarded as the vital motive forces of development in SSA nations in particular and in all countries in general. If SSA nations are able to formulate suitable SME policies and strategies, SMEs can beef up their contribution to economic development and corporate social responsibility. However SME promotional policies should be effective and result-oriented. The author hopes that the recommended elements of the policy implementation framework in this chapter will help Botswana and other SSA nations in their developmental endeavours. Effective and appropriate implementation strategies can help to bring a radical improvement in the activities of SMEs in SSA nations. SMEs in Botswana have continued to perform poorly despite government efforts (Ministry of Finance and Development Planning 2003, 2004). This is due to weaknesses in designing policy implementation strategies (Ministry of Finance and Development Planning 2004). Reporting failure does not help, but taking corrective action is vital to make sure that policy objectives are complemented by the appropriate policy implementation strategies. Therefore, the proposed elements (or ideal scenarios) of policy implementation can be instrumental for effective realisation of policy objectives. Concerned government organs and other stakeholders should revisit their policy implementation strategies for further improvement. The sky is the limit and this is a foundation paper. Other researchers are invited to propose numerous other SME policy implementation elements. The vital point is that, if policies and implementation strategies are formulated in congruence with the existing and forthcoming social and economic situations at national and global levels, the expected result will be undoubtedly fruitful. In sum, policy objectives should be achievable and through that SMEs should play their expected role in the socioeconomic development of Botswana and other SSA nations. Towards this end, concerned governmental organisations, commercial associations, public institutions, mass media, bilateral and international agencies, academic institutions, the financial sector and the business community representative agencies should play their expected role.

References

Araia, G. (2001) 'Development Policy Shift for Africa', *African Link Magazine* 10.3: 12-24.

BIDPA Briefings (2000) *The New Policy on Small, Medium and Micro Enterprises* (Gaborone, Botswana: BIDPA Publications): 1-8.

Briscoe, A. (1995) *Small Business Support in Botswana* (Gaborone, Botswana: Morula Press).

Chandrasekar, M. (2000) *Appropriate Technology Transfer for Botswana: An Overview* (Bonn, Germany: Friedrich Ebert Stiftung).

Chengeta, N.N. (2003) *The Technology Based Incubation in Botswana: Workshop Paper on Technology-based Business Incubators in SADC Countries* (Mauritius: WAIT).

Coskun, A. (2004) 'Motors of Innovation and Development', *The OECD Observer*, May 2004: 48-55.

Daniels, L., and Y. Fisseha (1992) *Micro and Small-Scale Enterprises in Botswana* (Gemini Technical Report No. 46; Bethesda, MD: Development Alternatives Inc.).

De, G., and S. Maria (2003) 'Mutual Guarantee Associations for Small and Micro-Entrepreneurs: Lessons Learned from Europe and Africa', *African Development Review* 15.1: 25-45.

Duncombe, R. (1999) *The Role of Information and Communication Technology for SMEs Development in Botswana* (Manchester, UK: Department for International Development).

Government of Botswana (1997) *National Development Plan 8, 1997/8–2002/3* (Gaborone, Botswana: Government Printer).

—— (1998) *SMEs Task Force Report* (Gaborone, Botswana: Government Publishing Services).

—— (1999) *National Policy on the Promotion of SMEs* (Government White Paper No. 1; Gaborone, Botswana: Government Printer).

—— (2001a) *National Development Plan 9, 2003/4–2008/9* (Gaborone, Botswana: Government Printer).

—— (2001b) *Vision 2016: Prosperity for All* (Gaborone, Botswana: Government Printer).

—— (2001–2004) *Botswana Statistical Reports for 2001, 2003, and 2004* (Gaborone, Botswana: Government Publishing Services).

Jalilian, H., M. Tribe and J. Weiss (2000) *Industrial Development and Policy in Africa: Issues of De-industrialization and Development Strategy* (Cheltenham, UK: Edward Elgar).

IISD (International Institute for Sustainable Development) (2004) *SMEs: Briefing Note* (Winnipeg, Canada: IISD Publications).

IMF (International Monetary Fund) (2002) *Country Reports on Economic Performance* (Washington, DC: IMF Publications).

Lebre La Rovere, R. (1996) 'IT diffusion in SMEs: Elements for Policy Definition', *Information Technology for Development, Amsterdam* 7.4: 169-82.

Liedholm, C. (2002) 'Small Firm Dynamics: Evidence from Africa and Latin America', *Small Business Economics* 18.1-3: 227-43.

—— and D.C. Mead (1999) *Small Enterprises and Economic Development: The Dynamics of Small and Micro Enterprises* (London: Routledge).

Luetkenhorst, W. (2004) 'Corporate Social Responsibility and the Development Agenda: The Case for Actively Involving SMEs', *Intereconomics* 39.3: 157-67.

Maini, Y. (2002) *The Progressive Path of Women Engineers in Botswana* (Swindon, UK: Halcrow Group Limited).

Maslow, A. (1968) *Reading in the Economics of Education* (UNESCO Report; Paris: UNESCO Publications): 623-35.

Ministry of Finance and Development Planning (2000) *National Economic Development Report* (Gaborone, Botswana: Government Printer).

—— (2003–2004) *Budget Speeches of 2002, 2003, 2004, Delivered to National Assembly* (Gaborone, Botswana: Government Printer).

Nugent, J.B., and Seung-Jae Yhee (2002) 'Small and Medium Enterprises in Korea: Achievements, Constraints and Policy Issues', *Small Business Economics* 18.1-3: 85-104.

Nwankw, S.O., and D. Richards (2004) 'Institutional Paradigm and the Management of Transitions: A Sub-Sahara African perspective', *International Journal of Social Economics* 31.1/2: 111-23.

Owualah, S. (1988) 'Providing the Necessary Economic Infrastructures for Small Businesses: Whose Responsibility?', *International Small Business Journal* 7.1: 10-30.

Rempel, H., *et al.* (1994) *The Place of Non-Formal Micro Enterprises in Botswana* (Gaborone, Botswana: University of Botswana).

Robertson, P.L. (2003) 'The Role of Training and Skilled Labour in the Success of SMEs in Developing Economies', *Education and Training* 45.8/9: 461-73.

Sunkel, O. (1972) 'Underdevelopment in Latin America Towards the year 2000', in J.N. Bahgawati (ed.), *Economics and World Order: From the 1970s to the 1990s* (New York: Macmillan).

Taylor, R.L. (2004) 'Pursuing the Global Economy: Assistance for Small Businesses', *Competitiveness Review* 14.1/2: 82-90.

Temtime, Z.T., S.V. Chinyoka and J.P. Shunda (2004) 'Decision Tree Approach for Integrating Small Business Assistance Schemes', *Journal of Management Development* 23.5/6: 563-84.

Tesfayohannes, M. (1998) *The Promotion of Small and Medium-Scale Enterprises Financing as a Contribution to Sustainable Industrial Development: The Case of Eritrea* (Aachen, Germany: Shaker Verlag).

Todaro, M.P. (2000) *Economic Development* (Reading, MA: Addison-Wesley, 7th edn).

Trulsson, P. (2002) 'Constraints of Growth-Oriented Enterprises in the Southern and Eastern African Region', *Journal of Developmental Entrepreneurship* 7.3: 331-40.

UNCTAD (United Nations Conference on Trade and Development) (2001) *Economic Development in Africa: Performance, Prospects and Policy Issues* (New York, United Nations).

UNDP (United Nations Development Programme) (2000) *Country Cooperation Frameworks and Related Matters: Country Review Report for Botswana* (New York: United Nations).

United Nations (2002) *Countries Development Reports* (New York: UN).

Visagie, J.C. (1997) 'SMEs' Challenges in Reconstructing South Africa', *Management Decision* 35.9: 660-67.

Wolgin, J.M. (1997) 'The Evolution of Economic Policymaking in Africa', *The American Economic Review* 87.2: 54-58.

World Economic Forum (2005) *Partnering Success* (Boston, MA: Harvard University Press).

Yumkella, K., and V. Jebamalai (2003) 'Leading Issues on Africa's Path to Industrialization: The Role of Support Systems and Instruments', *Journal of African Economies* 12.1: 30-40.

Part VII
Globalisation and conclusion

20

An overview of corporate globalisation and the non-globalisation of corporate citizenship in Africa

Rogers Tabe Egbe Orock

University of Buea, Cameroon

Rugman and Verbeke (2004: 3) observe that TNCs (transnational corporations), as 'key drivers' of the globalisation process, foster 'economic interdependence among national markets', suggesting that we are clearly in the era of corporate globalisation. Albeit being heralded as holding 'upcoming' opportunities for economic and sociopolitical development of the global society, such opportunistic undertones in corporate globalisation have materialised for the most in Northern countries. This chapter has one central thesis, that, from the perspective of corporate citizenship, such opportunities are slow in reaching Africa, arguing that one of the major obstructing elements excluding Africa from the benefits of corporate globalisation is the unwillingness of most TNCs to globalise the good corporate citizenship they exhibit in their Northern 'home' countries while operating in their African 'host' countries, as exposed by the history of transnational corporate activity in Africa.

By means of documentary research the chapter examines in general the actions of TNCs in Africa, from a corporate citizenship perspective, demonstrating that genuine promotion of the concept of corporate citizenship in the continent by TNCs is still to effectively take root, as the nature of their transactions with African governments is usually unethical, their response to social needs in the continent is insufficient while labour and environmental standards are at a low ebb in comparison to the situation in their Northern 'host' countries. The chapter begins by revisiting the main challenge of corporate globalisation as a whole. It proceeds to a brief historical overview of transnational corporate activity in Africa and the ideology that has since been framing such activities. Through the use of some pertinent cases around the continent, the chapter exposes the socially irresponsible actions of TNCs in Africa.

Instrumentalising TNCs for Africa's social development

Globalisation is seen by many as the basic defining element of the 'New World Order' (Owolabi 2001: 71), seeking to project a notion of a global cultural economy (Appadurai 1990: 2), marked by the prevalence of a liberal capitalist economic ideology and values of competition, suggesting the existence of 'markets' in lieu of nations (Sivandan 1998/1999: 6). As the figures suggest, there has been a rise in transnational corporate power. By 2000, on a global scale, 63,000 parent firms with almost 690,000 foreign affiliates were recorded, and the foreign affiliates of the top 100 TNCs had assets of US$2 thousand billion (UNCTAD 2000). DFID (2000) indicates that many of these are based in developing countries, with the potential to enhance development efforts in their 'host' countries.

Many have highlighted the fact that market liberalisation can contribute to the alleviation of crucial concerns of poverty, especially in the Southern countries (Dollar and Kraay 2001; Christiaensen *et al.* 2002). Others such as Hirst and Thompson (1999) argue emphatically that the costs and benefits of economic globalisation are borne unevenly, as the benefits are largely 'held up' in Northern countries, even though Southern countries bear most of the costs. Indeed, accumulating evidence suggests that Africa is sidelined within transnational corporate dominance. For instance the world's 100 largest economies now count 50 giant TNCs, none of which is indigenously owned in Africa. The five largest global corporations count sales greater than the total incomes of the 46 poorest countries, and most of these poor nations are in Africa. Furthermore, the top 200 corporations' sales levels approximate 20 times the combined annual incomes of the world's 1.2 billion poorest people (DFID 2000: 15; Craig 2003: 50).

In this context, African states are confronted with the problem of making corporate globalisation more proactive and contributory to development. Indicatively, many countries in the North, such as the Netherlands, Denmark, the United Kingdom and others, have been adopting measures, including corporate citizenship, to 'watch' and 'guide' the actions of such TNCs operating in their countries (which are also, mostly 'home' countries to these TNCs). Citing HSBC and Dresdner banks as examples, Mathiason (2002) observes that there are signs that even investment banks in Europe are 'warming to socially and environmentally friendly investments'. In the United States, even religious groups have embraced the idea, illustrated by the creation of the Interfaith Center on Corporate Social Responsibility, which is pressing for corporate accountability and stronger links between Northern shareholder groups with shares in TNCs and Southern groups that bear the impact of such corporate activities (Bendell 2004: 45; Charkiewicz 2005: 76). In another example, Morley Fund Management, an investment firm in the UK, has incorporated a socially responsible investment (SRI) perspective into its company-wide voting policy in the UK Stock Exchange (FTSE). Clare

Brook, director of SRI, believes Morley's voting policy on SRI to have been instrumental in inducing the FTSE to issue environmental impact reports one year later (Mathiason 2002).

The discourse and practice of corporate citizenship in the North has been widening, and has attracted special government policy focus on its developments in European countries. For example, in the UK, within the Department of Trade and Industry there is a Minister for Corporate Social Responsibility. The European Union (EU), for its part, has published a 'Green Paper on Corporate Social Responsibility' (CSR) and 2005 has been declared the EU year of CSR (UNIDO 2002: 1). All do not acclaim the corporate citizenship movement. It is even seen with suspicion by some (Marsden 2000; Vidaver-Cohen and Altman 2000), who are sceptical about the potential of corporate citizenship to change much of what exists presently. Yet we must recognise that the corporate citizenship project is one policy option that has been enabling Northern countries to manage globalisation, particularly corporate globalisation and corporate power. Evidently, for every country, the outcomes from globalisation depend on how it perceives and manages it. Thus, the most arduous challenge of corporate globalisation is that of management, for compatibility with development goals. As DFID makes clear,

> Managed wisely, the new wealth being created by globalisation creates the opportunity to lift millions of the World's poorest people out of poverty. Managed badly, it could lead to their further marginalisation and impoverishment. Neither outcome is pre-determined; it depends in the policy choices adopted by governments, international institutions, the private sector and civil society (DFID 2000: 15).

This explains why, in spite of the fact that corporate globalisation is seen by many as a seemingly unlevelled ground, many still believe that, in developing countries, corporate citizenship by TNCs is making a difference to efforts for sustainable development (UNRISD 1995; Murphy and Bendell 1999; Hansen 1999a, 1999b; Utting 2001, 2002; UNIDO 2002). Consequently, arguments have swung from confrontational to partnership, regarding the relationship that states and civil-society groups should adopt to achieve the best results from TNCs. Unfortunately, as examined below, the history and ideology guiding the actions of most TNCs in Africa diminishes the hopes one could nurse on scaling up opportunities from corporate globalisation. This makes consideration of the promotion of corporate citizenship by all actors an urgent requirement, as a policy option to enable the instrumentalisation of TNCs in Africa's social development.

Brief history of TNCs' activities in Africa and their ideology

Greer and Singh (2000) contend that TNCs did not really appear until the 19th century, following the breakthrough of industrial capitalism, which engendered the factory system and created more capital-intensive techniques, as well as more rapid transportation. This forced industry out of their 'homes' to these 'host' countries because of the demand for natural resources, especially in the petrochemical, food, furniture and textile sectors. Indeed, by the 19th century, 60% of these corporations' investments had shifted to Latin America, the Middle East, Asia and Africa (Greer and Singh 2000).

European presence in Africa during the pre-colonial and colonial period was marked by such names as the Berlin West African Plantation Company (for the Germans), the Royal Niger Company and United African Company (in many English-speaking African countries), the Société Générale and the Compagnie Française d'Afrique Occidentale (in many French-speaking African countries), existing with responsibility for the expatriation of African wealth which the peasants had created with immense suffering (Rodney 1972: 169). These companies were mostly concentrated within the primary sector, especially in the areas of agriculture and mining.

Neo-colonial Africa, with its increasing embrace of what it has been made to see as 'modernity', has given itself naively to a culture of immense consumerism (Sklair 2004). The lure of such modernity, with the consequence of heightened consumerism, makes Africa one of the largest markets for TNC manufacturing activities. For example, Jenkins (1987: 9, cited in Iyayi 2001), shows that by 1974 50% of Ghana's manufacturing was controlled by foreign firms; by 1976, in the case of Kenya the figure was 30% and 70% for Nigeria. These figures indicate the pace with which the lure of modernity and zeal to consume (especially what they do not produce) has delivered Africa even further into the grips of Northern capitalist imperialism through foreign direct investment (FDI), even though Zammit (2003: 16) argues that FDI in Africa has fallen.

TNCs in Africa are guided by a very capitalist ideology. Iyayi (2001) has argued that it is an ideology that rationalises the 'criminal actions' of TNCs. Korten (1996: 70-71, 131) advances some key elements of this ideology as including the belief that: the gigantic global corporations should be legitimate managers and authorities of the world's financial and technological resources, as well as its markets; profitability should be the sole basis of free corporate actions, in disregard for national or local consequences or needs; no loyalties are due local communities; people are generally motivated by ambition and an uncontrolled pursuit of such ambitions; and accumulative spirit (inherent in capitalist relations) necessarily optimises social outcomes.

In a similar light, Iyayi (2001) has indicated that the quickness and ingenuity with which TNCs in the oil sector exploit the undemocratic and corrupt contexts in developing-world countries makes them accomplices in the generation of precarious conditions in these countries. Supporting this view, Ashton-Jones *et al.* (1998) observe that such actions are rooted in an entrenched 'oil industry culture' that defines the relationship of Western oil companies with developing-world countries. Indicatively, Ashton-Jones *et al.* (1998: 30) argue that such an oil industry culture is grounded on assumptions that profit maximisation is the sole object of corporate existence and actions (*à la* Milton Friedman), such that any expenditure beyond that necessary is not welcomed. Also, such TNCs hold the misguided view that 'markets' (to mean the industrialised world) possess the rights to obtain the resources they want, at the cheapest cost, irrespective of the cost to the local people who are obliged to play 'hosts' to mining companies, and 'they' (the mining companies) 'know best and act responsibly' (Ashton-Jones *et al.* 1998). To these ends, neither the companies nor the governments with whom they work, especially in the sub-Saharan African countries, are willing to support any divergence from this culture, which is reinforced by 'cosmetic' public relations schemes and deep intimidation (Ashton-Jones *et al.* 1998: 31). Such is the immoral and irresponsible ideology framing the actions of TNCs especially in Africa, and these actions betray their unwillingness to globalise the values of corporate citizenship, which they uphold in their Northern home countries, to Africa, as the next section examines.

Social irresponsibility of TNCs in Africa: non-globalisation of corporate citizenship

By their profit-maximising and capitalist ideology, many TNCs have largely been responsible for increasing poverty and 'constructing' despicable conditions of labour in Africa. Complicit with several African governments, they have helped to institutionalise destructive conditions ranging from 'high place' corruption to political 'hijack' of basic rights, in order to secure their interests. Consequently, the charge on TNCs as accomplices in the misery of Africans is very often legitimated by such reflections, exposing them as socially irresponsible, as elaborated below.

Undermining governance capacities, fanning corruption in Africa

The large capital base and prominence of some TNCs makes them more powerful than many African states, implying that they have stronger bargaining power than these governments, which, more often than not, are most concerned with the goal of attracting the requisite foreign direct investment for economic growth (?) in their poor countries. These African countries therefore gullibly or knowingly accept very exploitative terms from TNCs' FDI. Indeed as Madeley (2003) sees it, FDI in Africa is dominated by TNCs, and the relationship between such TNCs and the governments of developing countries is largely unequal. They have the tendency of not consulting such governments and their local people before making most of their vital decisions.

The efforts of African governments to attract FDI from TNCs often require a reallocation of resources to provide the basic infrastructure necessary for industrial activities, implying a reduction of resources from other sectors of the economy such as agriculture, education and healthcare. In addition, the competition to attract FDI has led many African governments to offer very long tax holidays, ranging between five and ten years (Madeley 2003). These competitions often lead the countries to propose conditions that can be seen as devastating and unproductive for African economies. For example, in Cameroon, following the Presidential decision by Ordinance No. 90/001 of 29 January 1990, the country's Industrial Free Zone Legislation was passed, which sought to encourage the establishment of industries (principally from TNCs, given the trend in Cameroon). In the provisions of this legislation, investors were to benefit from commercial incentives such as exemptions from all margins and price controls, fiscal benefits such as a ten-year tax holiday on all taxes and profits, financial concessions such as the right to hold foreign exchange accounts and the guaranteed right to transfer abroad all funds earned and invested in Cameroon, in addition to labour-related concessions among others.

In another dimension, Soros (2003) has strongly and rightfully argued that there is a close link between TNCs' exploitation of natural resources, oppressive or undemocratic regimes and the prevalence of corruption. The 'secured revenue' from such TNCs in the form of bribes enables such governments to stay in power and they in turn allow TNCs a free hand in their exploitation of African natural resources. Even though OECD countries signed a convention in 1997 outlawing bribery by TNCs, the tendency has been that of heightening TNC involvement in corruption in African countries. Moreover, such a convention has not produced any record of prosecution. In Cameroon, for instance, as a result of the intense personalisation of power in the hands of President Paul Biya and his political and military elite (especially within his ruling CPDM party), the TNCs in nearly all sectors have exploited this undemocratic and unaccountable context (due to the existence of a frail civil society) to fan corruption. Illustratively, the forestry sector in Cameroon, dominated by TNCs' subsidiary firms, is exhibiting the normal confusion between the 'public' and 'private', characteristic of a neo-patrimonial state. Corruption permeates the forestry sector in Cameroon, especially with respect to the granting of forestry exploitation rights, the control of forestry activities and management of forestry revenues (Nguiffo 2005). In Lesotho, one of the 14 TNCs facing charges for bribing a government official to win contracts in the Lesotho Highlands Water Project, a Canadian engineering consultancy, Acres International, was convicted on two counts of corruption involving US$431,000 (Eigen 2002). TNCs seem to thrive and be comfortable in such a context of deep 'public official' corruptibility.

Unfortunately, as Eigen (2002), chairman of Transparency International, argues simply, 'corruption distorts economic decision-making as kickbacks prevail over quality, particularly in tenders and privatisation'. Understandably, many such TNCs are being strongly derided by activists who see them as part of the problem of misappropriation of state revenues in Africa by government officials. In an indication of this, Soros (2003) shows that, in recent years, lobbying and pressure groups have campaigned against Royal Dutch/Shell in Nigeria, ExxonMobil in Acertners in Equatorial Guinea, ChevronTexaco in Angola and Talisman in Sudan. He proposes a solution to these TNCs that seems quite simple and transparent enough: 'publish what you pay' to these African governments. But self-publication of payments by such TNCs is proving hard to come by.

Insufficient response to Africans' social needs

The partially true idea of Milton Friedman, that the responsibility of business is profit, can be accepted when appropriately qualified. He understood profit as limited only to economic performance. Today the notion of profit has widened to include two other elements: meeting social needs and ensuring environmental protection. This expanded vision of profit today is built into the concept of the 'triple bottom line', in the jargon of corporate citizenship and CSR, which is made up of the economic, social and environmental bottom lines.

Essentially, in Western countries, TNCs are scaling up to these 'new' corporate requirements. Undoubtedly, in Africa, TNCs have been 'over'-successful with the first bottom line of economic performance. But TNCs in Africa display a nonchalant and often insensitive ear to the social malaise of people living in the local environments in which they operate. Yet, as Cushman (1978, cited in Carroll 1981: 184) contends, business today 'must . . . for its well-being be willing to give serious consideration to the human needs as it does to the needs for productive profits'. In return for the resources and environments from which TNCs generate profits, they are expected by society to be good corporate citizens by adhering to the laws of the land and refraining from activities that have negative social consequences. In addition to this, they are expected to be proactive, and involved in 'finding solutions to society's problems and improving the quality of lives for their workers in particular and the community as a whole, if possible' (Maphosa 2003: 57).

Within the general picture in Africa, most TNCs in the past have displayed an 'escapist' culture in response to calls for their participation in solving social problems in the continent, although some are changing in their response to some social problems, as, for example, in the tragedy of HIV/Aids. For example, many companies are increasingly developing and implementing workplace and community HIV/Aids programmes, with the aim of mitigating the effects and spread of HIV/Aids in Africa. It is today common to see companies engaging to form national, regional or global coalitions (by a pooling of resources) to help respond to the pandemic. Such are the cases of the Global Business Council on HIV/Aids and the Corporate Task Force on Aids in Africa. Though encouraging, even such corporate response to Aids in Africa can still be argued to be a result of its direct links to productivity and profitability (Maphosa 2003).

Overall, there has not been sufficient response from TNCs with respect to social needs in Africa. Generating huge profits on a daily basis from their investments in Africa, TNCs are failing to make a plausible case for their social relevance in such a way as to be directly felt by most of the people at the grass roots. It has been convincingly argued that, rather than alleviating poverty, FDI in Africa by most TNCs is rendering Africans poorer and widening income inequalities between the generally 'stealing' elite and the masses in African countries, as previously shown (Madeley 2003).

For instance, in Chad, living conditions are very precarious, especially for the ordinary Chadian, as a result of 'threatening darkness' from an inadequate supply of electricity. In this picture, we have a TNC, Esso—a consortium of ExxonMobil, ChevronTexaco and Petronas of Malaysia in Chad—which has a power station generating up to 120 megawatts of electricity, approximately five times Chad's entire national capacity. All Esso says about the electricity situation in Chad is that its power station is meant to 'pump out crude oil from the ground and down the pipeline to the coast of Cameroon, not providing electricity to the local population'.[1] But this is a country from which Esso draws out 225,000 barrels of oil per day.

In the case of Cameroon itself, concerning this very oil project in Chad, it has recently been observed that the approximately 880 km of pipeline traversing the Cameroonian fragile ecological zones has seen a massive expropriation of land and destruction of plants and crops, as well as pollution of water resources. Driven by their usual ethos of cost minimisation for profit maximisation, the consortium provided minimal individual and communal compensation to the indigenously displaced people to restore or improve their broken livelihoods (Ndika 2004). Similarly in 2002, the Swiss-based TNC food giant Nestlé defended its demand for US$6 million from famine-stricken Ethiopia, following a dispute with the Ethiopian government after a former communist regime

1 UN Integrated Regional Information Network (IRIN) at IRINNews.org, 28 October 2003. See also *Alexander's Gas and Oil Connections News and Trends: Africa* 8.22 (13 November 2003), at www.gasandoil.com/goc/news/nta34660.htm, accessed 22 May 2005.

way back in 1975 nationalised a livestock firm owned by a German subsidiary of Nestlé. The Ethiopian government offered to pay US$1.5 million, but Nestlé insisted on complete payment of the US$6 million. This is a country that is battling with threats of thousands of deaths yearly from famine. Consequently, such obstinacy from Nestlé was so exasperating as to attract a condemnatory statement from Oxfam, a poverty relief organisation, which stated that there was no justification for diverting 'needed' money to a multinational which made profits of approximately US$3.9 million in the first six months of the same year (for details, see BBC 2002).

All these illustrative cases are merely a glimpse of how, wielding enormous power, TNCs have been carrying themselves with an apparent determination to be socially irresponsible and insensitive to the needs of the people in their 'host' countries. Many have principally been concerned with making profits, irrespective of the human conditions accompanying these profits.

Eroding environmental capacities in Africa

By now, we are familiar with the link between poverty and the environment, which has been well established in both Northern and Southern countries. Yet African countries have been and still are being subjected to huge amounts of environmental damage, especially from TNCs and local small and medium-sized enterprises (SMEs) involved in the extractive and heavy industrial manufacturing sectors. African countries, in a bid to 'keep their investors' have mostly been very complaisant. Nevertheless, all along, even if ignored by their governments, Africans at the grass roots understand that they are losing much from such environmental degradation.

We are acquainted to such slogans as 'environmentally friendly', 'sustainable wage', or 'on recycled paper' on goods from many Northern countries, as signs of a good corporate image and citizenship by the companies involved. In Africa, the picture is very different. TNCs have been and still are degrading the land, polluting waters and air, all of which are the principal environmental and health resources that a community must strive to secure.

In a case from Liberia, four former iron ore mining companies, Bong Mining Company, Liberian Mining Company, LAMCO Joint Venture Co. and the National Iron Ore Company, all formerly operated by TNCs, polluted waters by dumping their tailings directly into rivers, lakes and creeks. Iron oxide led to water pollution by brick-red coloration of the rivers, in addition to extensive destruction of fauna and flora (Shannon 1992). In another instance, Ghana has sustained major environmental degradation from the dumping of untreated waters into adjacent waters (Shannon 1992). Often, such waters become unfit for drinking and domestic uses, forcing the local people to travel long distances to obtain potable water.

Similarly, Iyayi (2001) observes that the activities of logging companies in Cameroon (most of which are TNCs) have caused severe damage to the land, dramatically altering the ecosystem. Such environmental malpractices pose threats to people's health within the local communities in which such TNCs operate. But, as Greer and Singh (2000) remind us, such social irresponsibility of TNCs in Africa also results in inherent harm to the planet and its inhabitants.

Lagging labour standards: a product of TNCs' over-zealousness for profit maximisation in Africa

It is evident that the availability of cheap labour is one of the principal factors attracting TNCs in Africa, especially for those that are labour-intensive. It is therefore not surprising that real wages have lagged largely behind growth in productivity in many African countries. In addition, against claims by some that TNCs are the principal source of employment in Africa, a report by UNRISD (1995: 154) shows that, by 1995, of the 73 million jobs created by TNCs, only 15 million went to developing countries (including Africa). Moreover, the nature of such jobs is such that they are low-skilled, low-paid and quite transitional (Madeley 2003). Illustratively, the promised jobs from the Chad/Cameroon oil project have turned out to be temporary, disappearing after each stage is completed (Silverstein 2003).

In addition to its temporal and unsustainable nature, TNC employment is noted to be associated with problems of despicable working conditions, a source of concern to a multitude of local Africans. These despicable working conditions maintained by many TNCs' subsidiaries in 'host' (African) countries have been compared with those in their Northern 'home' countries, and found to be far worse (Castleman 1995). Yet, such dehumanising, exploitative and risky working conditions have always been a source of pain and misery for many Africans, who can no longer distinguish whether they are fortunate or unfortunate to be employed.

Greer and Singh (2000) documented an illustrative case of the German TNC Bayer's chromate production factory, known as Chrome Chemical in South Africa. Chromate, a very corrosive chemical compound, causes respiratory illness such as lung cancer. This led a South African government report in 1976 to note health problems in nearly half of the plant's employees, which were related to their work. As the report observed, this was 'extremely disturbing and appeared to indicate a lack of concern regarding the physical welfare of the workers' (Greer and Singh 2000). Following observations by a trade union in 1990 that several workers at Chrome Chemical were affected by lung cancer, and the fact that none of them was aware that this disease might be related to the working conditions at the plant, the union proposed to review the factory's industrial hygiene records. Chrome Chemical's management objected to this and, in 1991, the firm opted to shut down much of its operations and lay off its workers; its parent firm, Bayer, refused to pay compensation to many former employees of Chrome Chemical, affected by the disease. As Castleman (1995) pointed out, 'Bayer could not get away with this in Germany.' This case from South Africa is reflective of the African workers' predicament. Most of them, working under very hazardous conditions, often ignorantly, have become very grateful for the occasional few tins of milk offered to them (when such companies are considerate) as preventive to these health hazards.

Conclusion

This chapter has shown that by itself corporate globalisation is not an *a priori* exclusionary process. Rather it is the policy options adopted by various countries for its management and the behaviour of the corporate actors in the various contexts that could be making the difference. This argument is supported by the preceding argument that, while corporate citizenship is being adopted in the North as a policy option, the unwillingness of TNCs to globalise the values of corporate citizenship in Africa is a principal cause for the continuous marginalisation of the continent from the benefits of corporate globalisation. Indicatively, Shannon's observation that 'transnational corporations maintain different standards and practices in their home and host countries . . . in their home countries there are strict environmental regulations and legislation which must be adhered to, otherwise they face serious penalties' (Shannon 1992: 684) should provoke further concern and reflection on the prospects that exist in sustaining and maintaining a strong culture of corporate citizenship in Africa.

References

Appadurai, A. (1990) 'Disjuncture and Difference in the Global Cultural Economy', *Public Culture* 2.2: 1-24.

Ashton-Jones, N., S. Arnott and D. Oronto (1998) *The Human Eco Systems of the Niger Delta: An ERA Handbook* (Ibadan, Nigeria: Kraft Books).

BBC (2002) 'Nestle insists on Ethiopian refund', BBC News World Edition, 19 December 2002, news.bbc.co.uk/2/hi/business/2589745.stm, accessed 22 May 2005.

Bendell, J. (2004) *Barricades and Boardrooms: A Contemporary History of the Corporate Accountability Movement* (Programme Paper Series Technology, Business and Society No. 13; Geneva: UNRISD).

Carroll, A.B. (1981) *Business and Society: Managing Corporate Social Performance* (Boston, MA: Little, Brown).

Castleman, B. (1995) 'The Migration of Industrial Hazards', *Third World Resurgence*, April 1995.

Charkiewicz, E. (2005) 'Corporations, the UN and Neo-Liberal Bio-Politics', *Development* 48.11: 75-83.

Christiaensen, L., L. Demery and S. Paternostro (2002) *Growth, Distribution and Poverty in Africa: Messages from the 1990s* (World Bank Policy Research Department Working Paper no. 2810; Washington, DC: World Bank).

Craig, G. (2003) 'Globalisation, Migration and Social Development', *Journal of Social Development in Africa* 18.2: 49-76.

DFID (Department for International Development) (2000) *Eliminating World Poverty: Making Globalisation Work for the Poor* (London: DFID).

Dollar, D., and A. Kraay (2001) *Trade, Growth and Poverty* (World Bank Policy Research Department Working Paper no. 2675; Washington, DC: World Bank).

Eigen, P. (2002) 'Multinationals bribery goes unpunished', *International Herald Tribune*, 12 November 2002.

Greer, J., and K. Singh (2000) 'A Brief History of Transnational Corporations', *Corporate Watch 2000*, retrieved from Global Policy Forum: www.globalpolicy.org/socecon/tncs/historytncs.htm#bk2_ft22, accessed 26 May 2005.

Hansen, M. (1999a) *Environmental Management in Transnational Corporations in Asia: Does Foreign Ownership Make a Difference? Preliminary Results of a Survey of Environmental Management Practices in 154 TNCs* (Occasional Paper; Copenhagen: Copenhagen Business School; UNCTAD Cross Border Environmental Management Project).

—— (1999b) 'Environmental Regulations of Transnational Corporations: Needs and Prospects' (mimeo; Geneva: UNRISD).

Hirst, P., and C. Thompson (1999) *Globalisation in Question* (Cambridge, UK: Polity Press).

Iyayi, F. (2001) 'Ecological Debt and Transnational Corporations in Africa', article presented at *Globalisation, Ecological Debt, and Climate change and Sustainability: A South-South Conference*, Berlin, November 2001.

Korten, D.C. (1996) *When Corporations Rule the World* (London: Earthscan).

Madeley, J. (2003) 'Transnational Corporations and Developing Countries: Big Business, Poor People', *The Courier* 196 (January–February 2003): 36.

Maphosa, F. (2003) 'HIV/Aids at the Workplace: A Study of Corporate Responses to the HIV/Aids Pandemic in Zimbabwe', *CODESRIA Bulletin* 2, 3, 4 (special issue): 56-58.

Marsden, C. (2000) 'The New Corporate Citizenship of Big Business: Part of the Solution to Sustainability?', *Business and Society Review* 105.1: 9-25.

Mathiason, N. (2002) 'Company Ethics? They're not our Business', *The Observer* 17 November 2002; observer.guardian.co.uk/business/ethics/story/0,,848098,00.html, accessed 5 June 2005.

Murphy, D., and J. Bendell (1999) *Partners in Time? Business, NGOs and Sustainable Development* (Discussion Paper 109; Geneva: UNRISD).

Ndika, A.C. (2004) 'A Happy Birthday? The Chad/Cameroon Oil Pipeline One Year On', *Pambazuka News* 23 September 2004; www.pambazuka.org/en/category/comment/24822, accessed 22 May 2005.

Nguiffo, S. (2005) 'The goat grazes where it is tied: Remarks on the Neo- patrimonial Administration of Cameroon's Forestry Sector', www.forestsmonitor.org, 15 March 2005.

Owolabi, K.A. (2001) 'Globalisation, Americanization and Western Imperialism', *Journal of Social Development in Africa* 16.2: 71-91.

Rodney, W. (1972) *How Europe Underdeveloped Africa* (London: Bogle-L'Ouverture).

Rugman, A.M., and A. Verbeke (2004) 'A Perspective on Regional and Global Strategies of Multinational Enterprises', *Journal of International Business Studies* 35.1: 3-18.

Shannon, E.H. (1998) 'The Role of National and Transnational Corporations in the African Mining Sector and the Environment: The Case of Noncompliance and Enforcement', INECE conference proceedings, www.inece.org/5thvol1/shannon3.pdf: 672-92.

Silverstein, K. (2003) 'With War, Africa Oil Beckons', *Los Angeles Times*, 21 March 2003; www.globalpolicy.org/socecon/tncs/2003/0321beckon.htm, accessed 5 June 2005.

Sivandan, A.A. (1998/1999) 'Globalisation and the Left', *Race and Class* 40.2/3.

Sklair, L. (2001) *The Transnational Capitalist Class* (Oxford, UK: Basil Blackwell).

Soros, G. (2003) 'Transparent Corruption', *Debtchannel*, February 2003.

UNCTAD (2000) 'World Investment Report 2000', www.unctad.org, accessed 5 June 2005.

UNIDO (2002) *Corporate Social Responsibility and Developing Country SMEs* (Vienna: UNIDO, www.unido.org/doc/511807.htmls).

UNRISD (1995) *States of Disarray: The Social Effects of Globalization* (Geneva: UNRISD).

Utting, P. (2001) 'La responsibilité des Entreprises dans la Perspectives du Developpement Durable', in IEUD (ed.), *Annuaire Suisse-Tiers Monde* (Geneva: IEUD).

—— (2002) *The Greening of Business in Developing Countries: Rhetoric, Reality and Prospects* (London: Zed Books/UNRISD).

Vidaver-Cohen, D., and B.W. Altman (2000) 'Corporate Citizenship in the New Millennium: Foundation for Architecture of Excellence', *Business and Society Review* 105.1: 145-68.

Zammit, A. (2003) *Development at Risk: Rethinking UN–Business Partnerships* (Geneva: South Center/UNRISD).

21

Treading lightly

CREATING HARMONY AND CO-OPERATION IN AFRICA

Malcolm McIntosh

Universities of Bath, UK, and Stellenbosch, South Africa

> I am convinced that a non-violent society can be built only on the foundation of harmony and co-operation, without which society is bound to remain violent. If we argue that cannot be done it will mean that a non-violent society can never come into being. In that case our entire culture would be meaningless (Mahatma Ghandi, October 1941).

Our Common Interest, the Report by the Commission for Africa, called for a dramatic increase in overseas aid but only if coupled with improvements in internal governance, and these too were the basis of the US new aid programme in 2005. Overseas debt amounts to the same amount as that stolen over the years by corrupt leaders in complicity with business and banks around the world. Rooting out 'systemic rot' is at the heart of the problem: systemic rot in Africa and in global trade rules and in the way we all see Africa. As *Our Common Interest* says on corporate citizenship issues:

> The international community has a role to play in maintaining high standards of governance. If it does so in its own activities—and demands it in activities of its private sector agents, like the multinational companies in developing countries—then it will be better positioned to encourage similar high standards in the way African countries manage the cash from their natural resources.

The Report says that business has a significant role to play:

- By understanding its own history in Africa

- By fostering peace and conflict resolution
- By acknowledging the role that business can play in promoting healthcare and education
- By recognising that agricultural subsidies in the US, Europe and Japan help to keep African farmers poor
- By accepting that the wealth extracted by business over many years has damaged personal relations between men and women and this coupled with poverty, lack of education and healthcare has caused the highest rates of HIV/Aids in the world

The key recommendations of *Our Common Interest* concern capacity building and accountability in Africa, strengthening civil-society institutions, rooting out corruption, preventing and managing conflict, providing basic education and health services coupled with clean water and sanitation, giving Africa the capacity to trade by changing subsidies and tariff barriers, and by giving more targeted aid based on projects that actually work.

It is strange, given the fact that Wayne Visser has noted in this book the comparative dearth of scholarly work on Africa from within Africa, that neither *Our Common Interest* nor the UN Millennium Development Goals[1] contain a reference to the need for greater vocational and tertiary education. At the moment those lucky enough to gain a good tertiary education or train in a profession in Africa often seek work in the US or Europe. Two strategies are needed: first, to build capacity in many more universities and further education and training institutions across Africa and fund them with endowments that will last for decades; and, second, to devise a way of getting Africa's professional diasporas back to Africa—forever or for a year or five. In 2003 Africa's 5 million dispersed people remitted back home some US$45 billion, which is nearly a quarter of some African countries' GDPs, and only just second to FDI (foreign direct investment) and external funding as sources of revenue[2] for Africa as a whole.

Various commentators have pointed out that, despite the best efforts of Europeans and white South Africans to ignore or destroy traditional ethnic, tribal and local allegiances, these flourish across Africa providing support, love, help, investment, networks, nourishment, communication systems and entrepreneurship. If, as Wolfgang Sachs said many years ago, that enterprise is as everyday for everybody as conversation, then there is no lack of it in any part of Africa (Sachs 1992). One issue is lack of access to title, money and markets that keeps Africans poor. It is this issue that Hernando do Soto addresses in *The Mysteries of Capital: Why Capitalism Triumphs in the*

1 'We will have time to reach the Millennium Development Goals—worldwide and in most, or even all, individual countries—but only if we break with business as usual. We cannot win overnight. Success will require sustained action across the entire decade between now and the deadline. It takes time to train the teachers, nurses and engineers; to build the roads, schools and hospitals; to grow the small and large businesses able to create the jobs and income needed. So we must start now. And we must more than double global development assistance over the next few years. Nothing less will help to achieve the Goals' (United Nations Secretary-General Kofi A. Annan, www.un.org/millenniumgoals).

2 *Africa Diaspora Investment Report*, London, 19–20 November 2004.

West and Fails Everywhere Else (De Soto 2000). Africans do not suffer from a lack of some forms of social capital but they have not been able to develop inter-African trade networks to any great extent and they have not been able to break entrenched colonial trading relations. But capitalism, or open markets as it is now called after the end of the Cold War, is not everything that Africa needs. More than anything it needs integrity and dignity. As Amartya Sen says in *Development as Freedom*, development can have many faces and growing economic enterprises is but one form of development (Sen 1999). De Soto argues that Western models of growth feature ownership of assets and property rights and Sen points out that it is possible to have these features as well as greatly enhanced levels of health, well-being and social prosperity within non-democratic political systems—witness Cuba and China which have very high rates of literacy and numeracy and low levels of infant mortality and malnutrition.

One of the companies that has profited most from Africa is Shell, and its charitable arm, the Shell Foundation, has a prescription for 'pro-poor' developmental enterprise with five principles (Shell Foundation 2005):

- Owned by poor people, sells to poor people, employs poor people
- Long-term viability of assisted enterprises and not permanently dependent on subsidy
- Financially viable business propositions that can scale up using local resources
- The application of the business model: risk assessment, market knowledge, customer-facing and low-cost production
- MNCs (multinational corporations) can offer 'value creating resources . . . *if assessed and deployed appropriately* can add enormous social value'

Some would argue that it is former colonial powers, and since then MNCs, that have kept local producers and workers poor because to do otherwise would be to deny MNCs their profit margins. Perhaps, and this is reflected in the renewed interest in corporate citizenship globally and recently in Africa, MNCs have seen the wind of change, as they did immediately prior to the fall of apartheid in South Africa, and are now able to see the benefits for themselves of stable political regimes, educated and conflict-free local communities and local markets for their products through pro-poor enterprise development. As the Shell Foundation says:

> Donors [of charitable support or aid] are encouraged to enter into new arrangements with big business in order to enlist its support in 're-engineering' the international development supply chain via the injection of business thinking along its entire supply chain.

On a slightly more radical note, the International Business Leaders Forum advocates exactly this. Many of its members are already attempting to put these principles into practice (Nelson 1996):

- Apply the highest international standards in workplace ethics, health and standards
- Employ and upgrade local people

- Develop locally needed and useful products and services
- Add value to exports locally
- Enhance local supply chains
- Support local education institutions
- Support and work with civil-society organisations that promote development in health, human rights, education and enterprise
- Work to increase 'positive inward investment'
- 'Promote better international trade terms and access to markets'

In *The End of Poverty* Jeffrey Sachs makes the point that we now know enough about economics, technology and trade to end poverty in our lifetime (Sachs 2005). Not that there is necessarily agreement between him and de Soto and Sen on all points, but they would all support the *Make Poverty History* campaign around the world which saw millions of people wearing rubber bracelets with that logo inscribed on them, because, perhaps in their naivety, they thought it was possible to achieve this goal. If, as I know it was, sniffed at by some people in Africa, particularly in South Africa, it must be remembered that in order to change the current trade rules there must be an understanding of history and there must be moral outrage about the current situation. As Tony Blair said: 'The developed world has a moral duty as well as a powerful motive of self-interest to assist Africa . . . A changed Africa could change the face of the world.' Or, as Nelson Mandela put it on a higher moral tone: 'Like slavery and apartheid, poverty is not natural. It is man-made and it can be overcome and eradicated by the actions of humans' (Mandela 2005).

The challenge for the corporate citizenship community, and those engaged in theorising or reflecting on practice, is to understand how this wave of globalisation has captured us all. All markets are connected, all telecommunications systems are connected, all weather systems are connected, our planet is home to us all. And now we can recognise that our largest economic institutions are companies, apart from nation-states. Our nation-states are not dead but they are in competition with supra-territorial corporations (STCs). The most urgent priority is to regain control of our STCs in order that we can direct their resources, financial and social, to helping solve, in partnership with government and civil society, the world's most pressing social and ecological problems (McIntosh 2003). In *Empire* Michael Hardt and Antonio Negri said that:

> Some claim that these have merely come to occupy the place that was held by the various national colonialist and imperialist systems . . . but the new reality of capitalism is that corporations are no longer defined by the imposition of abstract command and the organisation of simple theft and unequal exchange . . . but they directly structure and articulate territories and populations and make states merely instruments to record the flows of commodities, monies and populations that they set in motion (Hardt and Negri 2000).

So what does the future hold? While Africa is unique in having gone backwards in terms of economic growth in the last 50 years, there are many signs of positive change in recent years which include significant moves towards citizen participation through the development of democratic institutions, and the slow, but steady, development of post-apartheid South Africa. Countries such as the UK, despite their championing of *Our Common Interest*, need to stop selling arms into conflict areas even if it is a growth industry for the UK. Aids, malaria, war and poverty mean that life expectancy in Africa is expected to decline to 42 on average over the next ten years, the same as in Europe one hundred years ago. Compare this to Japan, for example, where life expectancy is more than double this at 88, where the population density is one of the highest in the world and where there is a lack of natural resources—just ingenious, creative, cohesive, well-educated people.

Finally, the Millennium Ecosystem Assessment Report[3] highlighted for the world the coming dangers associated with climate change, many of which will affect Africa more than other parts of the world because of poverty, geography, climate and poor infrastructure. One startling result of this work is that malaria accounts for 11% of disease in Africa, and this is likely to increase in the next few years. But if this disease had been eradicated, as it has been in many other parts of the world, Africa would have been US$100 billion better off over the last 35 years. This too is one of the five 'easy'-to-solve recommendations of the Copenhagen Consensus.[4]

As the world rethinks its relationship to planet Earth the last word goes again to Wolfgang Sachs from the Wuppertal Institute: 'Eventually, the world will no longer be divided by the ideologies of "left" and "right", but by those who accept ecological limits and those who don't.' The same applies to Africa as everywhere else. And this applies to how STCs think, breathe and act in Africa and elsewhere.

References

De Soto, H. (2000) *The Mysteries of Capital: Why Capitalism Triumphs in the West and Fails Everywhere Else* (London: Bantam Press).

Hardt, M., and A. Negri (2000) *Empire* (Cambridge, MA: Harvard University Press).

Mandela, N. (2005) 'Make Poverty History Speech, Trafalgar Square, London, 3 February 2005', *Journal of Corporate Citizenship* 18 (Summer 2005): 123-24.

McIntosh, M. (2003) *Raising a Ladder to the Moon: The Complexities of Corporate Social and Environmental Responsibility* (London: Palgrave Macmillan).

Nelson, J. (1996) *Business as Partners In Development* (London: IBLF, UNDP and World Bank).

Sachs, J. (2005) *The End of Poverty* (London: Penguin).

Sachs, W. (1992) *The Development Dictionary: A Guide to Knowledge as Power* (London: Zed Books).

Sen, A. (1999) *Development as Freedom* (Oxford, UK: Oxford University Press).

Shell Foundation (2005) *Enterprise Solutions to Poverty* (London: Shell Foundation).

3 www.millenniumassessment.org

4 www.copenhagenconsensus.com

Abbreviations

AA	Anglo American
ABB	Asea Brown Boveri
ABC	Attractive and new/Better quality/Cheaper offering
ABET	Adult Basic Education and Training
ABR	African Business Roundtable
ADB	Africa Development Bank
AICC	African Institute for Corporate Citizenship
Aids	acquired immuno-deficiency syndrome
ANC	African National Congress
APDF	Africa Project Development Facility
APEQUE	Association pour la Promotion de l'Eco-Association pour la Promotion de Efficacité et la Qualité des Entreprises (Algeria)
ART	anti-retroviral therapy
ASAP	Africa Sustainable Assistance Project (Ahold)
ASTD	Ahold Sustainable Trade Development
ATS	Alien Torts Statute (USA)
BASD	Business Action for Sustainable Development
BCSDZ	Business Council for Sustainable Development Zimbabwe
BEE	Broad-Based Black Economic Empowerment
BHPB	BHP Billiton
BMS	Bristol-Myers Squibb
BMSF	Bristol-Myers Squibb Foundation
BSR	Business for Social Responsibility
BUSA	Business Unity South Africa
CABEERE	Capacity Building for Energy Efficiency and Renewables Programme
CAIA	Chemical and Allied Industries Association
CBLA	Capacity Building, Leadership and Action
CBM	Consultative Business Movement
CBO	community-based organisation
CDM	Clean Development Mechanism

CEO	chief executive officer
CIRA	Center for Interdisciplinary Research on Aids (Yale University)
CMA	Capital Markets Authority (Uganda)
COE	community outreach and education
CR	corporate responsibility
CSI	corporate social investment
CSR	corporate social responsibility
DEAT	Department of Environmental Affairs and Tourism (South Africa)
DFID	Department for International Development (UK)
DGIS	Ministry of Development Co-operation (Netherlands)
DJSI	Dow Jones Sustainability Index
DME	Department of Minerals and Energy (South Africa)
DMSP	disease management service provider
DSL	digital subscriber lines
DSM	demand-side management
DTI	Department of Trade and Industry (South Africa)
EAP	Environmental Action Programme
ECGI	European Corporate Governance Institute
ECL	Exploration Consultants Limited
EIA	environmental impact assessment
EITI	Extractive Industries Transparency Initiative
EMCA	Environmental Management Co-operative Agreement (DEAT)
EMP	environmental management plan
EMS	environmental management system
ESCO	energy services company
EU	European Union
Eurep	Euro-Retailer Produce Working Group
FAP	Financial Assistance Program
FDI	foreign direct investment
FEMA	Forum Empresarial para o Meio Ambiente (Mozambique)
FFI	Fauna & Flora International
FPP	foetal protection policy
FTSE	Financial Times Stock Exchange
GAP	Good Agricultural Practices (Eurep)
GBC	Global Business Coalition
GDP	gross domestic product
GHG	greenhouse gas
GRI	Global Reporting Initiative
HBC	home-based care
HDI	Human Development Index
HDSA	historically disadvantaged South African
HIV	human immunodeficiency virus
ICC	International Chamber of Commerce
ICGU	Institute of Corporate Governance of Uganda
ICMM	International Council on Mining and Minerals
ICT	information and communications technology
IDC	Industrial Development Corporation of South Africa

IDP	Integrated Development Plan
IEA	International Energy Agency
IFC	International Finance Corporation
IMF	International Monetary Fund
IMO	International Maritime Organisation
IoDSA	Institute of Directors in Southern Africa
IPCC	Intergovernmental Panel on Climate Change
IPIECA	International Petroleum Industry Environmental Conservation Association
IRIN	Integrated Regional Information Network (United Nations)
IUCN	International Union for the Conservation of Nature (The World Conservation Union)
JBE	*Journal of Business Ethics*
JCC	*Journal of Corporate Citizenship*
JSE	Johannesburg Securities Exchange
KAP	knowledge, attitude and practice
LDC	less-developed country
MDGs	Millennium Development Goals
MNC	multinational corporation
MOH	Ministry of Health (South Africa)
MPP	Multi-Point Plan (South Durban Basin)
MPRDA	Mineral and Petroleum Resources Development Act (South Africa)
MR	medical research
MTCT	mother-to-child transmission
NBI	National Business Initiative (South Africa)
NEDLAC	National Economic Development and Labour Council (South Africa)
NEES	National Energy Efficiency Strategy (South Africa)
NEMA	National Environmental Management Act (South Africa)
NEPAD	New Partnership for Africa's Development
NGO	non-governmental organisation
OCC	Office of the Comptroller of Currency (Equatorial Guinea)
OECD	Organisation for Economic Co-operation and Development
OPEC	Organisation of Petroleum Exporting Countries
OSH	occupational safety and health
PEP	post-exposure prophylaxis
PFID-F&V	Partnership for Food Industry Development, Fruits and Vegetables (Michigan State University)
PGM	platinum group metals
PwC	PricewaterhouseCoopers
R&D	research and development
RFP	request for proposal
SA	South Africa
SATI	Southern African Tax Institute
SD	sustainable development
SED	socioeconomic development
SEIA	social and environmental impact assessment
SFU	Sustainable Futures Unit (NBI)
SHE	safety, health and environment
SIDA	Swedish International Development Co-operation Agency

SME	small or medium-sized enterprise
SMP	Staff Monitored Program (IMF)
SRI	socially responsible investment
SSA	sub-Saharan Africa
SSC	Species Survival Commissionn (IUCN)
SSCI	Social Science Citation Index
STC	supra-territorial corporation
STF	Secure the Future (BMSF)
STI	sexually transmitted infection
SUSG	Sustainable Use Specialist (SSC)
TAC	technical advisory committee
TB	tuberculosis
TI	Transparency International
TIPCEE	Trade and Investment Programme for Competitive Export Economy
TNC	transnational corporation
UDF	United Democratic Front (South Africa)
UN	United Nations
UNDP	United Nations Development Programme
UNEP	United Nations Environment Programme
UNITA	União Nacional pela Independência Total de Angola
USAID	United States Agency for International Development
USE	Uganda Securities Exchange
VCT	voluntary counselling and testing
VSAT	very small aperture terminal satellites
WBCSD	World Business Council for Sustainable Development
WRI	World Resources Institute
WSSD	World Summit on Sustainable Development, Johannesburg
WTO	World Trade Organisation
WWF	formerly World Wide Fund for Nature

About the contributors

Saleem H. Ali is Associate Professor of Environmental Planning at the University of Vermont's Rubenstein School of Natural Resources. His research focuses on environmental conflict resolution in the extractive industries. He is the author of *Mining, the Environment and Indigenous Development Conflicts* (University of Arizona Press, 2004).

saleem@alum.mit.edu

Corina Beczner has more than ten years of experience in environmental media. She is co-creator of GreenBiz.com, a leading information resource on aligning environmental responsibility with business success, and produced EcoTalk for CBS radio, covering green lifestyles with a focus on 'news-you–can-use'. Her broad environmental science and sustainability background includes geography, biomimicry, green design and industrial ecology. She has an MBA in Sustainable Management from Presidio School of Management and is co-editor of *The Dictionary of Sustainable Management*. Corina is the founder of Vibrant, a producer of organically inspired weddings and special events in California

cbeczner@presidiomba.org

Dr **Bruce M. Burton** is a Senior Lecturer in Finance in the Department of Accountancy and Business Finance at the University of Dundee in Scotland. Dr Burton has published many articles in the broad area of corporate financial management, and is an associate editor of *The European Journal of Finance*.

b.m.burton@dundee.ac.uk

Pierre Chantraine was born in Belgium in 1943. He holds a degree in Chemical Engineering from Queen's University (Kingston, Ontario, Canada). Over his 39-year career with DuPont Canada Inc. he held a variety of technical, staff and managerial assignments. From 1991 until his retirement in 2004 he was Manager for Energy and Environment at DuPont's Kingston site and was also very active in the Canadian Industry Program for Energy Conservation (CIPEC), a unique and successful government–industry voluntary partnership with the goal of reducing energy intensity in industry. Mr Chantraine is an energy management consultant whose work includes helping in the development of the South Africa National Energy Efficiency Accord signed in May 2005.

pchantraine@gmail.com

Larry M. Dooley is President of the Academy of Human Resource Development and Chair of the HRD Program at Texas A&M University. He has 16 years' experience as Chief Financial Officer of the university's College of Education. His research is in the foundations of HRD, leadership development, and technology integration in organisations.

l-dooley@tamu.edu

Niklas Egels-Zandén is a PhD student at the School of Business, Economics and Law at Göteborg University, Sweden. His areas of research are international business and corporate social responsibility, especially in relation to multinational corporations in developing countries. He has previously published in *The Journal of Corporate Citizenship*, *The Journal of Business Ethics* and *Business Strategy and the Environment*.

Niklas.Egels-Zanden@handels.gu.se

Bob Gower's background in marketing and design includes work on interactive projects for Newsweek, HBO and Discovery Channel. He is the former Director of Design of the *San Francisco Examiner* and holds an MBA in Sustainable Management from the Presidio School of Management. Bob is a founder of DriveNeutral.org, an organisation that offsets carbon emissions for individual car owners, and is co-editor of *The Dictionary of Sustainable Management*. He currently works with Eprida, a biofuels company, and Ursa Minor, an innovative digital media firm in Marin County California where he lives.

bgower@presidiomba.org

Angela R. Hansen is a consultant with Peacepath Consulting, a management consulting firm serving the international aid system. She has worked worldwide with clients in the business, government and social sectors and completed her MBA at the University of Cape Town in South Africa and Columbia University in New York.

Angela.R.Hansen@gmail.com

Kari Hartwig is Assistant Clinical Professor in Yale's School of Public Health and a researcher with the Center for Interdisciplinary Research on Aids (CIRA). She has worked in HIV/Aids research, intervention and evaluation activities in Africa, Asia and Latin America for more than 15 years.

Kari.Hartwig@yale.edu

Karen T.A. Hayes's background combines a degree in zoology, an MBA and qualifications in conflict resolution and law. Specialising in developing relationships with the private sector, Karen has worked with a range of organisations, including FFI and other NGOs, the UN and governments. This diversity reflects Karen's interest in the interface between sectors and her enthusiasm for finding common ground between different priorities, needs and constraints. Karen lives in Lubumbashi. Democratic Republic of Congo, where she now works for Pact, a US-based development NGO, funded by USAID, managing an initiative to address corporate responsibility issues in the Congolese mining sector.

office@hicksandhayes.com; www.fauna-flora.org

Professor **Christine V. Helliar** holds a chair in Treasury Management in the Department of Accountancy and Business Finance at the University of Dundee in Scotland. Professor Helliar is Director of Research at the Institute of Chartered Accountants of Scotland and has published widely in the areas of corporate finance, auditing and banking.

c.v.helliar@dundee.ac.uk

Suzanne 't Hooft is a former trainee at Ahold for the ASAP project and from these experiences she wrote a thesis on 'Public Private Partnerships and People Planet Profit: A Closer Look at Ahold's Triple P Initiative'. The thesis was written as a final part of her studies at the Nijmegen School of Management, part of the Radboud University of Nijmegen.

suushooft@hotmail.com

Assistant professor **Markus Kallifatides** is currently undertaking postdoctoral research at the Stockholm School of Economics focusing on historical and current social constructions of top management, highlighting themes of values, power and gender. Among his English-language contributions is co-authorship of *Invisible Management* (Thomson, 2001).

Markus.Kallifatides@hhs.se

Julia Kilbourne has a doctorate in public health and has a background in managing a range of in-country development projects in Africa and Latin America. More recently, she has been working for the business sector with responsibility for promoting ethical supply chain management. She is currently the Project Manager for the Ethical Tea Partnership.

JEKilbourne@aol.com

Susan A. Lynham is an assistant professor at Texas A&M University, has more than 18 years' experience as an HR/D professional in SA and the USA, and has a PhD from the University of Minnesota. Her scholarship focuses on strategic HRD and leadership, and applied theory.

slynham@coe.tamu.edu

Malcolm McIntosh PhD MA BEd FRSA is visiting professor at the Universities of Bath and Nottingham, UK, professor extraordinary at the University of Stellenbosch, South Africa, founding editor of *The Journal of Corporate Citizenship*, editor of *Visions of Ethical Business* from 1998 to 2002, Director of the Corporate Citizenship Unit at Warwick Business School, UK, from 1999 to 2001 and was a consultant and special adviser to the UN Global Compact from 2000 to 2005. He co-guest-edited a special edition of *The Journal of Corporate Citizenship* on Corporate Citizenship in Africa (Issue 18, Summer 2005).

malcolm.mcintosh@btinternet.com; www.malcolmmcintosh.org

Michael Merson is Director of CIRA, the Anna M.R. Lauder Professor of Public Health, and the former Dean of Yale's School of Public Health. His career in international public health spans nearly 30 years and includes serving as Director of the World Health Organisation's Global Programme on Aids.

Michael.Merson@yale.edu

Charlotte Middleton manages the Sustainable Futures Unit (SFU) at the National Business Initiative (NBI) in South Africa, ensuring the SFU's work plays a catalytic role in sustainable development and strengthening leadership in the area of corporate citizenship. She leads the partnership between the NBI and the World Business Council for Sustainable Development and is on the Sustainability Committee of the Institute of Directors in Southern Africa. She is also part of the South African interest group on the EFMD (European Foundation for Management Development)/UN Global Responsible Leadership Initiative. Charlotte edits *The Bottom Line*, a publication dedicated to issues of sustainable development. She is currently working towards her master's degree in corporate citizenship. She co-guest-edited a special edition of *The Journal of Corporate Citizenship* on Corporate Citizenship in Africa (Issue 18, Summer 2005).

charlotte@nbi.org.za; www.nbi.org.za

Judy Muthuri is pursuing doctoral studies at the University of Nottingham where she also attained her Masters of Research degree. She holds an MBA from the University of Nairobi and a BEd (Arts) degree from Kenyatta University, both in Kenya. Her research interests lie in CSR and international business management.

lixjnm@nottingham.ac.uk

Kiarie Mwaura is a Lecturer in Law at Queen's University Belfast. His research interests are in the fields of corporate law, CSR and human rights. He read law at Nairobi, Staffordshire and Wolverhampton and he is an Advocate of the High Court of Kenya.

j.mwaura@qub.ac.uk

Vassi Naidoo is the CEO of Deloitte, Southern Africa. He has a BCom and Diploma of Accounting from the University of Durban-Westville and is a chartered accountant (SA), providing active service to his profession. He also serves in a leadership capacity to numerous organisations, including the SA Colleges of Medicine and African Children's Feeding Scheme.

vnaidoo@deloitte.ac.za

Maresa Oosterman worked as a policy adviser for the Netherlands Ministry of Development Co-ordination (DGIS) and was seconded on a pilot programme to work for six months on Ahold's programme in Ghana. She is now first secretary at the Embassy of the Kingdom of The Netherlands in Kigali, Rwanda, where she is setting up a regional programme to contribute to stability in the Great Lakes Region through the sustainable development of natural resources.

maresa.oosterman@minbuza.nl

Rogers Tabe Egbe Orock is a development researcher and a graduate student of the Department of Sociology and Anthropology, University of Buea, Cameroon. He has written articles within the area of the politics of recognition, gender and poverty. He is currently interested in studies relating to the development of the 'ethnic question' within the corporate sector in Cameroon and its implications for Cameroon's development efforts.

rogerstabe@yahoo.com

Tracey Peterson has been the HIV/Aids Manager: Community Projects for De Beers since May 2005. Before this, Tracey managed the HIV/Aids workplace programme, responsible for crafting the HIV/Aids policy and strategy in collaboration with key stakeholders, and for managing implementation at the various mines and offices throughout South Africa. Tracey has been with De Beers for 13 years and has a communications background, being primarily responsible for media relations for the company before moving into HIV/Aids management.

tracey.peterson@debeersgroup.com

John Porter is a Reader in International Health at the London School of Hygiene and Tropical Medicine. His background is in medicine and public health and his research work concentrates on an interdisciplinary approach to the control of infectious diseases, in particular HIV and TB. Ethics and human rights remain the foundations of his approach to public health.

John.Porter@lshtm.ac.uk

José A. Puppim de Oliveira is Associate Professor at the Brazilian School of Public and Business Administration (EBAPE), Getúlio Vargas Foundation (FGV), Rio de Janeiro, Brazil. He specialises in the political economy of sustainable development and corporate social responsibility.

puppim@fgv.br

Dinah Rajak is a DPhil student in Anthropology at the University of Sussex. Her research focuses on the role of transnational mining corporations as agents of development. Before her DPhil she worked as a research officer for a project funded by the Department for International Development.

d.r.rajak@sussex.ac.uk

Cathy Reichardt started her career as a regulator in the United Kingdom and has worked as a consultant for mining projects throughout sub-Saharan Africa and the Asia–Pacific region. Thereafter she was AngloGold's Environmental Manager for East and West Africa region. She is currently a senior lecturer at the University of the Witwatersrand's School of Mining Engineering specialising in the integration of non-financial risk management into mining projects.

reichardt@egoli.min.wits.ac.za

From 1990, **Markus Reichardt** worked in a variety of operational and corporate environmental, small and medium-sized enterprise (SME) and community engagement positions in the South African-based Anglo American Group, culminating in his role as Corporate Environmental Manager for AngloGold. He co-founded and co-managed SR & I (Pty) Ltd, the data provider for the JSE Socially Responsible Investment Index, the first such index in a developing country. Since 2003, he has been a consultant to the southern African resources and financial sectors.

mrkusncathy@mweb.co.za

Alana Rosenberg is Research Associate in the Office of International Training at CIRA with experience in public health HIV/Aids research and evaluation activities in Western and Southern Africa.

Alana.Rosenberg@yale.edu

Victoria Ryan is an attorney, consultant and independent researcher in corporate governance. Prior to completing her MBA at the University of Cape Town in South Africa and London Business School, she practised environmental and corporate law at Werksmans Attorneys in Johannesburg.

VictoriaRyan@mweb.co.za

While working in global HIV/Aids management in De Beers, **Julie Shaw** became interested in the importance of problem definition and context when designing solutions. She built a model of psychological health for De Beers, which is captured in her 2004 book *Icebergs in Africa*, and now does freelance writing and wellness design while sidestepping traditional HR work.

rainbow@icon.co.za

Telita Snyckers has a master's degree in Law and has been admitted as Attorney of the High Court. She has had experience as a prosecutor, and subsequently as an attorney specialising in commercial litigation. She joined SARS as a senior legal adviser, and held a number of roles dealing with enforcement and compliance-related strategy and policy. She is currently focusing on corporate policy and strategy.

tsnyckers@sars.gov.za

Geoff Stiles is currently Managing Director, Southern Africa Office for Marbek Resource Consultants Ltd, a Canadian firm of energy and environment specialists. After receiving a PhD in Economic Anthropology from McGill University, Dr Stiles taught social and economic development at Memorial University in St John's, Canada, for 13 years before moving to the private sector where he developed a consulting practice in energy and environment. Since 1987, Dr Stiles has worked primarily in Southern Africa, managing a series of large multi-country projects in energy efficiency and greenhouse gas mitigation. In 2001, he moved to South Africa to manage the CBLA Greenhouse Gas Mitigation project, which included development of the National Energy Efficiency Accord. He is currently working on a number of projects in the area of CDM and GHG mitigation, including developing a CDM guide for the South African Chamber of Mines and managing a fund for CDM project development.

stiles@marbek.ca

Robert G. Taylor is Professor in the Faculty of Management Studies and Director of the Leadership Center at the University of KwaZulu-Natal, South Africa. He has previously worked in professional practice and in the private NGO sector. His research interests include organisational leadership and innovation practices relevant to African circumstances.

taylorr@ukzn.ac.za

Mengsteab Tesfayohannes (PhD) is research Associate Professor at the Department of Management, University of Waterloo, Canada. His research interests include: entrepreneurship and SME development; investment projects promotion; sustainable economic development; gender-aware business development in the global South; and technology and innovation promotional strategies. Before joining the University of Waterloo in 2002, he worked at the University of the Witwatersrand (South Africa), University of Botswana, University of Bayreuth (Germany), University of Asmara (Eritrea) and the University of Graz (Austria). He also worked as a short-term consultant for a number of private, governmental and international organisations including United Nations agencies.

haryohruth@rogers.com

Wayne Visser MSc BBusSc is completing doctoral studies at the International Centre for Corporate Social Responsibility (University of Nottingham, UK). He is author of *Business Frontiers: Social Responsibility, Sustainable Development and Economic Justice* (ICFAI University Press, 2005); *Beyond Reasonable Greed: Why Sustainable Business is a Much Better Idea!* (with Clem Sunter; Human & Rousseau Tafelberg, 2002); and *South Africa: Reasons to Believe!* (with Guy Lundy; Aardvark Press, 2003). Until 2003, he was Director of Sustainability Services at KPMG South Africa. He is also the External Examiner for the Postgraduate Diploma in Sustainable Business (University of Cambridge, UK) and Research Fellow at the Centre for Research into Sustainability (University of London, UK). He co-guest-edited a special edition of *The Journal of Corporate Citizenship* on Corporate Citizenship in Africa (Issue 18, Summer 2005).

wayne@waynevisser.com; www.waynevisser.com

Palma Vizzoni is experienced in cultural relations and on-the-ground environmental crisis management. For the past three years she has studied and worked with the Dagara people of Burkina Faso in West Africa while also drilling wells for drinking water. Palma completed her BA in International Environmental Policy at Colby College in Waterville, Maine. As part of her studies she spent a year abroad with the International Honors Program living in communities in several countries studying the implementation of proactive solutions to environmental and social problems. Palma earned an MBA in Sustainable Management from Presidio School of Management in San Francisco, California. Her current work is with a company called Eprida (www.eprida.com) which has created a technology that turns biomass into liquid diesel fuel and a fertiliser that builds topsoil. It is a climate change remediation process which has the net result of being carbon-negative.

pvizzoni@presidiomba.org

Simeon Wanyama is a former Senior Lecturer and Dean at the Uganda Martyrs University, and is currently studying for a PhD in the Department of Accountancy and Business Finance at the University of Dundee in Scotland. Mr Wanyama is a graduate of St John's University in New York.

simeon@accamail.com

Index